Studies in European Economic Law and Regulation

Volume 8

The series shall focus on studies devoted to the analysis of European Economic Law. It shall firstly embrace all features of EU economic law in general (e.g. EU law such as fundamental freedoms and their relationship to fundamental rights, as well as other economic law such as arbitration and WTO law) and more specifically (antitrust law, unfair competition law, financial market law, consumer law). This series shall cover both classical internal analysis (doctrine) as well as external analysis, where European Economic Law and Regulation is the subject of analysis (Law and Economics, Sociological Analysis, Comparative Law and the like).

The series accepts monographs focusing on a specific topic, as well as edited collections of articles covering a specific theme or collections of articles by a single author. All contributions are accepted exclusively after a rigorous double-blind peer-review process.

More information about this series at http://www.springer.com/series/11710

Gianluca Sgueo

Beyond Networks - Interlocutory Coalitions, the European and Global Legal Orders

Springer

Gianluca Sgueo
New York University
Florence, Italy

ISSN 2214-2037 ISSN 2214-2045 (electronic)
Studies in European Economic Law and Regulation
ISBN 978-3-319-28873-4 ISBN 978-3-319-28875-8 (eBook)
DOI 10.1007/978-3-319-28875-8

Library of Congress Control Number: 2016931368

Printed on acid-free paper

This Springer imprint is published by Springer Nature
The registered company is Springer International Publishing AG Switzerland

This book is dedicated to Maya and Bianca,
through whose eyes I see the future.

Acknowledgements

This book is the culmination of 6 years of work. It began back in 2010 with my doctoral dissertation on supranational democracy. As part of my PhD, I conducted a comparative study of different models of consultative democracy operating in the supranational arena. My research was supervised by Professors Giulio Vesperini from the University of Viterbo *La Tuscia*, Richard Stewart from the New York University and Jean Bernard Auby from the *Institut d'Etudes Politiques de Paris*. This book would not exist without their stewardship of that thesis project. In 2009, the project that produced this volume began as part of a joint research on "The Relationship Between the Global Administrative Law and the European Administrative Law". The project, taken on by the Universities of Rome *Tor Vergata*, Naples *Federico II*, Viterbo *La Tuscia*, Siena and Molise, culminated in a workshop at the Italian *Scuola Superiore della Pubblica Amministrazione* in Rome in June 2010. The project aimed to elucidate the interactions between European administrative law and the administrative law of global significance. In 2011, the result of that research appeared in a book published by Springer, titled *Global Administrative Law and EU Administrative Law*. I greatly benefited from insights and critiques provided by the coordinators of that research: Professors Edoardo Chiti (University of Viterbo) and Bernardo Mattarella (University of Siena). Between 2012 and 2014, I continued research on the role of global civil society in shaping principles of global and European law, a topic that I had only quickly analysed in the volume published in 2011. The *Centro de Estudos Sociais* (CES) of the University of Coimbra provided me with a postdoc fellowship. As postdoc researcher in democracy and globalisation at the CES, I devoted my research to understanding how and why interest groups operating beyond the national borders merge into organised networks. I classified these networks under the definition of "interlocutory coalitions", and I described its advocacy strategies. This book attempts to consolidate these complex issues in a coherent, and hopefully captivating, framework. Between 2014 and 2015, I had the opportunity to be teaching fellow in a course on globalisation and democracy at the Bocconi University, in Milan. The lectures were structured as ongoing discussions with the students, and I learned a great deal from these debates. I am also grateful to my students at the New York University in Florence, where I teach "activism and democracy", who inspired my research and helped me inch it forward. From September to November 2014, I also had the opportunity to undertake research on this subject as visiting scholar at the Amsterdam Centre of International Law.

I wish to thank those who contributed with their comments and suggestions to this work and helped me to avoid at least some of the errors that I would have otherwise made. For constructive comments, significant proposed amendments as well as encouragement, I would like to express my deep gratitude to Professor Giovanni Allegretti, my research supervisor at CES. An earlier version of the book benefited from the helpful comments and suggestions given by Professors Lorenzo Casini and Anne Peters. Professor Alberto Alemanno was also a source of inspiration. His provocative ideas provided a valuable contribution to the advancement of my research. Advice from Giulio Napolitano on written and oral incarnations of this research has been also a great help to its planning and development. But, mostly, this book has benefited intellectually and organisationally from the comments and suggestions provided by Professor Sabino Cassese: without his constant encouragement and advice, this research would probably never be concluded. To a minor extent, I benefited from the smart ideas that emerged during the 2011 IRPA lecture during which I had the opportunity to present an earlier version of this research. My grateful thanks are also extended to Nina Amelung and Britta Baumgarten who invited me to participate in the "Transnational Public Participation and Social Movement Activism" workshop held in 2013 at the *Universidade Nova de Lisboa*. All the participants in the workshop provided valuable comments on a previous version of this research. In addition to all of those named above, I was privileged to discuss portions of this works in many settings over many years with many intelligent people. While any listing of this group is sure to be incomplete, it does include (in no particular order) Dario Bevilacqua, Bruno Carotti, Josephine van Zeben, Pablo Meix, Ruairi O'Neill, Euan McDonald and Ingo Venzke. Everyone in this group has shared insights on early drafts of this book that I have tried to incorporate into the text. I owe my deepest debt to the people working for non-governmental organisations with whom I have interacted over the last 2 years, and I am indebted to the librarians at the many institutions that housed the works cited in this volume. I also want to extend my gratitude to the editorial team at Springer. In particular, I want to thank Neil Olivier and Diana Nijenhuijzen for their supportive and efficient handling of the book project. I also appreciated the thoughtful comments of the publisher's anonymous reviewers. A special thanks goes to the innumerable trains, airplanes and cafeterias where I had the occasion to sit, reflect and write over the last 3 years. A great deal of what has become part of this book was conceived while commuting from one place to another. A very special thanks also goes to Sarah Tighe, who has edited this research and helped with both the fluency of the English language and the contents. It is thanks to Sarah that this volume is now in its current form. Any remaining errors are mine alone.

Finally, I would like to offer my special thanks to Claudia Ascione for her interminable patience, assistance with the statistics used in this book and her unwavering support. Without her companionship along the way and constant encouragement, I would have not been able to overcome the intricacies of my research and finally put my ideas onto paper. I feel extremely lucky to be sharing my daily life with her.

All views expressed in this book are made at the sole responsibility of the author.

Foreword

What Role – If Any – For Civil Society Coalitions in Supranational Governance?

Policymaking has traditionally been tackled from the top down, that is to say, from the perspective of regulators, be they bureaucrats, officials, or politicians rather than from the perspective of the regulatees, such as citizens, businesses, and consumers. Before the last two decades, the debate about the virtues of participatory democracy, and in particular stakeholder engagement in government decision-making, was predominantly academic.[1] Today, amid contemporary challenges of representative democracies, such as civic disaffection and increased distrust of political parties, an increasing number of countries as well as international organisations are progressively recognizing the importance of public engagement in policymaking.[2] Participatory policymaking is sought at both domestic (municipal, local, national) and international (bilateral, plurilateral and multilateral) level. Yet in parallel to the multiplication of participatory opportunities the question arises as to whether citizens' and civil society organisations' greater involvement in both domestic and supranational policy-making is enhancing or weakening democracy.

While the immediate answer appears clear and undisputable – as governments as well as international organisations must be responsive and accountable to citizens –, an engaged civil society poses several well-known yet unsolved challenges to the democratic process: that of accountability (who are civil society organizations accountable to?), efficiency (what if the interests represented are too many to handle?), capacity (how can they keep up with all participatory opportunities?), and that of democratic deficit (how representative can they be?). As envisioned in *tempore*

[1] See, e.g., J. Dryzek, Deliberative Democracy and Beyond: liberals, critics, contestations (Oxford, OUP, 2000).

[2] A. Alemanno, Stakeholder Engagement in Regulatory Policy, in OECD, Regulatory Policy Outlook, OECD Publishing, 2015.

non suspecto by Ralf Dahrendorf,[3] all these challenges do not only persist but are also heightened when civil society actors operate transnationally. More critically, the commercialization of advocacy through astroturfs, i.e. fake grassroots efforts encouraged by the industry, and other forms of 'subsidized public' further complexify those challenges today.[4]

Gianluca Sgueo, in *Beyond Networks*, critically dissects and systematizes such a debate by providing an insightful, well-researched and elegantly written account of the democratic potential carried out by coalitions of civil society actors.

And he does so in a timely manner. Amid the negotiations of a new generation of trade agreements, such as the Transatlantic Trade and Investment Partnership (TTIP) and the Transpacific Partnership (TPP), the number of transnational systems of regulation and regulatory cooperation mechanisms is set to increase. Given the wider scope of policy areas covered by these new transnational regimes and cooperation mechanisms and their rather intrusive approach to domestic regulatory autonomy,[5] the interests at stake will not only be broader than in the past but also of constitutional significance, affecting third party States, private companies, civil society organizations as well as individual citizens. As a result, the overall inclusiveness of transnational regulatory policymaking is set to expand and translate into new participatory channels. According to such a transformative dynamic, the various principles of administrative law governing both domestic and transnational policymaking will continue to develop and transform – in a continuous and puzzling process of learning, borrowing, cross-referencing and cognitive influence.

Beyond networks provides a significant and original contribution to our understanding of such an ongoing globalization of administrative law by further unpacking its underlying dynamics. In building upon and contributing to the existing global administrative law literature, this book innovates it from at least three different perspectives.

First, rather than focusing on the interactions *between* domestic and supranational legal systems, along the typically vertical top-down and bottom-up perspectives, this book looks instead at the horizontal interactions between administrative rules *across* supranational systems. In particular, it chooses as its privileged area of investigation the linkages between European administrative law, notably the broader and more conceptualized European Administrative Space, and the administrative principles of law pertaining to other supranational regulatory regimes and regulators (generally referred as Global Administrative Law), such as the World Bank, the World Trade Organization, the United Nations, the Organization for Economic

[3] See R. Dahrendorf, The Third Way and Liberty: An Authoritarian Streak in Europe's New Center, Foreign Affairs, 16 (1999).

[4] E.T. Walker, Grassroots for Hire, Public Affairs Consultants in American Democracy, CUP 2014.

[5] The TTIP for instances ranges from general provisions in trade in goods and services to more specific chapters on public procurement, rules of origin, technical barriers to trade, food safety and animal and plant health, chemicals, cosmetics, information and communication technology, pharmaceuticals, energy and raw minerals, intellectual property, etc. For a complete list, see http://trade.ec.europa.eu/doclib/press/index.cfm?id=1230

Cooperation and Development, the Asian Development Bank and the Council of Europe. In discussing how administrative rules, mechanisms and practices converge, diverge and give rise to mutual learning, this volume considers all relevant legal formants, including the case of law produced by several international courts.

Second, while conventional global administrative law archetypally focuses on the nature and action of institutional players and informal networks of institutional actors, this volume extends its focus to non-state actors, notably to civil society organisations. With a turnover averaging 5 % of the Gross Domestic Product (GDP) in the majority of Western democracies, civil society organisations are understood and discussed as one of the central 'mechanisms supporting the interactions between supranational legal regimes'. Their multifaceted action in shaping transnational administrative regimes defines the scope of the book. But there is more.

Third, the volume does not look at *all* civil society organizations – and at their collective contribution in shaping administrative principles as originally conceptualised by Archon Fung[6] – but focuses instead on coalitions made of those organizations when acting transnationally. It examines them as a 'distinct actor in the supranational arena'. While the existing literature has considered transnational networks composed of inter alia non-state actors, the novelty of this book is to focus on coalitions and networks *exclusively* made of civil society organisations. In the author's view, those can be made of non-governmental organizations, think tanks, foundations, universities as well as individuals and include entities as diverse as the Alliance for Lobbying Transparency and Ethics Regulation (ALTER), a Brussels-based organization of civil society actors, the Asian Development Bank, the Transatlantic Consumer Dialogue, a EU-sponsored platform gathering EU and US consumer groups, or Avaaz, the not-for-profit petition platform enabling the emergence of ad hoc "virtual web" of citizens that tie together to support a cause through an online-petitioning platform.

While networks are nothing new, not even when they are formed among non-state actors, their connections, activities and impacts are unprecedented. This appears all the more true when one considers their defining features: the supranational vocation of their action, the public-private nature of their funding, and their deliberative capability. But there is more to make coalitions worth scrutinizing. To borrow from Jeremy Heimans and Henry Timms' most influential theorization, non-state actors increasingly embody a 'new power'.[7] When contrasted to the 'old power', the new one is open and accessible (as opposed to being closed), participatory (as opposed to being jealously guarded), peer-driven (as opposed to be held by a few) and often network-based. As such, civil society coalitions do call for – and do justify – some dedicated academic attention, closer inspection and a new, individual theorization.

---

[6] A. Fung, Associations and Democracy: Between Theories, Hopes, and Realities, 29 Annual Review of Sociology, 515 (2003).

[7] J. Heimans and H. Timms, Understanding New Power, Harvard Business Review, December (2014).

Once established a case for studying coalitions of civil society organization through the lens of Global Administrative Law, the book eventually unveils its underlying research question. This volume specifically attempts to explain *how* civil society networks – which are studied within the broader notion of Global Civil Society (GSC) – drive the development of principles of democratic value at the supranational level. It does so within the broader debate about new modes of global governance and in particular that of experimentalist governance. It proceeds to theorize an autonomous organization network model within GSC: the so-called 'interlocutory coalitions'. Those coalitions are typically made of diverse category of entities whose major – sometimes solely – common feature is the cross-border pursuit of a common cause. In order to build an original and valuable taxonomy of civil society networks, interlocutory coalitions must be contrasted to other forms of networks, including social networks, trans-governmental committees, think tanks, Parallel Summits and QUANGOs. After reconstructing their respective composition, membership, rules of governance and legal status, the book delves into interlocutory coalitions' decision-making. How do coalitions presenting high degree of variation when it comes to their mission, governance, funding and membership coalesce around one common cause? How do they come to existence and get along? How can such coalitions speak with one voice when representing and advocating their common position in front of the relevant international organizations? What kind of techniques and deliberative mechanisms are used to attain a common position and then convey it to the outside world?

There is one single explanation capable of addressing these multiple questions. This must be found in the inherent mission of any coalition, that of mediating. Mediation can be defined as a multi-level and multi-directional activity involving on the one hand the bargaining between the positions of participants (internal mediation), and on the other the negotiations with domestic and transnational regulators (external mediation).

It is against this conceptual understanding of civil society coalitions that this book explores and discusses their democratic potential in supranational governance. In particular, it discusses whether and how interlocutory coalitions may encourage the spreading of principles of administrative governance related in particular with participatory democracy across the European and global levels.

The claim, which is consistently argued along the book and finds support in the existing literature, is that while transnational activism from single civil society's actors fails to promote transnational democracy, the activism promoted by supranational coalitions of civil society actors opens up possibilities for more democratic supranational governance.

While this thesis is plausibly substantiated along the volume and corroborated by existing literature,[8] it remains unclear to whom this outcome must be ascribed to. In other words, is the resulting democratization the single civil society's actors fault or their coalitions' merit?

[8] See, e.g., B. Wejnert, Diffusion of Democracy. The Past and Future of Global Democracy, Cambridge (2014).

As hinted by the author, due to their analogous explanatory power, these two solutions are far from being mutually exclusive. On the one hand, competing interests, actual fragmentation, participatory overkill, weak accountability and limited legitimacy diminish the capability of single civil society's actors to democratize the supranational legal order. On the other, their common raison-d'être, non-exclusive and selective memberships as well as deliberative capability render interlocutory coalitions particularly well positioned to democratize transnational governance. In particular, the democratizing potential of the latter in supranational policymaking would emerge from the win-win encounters between supranational regulators and civil society. While the former finds in coalitions efficient, legitimate and accountable avenues when discharging their regulatory duties, the latter discovers in supranational actors an opportunity to participate in, and shape, the construction of supranational governance. Although instrumental and often utilitarian, the relationship between civil society coalitions and regulators is set to consolidate over time.

In the words of the author,

> At a time in which regulation increasingly concerns objects and situations whose heterogeneity and complexity escapes the cognitive capacities of supranational decision-making bodies, cooperation with large coalitions of civil society actors becomes fundamental for sound policy-making.

The thesis is as strikingly as provocatively clear. The world needs more – not less – coalitions of civil society actors. And that for two major reasons. First, interlocutory coalitions transfer epistemic legitimacy to transnational policymaking. Second, they assert and convey procedural transparency and accountability to supranational governance. It seems undisputable that transnational regimes need both today.

But how interlocutory coalitions do contribute to the construction of supranational governance? How do they democratize a typically technocratic, largely counter-majoritarian phenomenon such as supranational policymaking?

The democratizing potential of interlocutory coalitions translates – amid a broader phenomenon of policy diffusion – into cross-border administrative convergence. This can be conceived as a pattern of harmonization of principles of democratic governance across legal systems. In line with Olsen's theorization,[9] administrative convergence may result from two complementary mechanisms, that of attractiveness and that of imposition. While interlocutory coalitions may, by linking various actors and institutions across borders, mobilize good practices and standards from different legal arenas (convergence through attractiveness), they may also prompt a similar dynamic by relying – and often leverage – on IOs' leadership and authority (convergence through imposition).

In the light of the above, it seems plausible to claim – as the book does – that the ensuing, dynamic mix of attractiveness and imposition could lead to administrative convergence and possibly contribute to democratizing supranational governance.

[9] J.P. Olsen, Towards a European Administrative Space?, 10 Journal of European Public Policy, 506 (2003).

Yet, as partially recognized by the author, this process is far from being effortless. It rather unearths complex dynamics that – given the relatively young age and rapidly transformative nature of civil society coalitions – remain to be empirically examined and tested. The relationship between interlocutory coalitions and transnational regulators cannot but suffer of many of the problems faced by single civil society actors when interacting with regulators. Thus, for instance, it is well established that coalitions compete among themselves as much as single civil society actors do.[10] Likewise, coalitions cannot represent all interests, but only certain interests. Moreover, one cannot assume that – due to their heightened deliberative capacity – coalitions are inherently more representative than single civil actors of the interests they pursue. While coalitions' input is generally presumed to be representative of their cause, most coalitions organisations lack – as conceded by Gianluca Sgueo – adequate internal participatory mechanisms enabling that degree of representativeness. Yet no participatory mechanism could attain its goal unless the relevant stakeholder organisations are genuinely representative of the interests at stake.

In these circumstances, a normative – rather than an analytical stance – is required. The first question to be asked should therefore not be *how* but *whether* coalitions must play a democratizing role in transnational governance. In other words, given the inherent limits of their actions, how desirable is to have such a multitude of hybrid, often hetero-directed actors shape global governance? Can interlocutory coalitions realistically contribute to a global participatory democracy? And is such a thing even appropriate?

This is a difficult set of questions that calls for both a theoretical and real-world contextualization.

When measured against the realities of participatory practices, the democratic potential of civil society coalitions appears limited.[11] The dominant attitude vis-à-vis participatory engagement – at both domestic and international level – is instrumental rather than intrinsic, i.e. the degree to which decision-making processes live up to democratic principles.[12] This suggests that the actual commitment towards participation is more likely to contribute to the legitimacy of the policy process than to its overall democratic credibility and accountability. However, the two aspects of intrinsic and instrumental value are closely interrelated. Therefore without a broader commitment to the intrinsic value of public engagement, there is a risk that not only governments but also transnational regimes across the world will continue to fall short in reaping the instrumental benefits they seek.

While this book concludes that interlocutory coalitions appear as 'the best possible drivers of harmonization of principles of democratic governance at the supranational level', ultimately, the democratising potential of civil society coalitions lies

[10] S. Batliwala and D. Brown (eds.), Transnational Civil Society. An Introduction (Bloomfield, Kumarian Press, 2006).

[11] See, e.g., D. Klingemann and D. Fuchs (eds.), Citizens and the State (Oxford, Oxford University Press 1995).

[12] OECD (2009), Focus on Citizens: Public Engagement for Better Policy and Services, OECD Publishing, Paris, p. 27.

as much in the hands of the transnational regulators and their administrations as in those of the coalitions themselves. In particular, transnational regulators could proactively facilitate coalitions' building and, once those are set up and running, enhance their internal deliberative (or 'mediation' in Sgueo's terminology) capacity. For a start, this could be done by *inter alia* supporting financially weak groups (e.g. the introduction of consultation fees on corporate groups could be envisaged). The ensuing 'upgrading' of their internal mediation function would then spill over to their external activity so as to overcome some of the major obstacles they currently face. Given the instrumental nature of their relationship, which is largely driven by mutual interdependence, we might reasonably expect both transnational regulators and interlocutory coalitions to commit to deepen and inject trust into their interactions.

Their efforts should be directed to one single aim: to ensure equal representation of interests. This remains one of the – if not the one –fundamental pre-conditions for meaningful and effective interactions within the existing transnational governance. Instead of returning to the old recipes for enhancing civil society within the Nation state, time has come to think creatively about how those interactions can be organized so as to meet the radical different circumstances of the emerging transnational governance. This book provides a rigorous, constructive and promising stepping stone to embark on such a challenging journey. Yet the case for a global participatory democracy remains to be made.

New York University School of Law
New York, NY, USA

Alberto Alemanno

Introductory Remarks

As the scientific discourse over globalisation progresses, a growing amount of research expounds and discusses how the global legal arena influences – and, in turn, is influenced by – the domestic legal systems. Concepts such as "global governance", once vague and poorly understood, have grown in use and are now familiar to many. Globalisation has become such a powerful and diffuse concept in academic fields that the anti-globalisers have themselves gone global. Critics on globalisation have refocused on how globalisation should be, rather than on whether it should take place. Yet, the more the streams of academic concern on globalisation and its effects – and particularly on globalisation of administrative law – confluence, the less the framework for assessing this phenomenon shows coherency or rationality. Paradoxically, the more the term "globalisation" becomes difficult to escape, the more difficult it is to define. The key questions to be answered are manifold and include benefits and costs deriving from homogenisation of legal cultures, the unequal distribution of resources, the public-private hybridism and so forth. Indeed, this is the main dilemma (and, at the same time, challenge) currently faced within academic discourse on cross-border legal interactions and germination of principles of administrative governance.

This volume has an admitted affinity with the works of leading scholars on globalisation of administrative law, such as Sabino Cassese, Richard Stewart, Benedict Kingsbury, Eyal Benvenisti and Daniel Etsy. However, this volume does not attempt to rehash what are by now well-known principles of administrative law operating at the supranational level. Rather, it seeks to portray two of the most controversial aspects of globalisation of administrative law. The first relates to the convergence between administrative rules pertaining to different supranational regulatory systems. Traditionally, the spread of methods of administrative governance has been depicted primarily against the background of the interactions between the domestic and the supranational arena, both from a top-down and bottom-up perspective. However, the exploration of interactions occurring at the supranational level between legal regimes is still not grounded on adequate empirical evidence. This book attempts to supplement this angle of inquiry by focusing on the interactions between the European administrative law and the administrative principles of law pertaining to other supranational regulatory regimes and regulators such as the World Bank, the World Trade Organization, the United Nations, the Organisation for Economic Co-operation and Development, the Asian Development Bank, the Council of Europe and so forth. Factors of historical, political and legal significance drive the spillover of methods of democratic governance across these systems. The European administrative space relies on a set of principles and legal standards pertaining the Member States' legal systems. These include transparency, public liability, the granting of adequate procedural rights to the parties involved and judicial review. Increasingly, the same elements can be found in global regulatory regimes. Transparency in rule-making, due process in decisions affecting private parties and review mechanisms to ensure legality are considered key to promoting accountability and legitimacy of supranational regulators. At the political level, the array of contractual relations and political dialogues between the European institutions and their supranational partners – ranging from functionally specific terms that address specialised transnational goals to broad alliances which address general common needs – have encouraged the globalisation of certain European rules and at the same time have provided incentives for EU administration to act in compliance with global rules. A third crucial element that is driving interactions between the European administrative space and global administrative systems is the jurisprudence of the handful of courts and arbitration tribunals that currently reside and operate in the international and the European legal environments.

Yet these factors do not cover the whole spectrum of the relevant phenomena that encourage the convergence between European and supranational, or global, administrative rules. This volume argues that the role of civil society actors must also be addressed if a more representative picture of the spillover of methods of administrative governance across the European and the global arenas is to be achieved. Civil society actors operating at the supranational level are understood and described in this volume as one of the mechanisms supporting the interactions between supranational legal regimes. However, they are also portrayed as the second controversial aspect of globalisation. This book attempts to describe the importance of deliberative *fora* – or coalitions – of non-state actors for framing shared strategies towards European and supranational regulators. It is argued that transnational activism from single civil society's actors is not necessarily cosmopolitan in orientation and does not necessarily intend to promote transnational democracy, while the activism promoted by supranational coalitions of civil society actors opens up possibilities for more democratic supranational governance. However, this book explains that the reasons behind the existence of such coalitions have nothing to do with promotion of democratic governance. Supranational coalitions of civil society actors are born out of necessity. It is noted from the outset that coalitions of civil society actors could be viewed pragmatically as a necessity for both supranational regulators and the civil society actors themselves. The former need to efficiently address the topics they are demanded to regulate and to overcome issues of legitimacy and accountability. The latter are interested in searching for effective ways to participate in the construction of supranational governance. In many respects, coalitions of civil society actors can be understood as *loci* for fulfilment of both needs. On the one hand, they offer single civil society actors the opportunity to coalesce their interests – rarely identical, but nonetheless complementary – and thus enhance their impact on supranational governance as well as increase their chances to raise funds from donors. On the other hand, supranational coalitions of civil society actors help supranational regulators to increase their accountability and legitimacy. At a time in which regulation increasingly concerns objects and situations whose heterogeneity and complexity is beyond the reasoning of supranational decision-making bodies, cooperation with large coalitions of civil society actors becomes fundamental for sound policy-making. Aside from this, it may be suggested that supranational regulators find it easier to negotiate with a single coalition instead of managing multiple negotiations with a multitude of civil society actors.

Indeed, there are questions as to whether enough commonality exists between these coalitions to consider them as a distinct actor in the supranational arena. After all, transnational networks composed of a variety of members, including non-state actors, have already been accounted for in scientific debate. Already in 1996 Manuel Castells had conceptualised modern society as a "network society", where power is organised around networks programmed in each domain of human activity. Two years later, in 1998, Margaret Keck and Kathryn Sikkink described organised networks of civil society actors in a seminal research on cross-border activism. Anne-Marie Slaughter followed in 2004. She heralded a "new world order" in which government officials, financial regulators, judges and legislators were composed into networks to exchange information and coordinate activity across national borders. However, this volume is distinguished from the works of Castells, Keck and Sikkink and Slaughter in two important respects. Firstly, this book narrows the focus of civil society's networks, conceptually divorcing them from networks of different nature (e.g. those in which states, social movements or other public actors are also included). The sole members of the coalitions described in this volume pertain to the sphere of civil society. They include, inter alia, non-governmental organisations, think tanks, foundations, universities and individuals. In this sense, these coalitions are reminiscent of the "issue networks" theorised by Hugo Heclo. Because they are treated as distinctive actors, the coalitions described in this volume are also differentiated from other civil society actors who operate individually or under various forms of agreements (e.g. social movements, epistemic communities and parallel summits). As a second departure from the research of Keck and Sikkink (and that of Slaughter), this book specifically attempts to explain how civil society coalitions drive the development of principles of administrative governance at the supranational level. This also separates the coalitions described in this volume from Heclo's issue networks, since the latter are located, and operate, exclusively at the national level. To be more precise: this book analyses how coalitions of civil society actors encourage the spreading of principles of administrative governance related with participatory democracy across the European and global levels.

In order to understand whether supranational coalitions of civil society influence European and global decision-making processes, how this influence can be depicted and which kind of problems it raises, this book primarily focuses on the activities in which those coalitions are engaged. These include mediation, rule-making and implementation. Mediation consists of the discussion of the diverging positions carried out by the coalitions' participants and the promotion of policy alternatives to supranational decision-makers. From an early stage, coalitions of civil society actors mediate "internally" between the interests of the diverging members; later, they mediate between these interests and the representatives of supranational regulators. The lobbying pursued by the coalitions described herein into the official negotiations of supranational regulator – and/or into the other phases of the policy cycle – often results in them influencing the policies and shaping the strategic direction of European and global regulatory bodies. Coalitions of civil society, for instance, may influence the agenda setting of the supranational regulators; they may work as catalysts in calling for the revocation of rules that no longer work in the common interest; or they may deliberately shift from one legal regime to another (a practice known as "forum shopping") to stake their claims and influence the building of more amenable policies. Finally, the coalitions of civil society actors may have enforcement powers. They may monitor the compliance of specific norms and rules, they may evaluate the degree to which these rules are successful, and they may report the possible breaches of these rules to the competent bodies. Having described the activities of the coalitions of civil society actors, the focus of analysis is shifted to the opportunities that cooperation among such coalitions and supranational regulators may bring to their substantive goals: reliability and legitimacy, respectively. Particular attention is given to the consequences determined by these divergent expectations regarding cooperation.

The last part of this volume discusses the influence of supranational coalitions of civil society actors on the convergence of principles of administrative governance across the European and the global legal regimes. At first glance, the proposition that convergence of supranational governance may be achieved through the advocacy of supranational coalitions of civil society may strike many scholars as implausible. Not infrequently, scholarly observation of the involvement of civil society actors in supranational decision-making has stressed the variation – rather than the convergence – of participatory patterns in global legal regimes. This volume breaks with this interpretation of civil society's involvement in global governance. To this end, a distinction between the contribution given by single non-state actors and by coalitions of civil society actors to the evolution of the supranational legal order is presented (and, in doing so, this volume also takes into account the widespread disagreement as to whether civil society actors can be viewed as contributors to supranational policy-making). This volume suggests that two forms of convergence of administrative governance, namely, attractiveness and imposition, are encouraged by the cooperation between supranational coalitions of civil society actors and supranational regulators. Hence an important differentiation may be made between the described cooperation and what international legal doctrine commonly defines as "regime complexes". Regime complexes are described as higher-order governance arrangements that replace integrated international regimes in specific issue areas, e.g. refugee policy, anti-corruption, climate change and food security. Such regimes include various mixes of states, substate units, international organisations and civil society actors. Cooperation between coalitions of non-state actors and supranational regulators is tighter in its scope, since it refers to the area of activity of the given regulator, and broader in its effects, since it seems to drive harmonisation of administrative governance.

The effects on global governance as a result of the growing presence of networks of civil society actors are not entirely positive. The tensions related to networking in civil society are the object of analysis in the concluding remarks of this volume. These tensions raise doubts about network's desirability as drivers of harmonised principles of participatory democracy at the European and global levels. If that were the case, civil society networks may not be the brave new world they appear to be at first sight. They would better fit into the definition of a compromise between civil society actors, interested in increasing their fundraising capacity, and supranational regulators, concerned by the preservation of their, albeit only seemingly, legitimacy. As a further consequence, the leverage of such networks on global governance, if any exists, would at the best promote a "nominal democracy", as Robert Keohane names it – i.e. a democracy that meets democratic standards on the surface and embodies the rhetoric of democracy, but lacks the content. The most evident tension is related to the functioning of coalitions of civil society actors. Holding civil society actors together in a coalition constitutes a complicated enterprise. This is especially apparent when coalitions grow bigger. When networks expand into hundreds of participants, the likeliness of controversial opinions increases. Thus, larger coalition may be considered weaker coalitions, due to the wide range of adherents with different views, sizes and strategies. Furthermore, a bigger network is also a more formalised network, since it is obliged to sacrifice some flexibility and to adopt formal procedures, in order to reflect the views of all its constituents. Competition among different coalitions represents the second tension that, according to this volume, challenges networking in civil society. This book assumes that the presence of a large number of civil society actors in the policy arena creates not only the basis for cooperation but also (and perhaps more frequently) for competition. This is the case of bigger coalitions, encompassing a great diversity of actors in a constant struggle to be guided by clear leadership. But it may also be the case for smaller coalitions, motivated by the necessity to remain competitive in order to gain attention and associated advantages in terms of funding and accessibility to supranational policy-making. A third tension may occur when a given supranational regulator refuses to cooperate with a coalition of civil society actors on the basis of rules or standards formerly approved by a different regulator, assuming their uniqueness. Richard Stewart recently exemplified this point by describing competition among global regulatory bodies in providing regulatory standards to firms, governmental bodies and other global regulatory bodies. In Stewart's analysis, such competition is regarded as beneficial, because it can generate powerful incentives to respond to the interests and concerns of consumers of regulatory standards. However, the opposite is also true. Competition among global regulatory bodies may hamper or delay the process of harmonisation of regulatory standards, including those of interest to this volume, i.e. those concerned with transparency, participation and reason giving. A last tension accounted for in the concluding remarks of this volume relates to the loss of creativity and experimentation that might occur when the same standards and practices are massively recycled from different coalitions of civil society actors. Organised networking in civil society may hamper cultural diversity and ultimately produces anonymous standards and undistinguished convergence. Finally, two more areas of concern are discussed in the conclusion of this volume. The first relates to the concrete impact of civil society's networks on the evolution of democratic governance at the supranational level. The second is concerned with the consequences that networks of civil society actors may have on the relationship between supranational regimes of administrative law.

Two last points remain to be clarified. First, this volume does not seek to answer all the challenges and problems regarding civil society coalitions in the global legal order. Rather, it focuses on a very specific aspect of their activity. More research and debate will be needed to complete the puzzle. Second, and relatedly, this volume does not argue that supranational coalitions of civil society currently solve the problem of participatory democracy at the supranational level. The issues contained herein are so new that changes will occur even as this book goes to press or soon thereafter. Nevertheless, it is hoped that this volume will provide some useful insights and clarity on the topic of globalisation of administrative governance as well as on the democratic potentials possessed by coalitions of civil society and that it will help to reframe ongoing debates on this fascinating topic.

Contents

About the Author

Gianluca Sgueo, PhD administrative Law (University of Lecce, Italy), LLM in European Public Law (European Public Law Academy, Greece) is Professor in *Media, Activism & Democracy* at the New York University, Florence, and post-doc researcher in *Democracy and Globalization* at the Centre for Social Studies of the University of Coimbra. He is also Department Director (Area "Institutions") at I-Com, the Institute for Competitiveness, Italy, and policy analyst at the European Parliamentary Research Service, Brussels.

Abbreviations

AB	Appellate Body
ADB	Asian Development Bank
ALNAP	Active Learning Network for Accountability and Performance in Humanitarian Action
ALTER-EU	Alliance for Lobbying Transparency and Ethics Regulation
ATM	Alternative Trade Mandate
BINGO	Business-friendly international non-governmental organisation
BONGO	Business-organised non-governmental organisation
CAN	Climate Action Network
CCUPU	Consultative Committee of Universal Postal Union
CERES	Coalition for Environmentally Responsible Economies
CINGO	Conference of International Non-Governmental Organisations
CITES	Convention on International Trade in Endangered Species of Wild Fauna and Flora
CPDE	Civil society organisation partnership for development effectiveness
COE	Council of Europe
CONGO	Conference of NGOs in Consultative Relationships with the United Nations
CSO	Civil society organisation
EAL	European administrative law
EAS	European administrative space
ECB	European Central Bank
ECHR	European Court of Human Rights
ECJ	European Court of Justice
ECOSOC	United Nations Economic and Social Council
EEB	European Environmental Bureau
EFSA	European Food Safety Authority
EPHA	European Public Health Alliance
EPLO	European Peacebuilding Liaison Office
EU	European Union

EUEB	European Union Eco-Labelling Board
GAL	Global administrative law
GAP	Global Accountability Project
GATT	General Agreement on Tariffs and Trade
GCAP	Global Call to Action Against Poverty
GCS	Global civil society
GDP	Gross domestic product
GONGO	Government-organised non-governmental organisation
GRID	Global reflexive interactive democracy
HAP	Humanitarian Accountability Project
HRDN	Human Rights and Democracy Network
IC	Interlocutory coalitions
ICJ	International Court of Justice
IFC	International Finance Corporation
ICSID	International Centre for Settlement of Investment Disputes
ILO	International Labour Organisation
IMF	International Monetary Fund
INGO	International non-governmental organisations
IO	International organisation
IP	Inspection Panel
IPCC	Intergovernmental Panel on Climate Change
ISO	International Organization for Standardization
ITLOS	International Tribunal of the Law of the Sea
JTR	Joint transparency register
LSE	London School of Economics
MB	Management board
MOP	Meeting of the parties
NATO	North Atlantic Treaty Organisation
NFPO	Not for profit organisation
NGO	Non-governmental organisation
NNGO	Northern NGO
OECD	Organisation for Economic Co-operation and Development
OECD DAC	Organisation for Economic Co-operation and Development Development Assistance Committee
OMC	Open method of coordination
PBS	Public Broadcasting Service
PPP	Public-private partnership
QUANGO	Quasi-autonomous non-governmental organisation
RINGO	Religious international non-governmental organisations
SIGMA	Support for Improvement in Governance and Management in Central and Eastern Europe
SM	Social movement
SMO	Social movement organisation
SNGO	Southern NGO
TNC	Transnational corporation

TNGO	Transnational NGOs
TSMO	Transnational social movement organisation
UN	United Nations
UNCAC	United Nations Convention against Corruption
UNCLOS	United Nations Convention on the Law of the Sea
UNECE	United Nations Economic Commission for Europe
UPU	Universal Postal Union
US	United States
YWCA	Young Women Christian Association
WHO	World Health Organization
WIPO	World Intellectual Property Organization
WB	World Bank
WBG	World Bank Group
WTN	World Third Network
WTO	World Trade Organization

Chapter 1
A Framework for Interactions Between National, European and Global Administrative Systems of Law

1.1 Civil Society Networks and Supranational Democracy

According to Diogenes Laertius and Athénaios Naukratios, the Greek Ktesibios was one of the most prolific inventors of his times. Known as the "father of pneumatics", Ktesibios invented the clepsydra and the hydraulis, the precursor of the modern water pipe. Also attributed to Ktesibios was the siphon,[1] a device enabling liquids to drain from a reservoir through a higher point, the flow being driven only by the difference in hydrostatic pressure thus eliminating the need for pumping. Throughout history, siphons have been used as weapons as well as in agriculture and industry.

In March 2014, almost twenty-three centuries after Ktesibios, the Alliance for Lobbying Transparency and Ethics Regulation (ALTER–EU), a Brussels-based organization of civil society actors, petitioned future members of the European Parliament to "stand-up for citizens and democracy against the excessive lobbying influence of banks and big business". Of the 1100 candidates that signed the petition, 165 were elected. They declared their commitment to cooperating with ALTER in tackling the problems of corporate lobbying and to promoting a European parliament that operates in the public interest with strong ethics and transparency rules. The ALTER case is not unique. Since 1978 approximately 1000 legislators in 139 elected parliaments around the globe have joined Parliamentarians for Global Actions, a non-profit, non-partisan international network aimed at promoting peace, democracy, the rule of law, human rights, gender equality and population issues by informing, convening, and mobilizing parliamentarians to realize these goals.

Halfway across the world, another supranational institution, the Asian Development Bank (ADB), has committed to promote economic and social progress in the Asia-Pacific region. The governing board of the Bank is not elected, nor does it have a direct mandate to represent citizens. Yet, it has decided to operate within a

[1] See Heron of Alexandria, *Pneumatica*, ca 50 AD.

G. Sgueo, *Beyond Networks - Interlocutory Coalitions, the European and Global Legal Orders*, Studies in European Economic Law and Regulation 8,
DOI 10.1007/978-3-319-28875-8_1

framework of informal agreements with civil society organizations and community groups. Under Strategy 2020, ADB's partnerships with nongovernment organizations (NGOs), community-based organizations, labour unions, and foundations have become even more central to the planning, financing, and implementing of ADB operations. The ADB reports that, in 2010, 81 % of approved loans, grants, and related technical assistance, and 37 % of approved stand-alone technical assistance, included some form of civil society participation. Among the many interlocutors of the ADB is the NGO Forum. The Forum, an alliance of civil society actors, monitors the policies, projects and programs of the Bank. Closely resembling the NGO Forum, i.e. a network of civil society actors operating at a supranational level and devoted to advocacy on given issues, is the Global Academy of Liberal Arts. The first network of this kind, the Academy was born in June 2014 and now includes 16 universities from China, South America, the United States (US), Europe and Australia. As members of the network, these universities are committed to defending liberal arts in higher education. Activities of the network also include joint programme development, comparative research, student exchange, remote teaching, and visiting lecturers.

In concomitance with the abovementioned initiatives, Avaaz and Change.org, probably the most-well known platforms for online petitioning, have been used by million people worldwide. Avaaz is a virtual campaign platform whose claim is to provide a direct way for concerned citizens to make their voices heard while bypassing issue-specific organizations. Thus far, Avaaz has been the electronic conduit for more than 30 million members and 50 million actions since 2007. Change.org stated mission is to "empower people everywhere to create the change they want to see". Not surprisingly, it is growing at a striking rate. Every month Change.org launches thousands of new campaigns promoted by individuals and not-for-profit organizations, on a wide range of issue, including economic and criminal justice, human rights, the environment, and food sustainability. With more than 170 staff in 18 countries and operating in several languages, including Arabic and Chinese, it is estimated that Change.org has mobilized an average of 500 petitions per day since its creation, in 2007.

At this point, readers may be wondering what a NGOs petition to European Parliament candidates has in common with an international development bank collaborating with an Asian-led coalition of NGOs; not to mention 1100 parliamentarians, 16 universities across the globe and millions people connecting to online-petitioning websites. There may also be questions regarding their relationship with Ktesibios' siphon. The immediate, and predictable, response is simple: nothing at all. Admittedly, geographical, topical and structural variations of the events are manifest. However, readers may be relieved to discover at least three common elements between these parties.

First is the fact that all the individuals, organizations and institutions mentioned above engage in activities held "upon an international plane", to use the celebrated words of the International Court of Justice (ICJ) in the *Reparations for Injuries* Opinion. Not that the domestic sphere is negligible. On the contrary, states remain predominant actors of all the described events. But the focus of these events, at least in their essential aspects, crosses national borders and can be found at the supranational level. The current world is driven by more global policy making, in more varied form, writes Mark Marzower (2013), and this provides the neutral framework to the interactions of diverse societies, adds Henry Kissinger (2014). "Willingly or unwillingly" – reminds Eyal Benvenisti (2014) – "sovereigns surrender their monopoly on regulatory power to actors whose reach defies political boundaries". This, after all, reflects the complexity of the era we are currently living in. An era in which nation-states are no longer the sole or dominant players, and almost any contemporary phenomenon of importance transcends some kind of border. When the United Nations (UN) was formed, some 70 years ago, there were only 51 states, few international organizations and a world population of around two billion people. Today there are almost seven billion people, nearly 200 states and an estimated 60,000 international organizations. Multilateralism is perceived as a necessity by states: treaties and conventions are often too slow for immediate issues. Cooperation at the supranational level is thus needed to reach effectively a multitude of goals, including the fight to global warming and terrorism, the liberalization of economy, the integration of communication, and the standardization of goods and services.

Secondly, the abovementioned cases involve a public body partnering with a private body. While distinct analytically, civil society is never wholly autonomous or completely separate from domestic or supranational public powers. Nor are public powers insensitive or invulnerable to the actions of non-state actors.[2] "No governor governs [*the globe*] alone", notes Deborah Avant (2010). Or, as Robert Keohane and Joseph Nye (1977) argued almost 40 years ago, in world politics public and private powers are necessarily interdependent. "Growing interdependence" is also the descriptive label used by Charles Kegley and Eugene Wittkopf (1995), and further developed by Jhon Ruggie (2004). Visions diverge for how the interdependence public-private in the global landscape has to be interpreted. Some view a constitutional order in progress,[3] and envisage a "subjectivation" of supranational law (i.e. the progressive extension of rights and participatory opportunities to private actors in the global arena).[4] Other scholars see further fragmentation taking hold.[5] However, agreement exists upon the fact that such alliances, or public-private partnerships – PPPs, multi-stakeholder initiatives or even, more generally, networks – entails a power shift, a role shift and a responsibility shift. The "power shift" leads towards more synergetic relationships between public and private actors. The "role shift" implies that non-state actors perform regulatory functions that were tradition-

---

[2] For a critique on the distinction between the concepts of public and private in global governance See S.S. Eriksen, O.J. Sending, "There is no global public: the idea of the public and the legitimation of governance" (2013) 5 *International Theory* 213.

[3] See, for instance, N. Krisch, *Beyond Constitutionalism: The Pluralist Structure of Postnational Law* (Oxford, Oxford Constitutional Theory, 2010).

[4] See M.P. Maduro, *We the Court: The European Court of Justice and the European Constitution* (Oxford, Hart Publishing, 1998).

[5] See, for instance, T. Isikel, "Global Legal Pluralism as Fact and Norm" (2013) 2 *Global Constitutionalism* 160.

ally in the responsibility of states. Hence, by assumption the role shift goes along with a "responsibility shift" (with consequences on the legitimate use of authority). PPPs may vary in nature and scopes. Some contain measures that are legally binding upon their members; others are based on mutual trust and recognition. Further, depending on the case, civil society actors involved in such networks may strategize, lobby, advocate, complain, monitor and collaborate; whereas public powers may negotiate, give financial and/or logistic support and, at times, resist stakeholders' pressure. In any case, PPPs overcome the classic divide between state regulation, on the one hand, and self-regulation, on the other hand, and encourage the birth of hybrid forms of co-regulation. They capture the crucial changes that the exercise of political authority is experiencing in the global arena.

A third common feature of the events described above relates specifically to the civil society, and pertains again to networks. Bearing in mind the differences in terms of volume, length, legal nature and aims, all the initiatives presented are indicative of the presence of an organized network of civil society actors, where "organized" stands chiefly for an administrative, hierarchical structure to support the network's members, and foster its commitment to a set of common values. Such networked civil society seems to show a reverse trend to that commonly associated with representative democracy, and exemplified by drops in voter turnouts, waning party membership, and citizens' alarmingly low levels of trust and satisfaction in politics. As Rodney Hall and Thomas Biersteker (2002) note in the introduction to their edited volume on the emergence of private authority in global governance, civil society actors "appear to have taken on authoritative roles and functions in the international systems". Their connections, notes Jan Scholte (2014), are experiencing historically unprecedented quantities, scopes, frequencies, velocities, intensities and impacts. From the "virtual web" of citizens that tie together to support a cause through an online-petitioning platform, passing through an informal alliance of universities, up to more formalized coalitions of non-State actors operating in Europe and Asia, an associative spirit puts the basis for cooperation that, albeit apparently, may offset the much debated decline in representative democracy.

It is these three elements, i.e. the supranational legal sphere, the public-private liaison, and civil society actors coalescing into networks, that the present volume aims to explore. This book regards the emergence of formalized networks of civil society actors as a momentous phenomenon currently occurring at the supranational level. Let there be no mistake: networks are nothing new. There are plenty of examples of networks spanning continents and millennia. These include the 1888–1928 international suffrage movements to secure voting rights to women, or the 1833–1865 Anglo-American campaign to end slavery in the US. But what is novel about the networks of our age is that they, and the effects they produce, are increasingly global in nature. Among the many effects produced by the rise of globalised civil society networks, one effect is considered by this book as particularly important. This is the capacity of networks to host deliberative dialogues amongst large groups of individuals and institutions, improving standard consultation and engagement practices at work in their counterparts: the supranational institutions. While Margaret Keck and Kathryn Sikkink (1998) already approached this topic in 1998 (following on 1996 Manuel Castells' conceptualisation of a "network society") in a seminal research on cross-border activism, this book is distinguished from Keck and Sikkink in two important respects. First, this book narrows the focus of civil society's networks, conceptually divorcing them from networks of different nature (e.g. those in which states, social movements, or other public actors are also included). In so doing, this book describes the interactions between civil society actors and supranational regulators not in terms of a network (as Keck and Sikkink did in 1998, followed by Anne-Marie Slaughter in 2004) but in terms of a partnership. This brings us to a second, crucial, difference. This book specifically attempts to explain how civil society networks drive the development of principles of democratic value at the supranational level, which indeed is a simplification of a much more complex reality – i.e. the relations between civil society associations and democracy, masterfully described by Archon Fung and Mark Warren.[6]

Two legal regimes are particularly relevant: the European and the global ones (which in effect include a number of supranational legal systems). This is where the siphon metaphor comes into play. For the purpose of the analysis of this book, the European and the supranational legal systems, as well as the various transnational networks of civil society actors, are considered as being distinct normative communities, in accordance to the description offered by Paul Berman (2007). Such normative communities are not independent of each other. They are interdependent – and the interactions between them can be described using the metaphorical posture of the Ktesibios' siphon. As liquids stream mechanically from one point to another due to hydrostatic pressure, so does the "spill-over" of principles, good practices, and policy standards – in a nutshell: methods of administrative governance[7] flows between the European and other supranational regulatory systems. Sandra

[6] Archon Fung describes six paths through which associations sustain democracy, namely: (1) through the intrinsic value of associative life; (2) through fostering civic virtues and teaching political skills; (3) through offering resistance to power and checking governments; (4) through improving the quality and equality of representation; (5) through facilitating public deliberation; (6) and, finally, through creating opportunities for citizens and groups to participate directly in governance. For further details See A. Fung, "Associations and Democracy: Between Theories, Hopes, and Realities" (2003) 29 *Annual Review of Sociology* 515. Mark Warren distinguishes the functions of association into three broad categories: the developmental effects they may have on individuals; their role as medium for broad political discourse; and the institutional effects of their active presence in a democracy. See M.E. Warren, *Democracy and Association* (Princeton, Princeton University Press, 2001).

[7] A definition used in this volume in the specific sense of governance without governmental involvement. This includes all forms of cooperative relationship between public and private bodies to fulfil a policy function. See E.O. Czempiel, J. Rosenau, *Governance Without Government: Order and Change in World Politics* (Cambridge, Cambridge University Press, 1992). Rosenau and Czempiel's thinking of the concept of global governance denotes all types of control in transnational politics at all levels of social interaction. On governance See also K. Dingwerth, P. Pattberg, "Global Governance as a Perspective on World Politics" (2006) 12 *Global Governance* 189; D. Held, M. Koenig-Archibugi, *Taming Globalization: Frontiers of Governance* (Oxford, Polity Press, 2003); D. Held, A. McGrew (eds.), *Governing Globalization* (Cambridge, Polity Press, 2002); A. Heritier (ed.), *Common Goods: Reinventing European and International Governance* (Lanham, Rowman & Littlefield Publishers, 2002); P. Moreau Defarges, *La gouvernance* (Paris, Presses Universitaires de France, 2003); P. Lascoumes, P. Le Galès, *Sociologie de l'action publique* (Paris, Armand Colin, 2009).

Lavenex and Frank Schimmelfennig labelled as the "governance" model of democracy promotion the transfer of democratic principles related to accountability, transparency and participation in the context of sectorial cooperation arrangements between the European Union (EU) and domestic administrative actors. They identify the notion of "democratic governance" at the level of the principles that guide administrative rules and practices in the conduct of public policy. Hence, they focus less on specific democratic institutions such as elections or parliaments, and more on the principles underlying democracy that are applicable to all situations in which collectively building decisions are taken. This book attempts to supplement this perspective by transposing this model of democracy promotion from the European domain to the global arena. The spill over of methods of democratic governance, proposed in this book, is primarily driven by factors of historical, political, and legal significance. Yet these factors, it will be also argued, do not cover the spectrum of the relevant phenomena that emanate from the grey zone between European and supranational, or global, law. To obtain a more representative picture of the spill over of methods of administrative governance across the European and the global arenas, the above-mentioned networks of civil society actors, and the influence they exert on the scope and dictates of supranational legal systems, must be addressed.

The following sections will illustrate the historical, political and legal factors that drive the interactions between the European legal order and other supranational systems of norms. The first part of this chapter will address the role of civil society in the supranational legal arena, when relevant to the discourse. From Sect. 1.6 onward, the role of civil society will be illustrated in more detail. The chapter will conclude by detailing the structure and argument contained within this book.

1.2 The European Administrative Space

A historical perspective may suggest that the shift of the EU from a single integrated market towards a complex legal system, composed of a plurality of actors on different levels that interact in order to achieve common objectives, has contributed to the formation of an extensive body of administrative law. This is the "European administrative space" (EAS), to use Martin Shapiro's terminology (2001).[8] Once a

[8] See also J.P. Olsen, "Towards a European Administrative Space?" (2003) 10 *Journal of European Public Policy* 506; H.C.H. Hofmann, "Mapping the European Administrative Space" 31 *West European Politics* 662; E.G. Heidbreder, "Structuring the European Administrative Space: Policy Instruments of Multi-Level Administration" (2011) 18 *Journal of European Public Policy* 709. More generally on European administrative law See S. Cassese, "European Administrative Proceedings" (2004–2005) 68 *Law & Contemporary Problems* 21; M.P. Chiti, "Forms of European Administrative Action" (2004) 68 *Law and Contemporary Problems*, 37; F. Bignami, "Creating European Rights: National Values and Supranational Interests"(2004–2005) 11 *Columbia Journal of European Law* 241. For more general discourse on the evolution of modern administrative law See M. Loughlin, *The Idea of Public Law* (Oxford, Oxford University Press, 2003). Loughlin's assumption is that the causes of the extension of the interests of government both for the welfare

quickly glossed-over section in European law textbooks – for almost 30 years after the Treaty of Rome the common wisdom was that European administrative law did not exist – the EAS is nowadays at the centre of a vigorous academic debate. The EAS is the area in which increasingly integrated administrations jointly exercise powers delegated to the EU in a system of shared sovereignty. European administrations allocated with new powers and duties are subjected to elaborate statutory codes of procedure. The EAS – a "new form of synarchy", in the words of Dimitris Chryssochoou (2009)[9] – arises as a consequence of a transition from the classical model of interstate relations to a system of shared rules operating within the structural logic of co-governance. Interestingly, a body of principles and rules originally conceived to govern the action of the EU public powers and the activity of the national administrations operating as decentralized EU agencies, has gradually established a policy system made up of national, European and mixed authorities that are jointly responsible for the administrative implementation of EU rules.

In the EAS, the role of states has been, and continues to be, transformed, i.e. the distinction between the inner sphere of the Member States and its outer space has become less prominent – even fuzzy at times – and the exercise of public law deterritorialized. The function as well as the extent of the power that European Member States exercise is integrating and, at the same time, lengthening, the EAS. These transformations notwithstanding, the EAS relies on a set of principles and legal standards scattered throughout a variety of sources of EU law and the legal systems of Member States. These include transparency, public liability, the granting of adequate procedural rights to the parties involved, and judicial review. In primary law, for instance, Article 41 of the Charter of fundamental Rights of the EU establishes the right to fair and impartial administration. At the level of secondary law, a variety of binding and nonbinding instruments regulate administrative procedures. Exemplary is Regulation No. 1/2003 which regulates the Commission's procedures on competition law. The jurisprudence of the European court of Justice (ECJ) also established several principles of good administration, including the right to a hearing, and the duty of transparency.

---

of the individual citizen and for the corporate well being of the nation is inextricably bound with what he calls the "*rise of the masses*". In Loughlin's opinion, the powers of modern governments impact not only on the individual citizen but also on business organizations of every type. Thus the concern of government extends not only to the welfare of the individual but also to the performance of the economy and prosperity of the nation. As a further consequence, he observes that an extensive body of administrative law has grown rapidly.

[9] See also L. Hooghe, G. Marks, *Multi-level governance and European integration* (Oxford, Rowman & Littlefield Publishers, 2001); A. Littoz-Monnet, "Dynamic Multi-Level Governance – Bringing the Study of Multi-Level Interactions into the Theorising of European Integration" (2010) 14 *European Integration Online Papers* (*EIoP*) article 14, available at www.eiop.or.at/eiop/texte/2010-001a.htm.

1.3 Global Administrative Law

Over the last 20 years, principles similar to those elaborated by the EAS have been acknowledged in the global arena by a number of International Organisations (IOs) to whom sovereign decision-making authority has been relocated from states.[10] The identification and description of these principles has become known as "global administrative law" (GAL). Already in the early 1980s political scientists as Stephen Krasner (1983) started to speak of "international regimes" to address the convergence of principles, norms, rules and procedures in given areas of international relations. Legal scholarship has borrowed the concept of international regimes, and adapted it to the study of global institutions that hold regulatory powers. Hence the choice of global, rather than international, is not a matter of mere terminology. In an essay that lays the foundations of GAL, Sabino Cassese (2009) reflects on the difference between international and global law. Only the latter, warns Cassese, captures the identity of a world as an interconnected whole.[11] Benedict Kingsbury, Nico Krisch and Richard Stewart (2005) describe GAL as the whole array of "mechanisms, principles, practices, and supporting social understandings that promote or otherwise affect the accountability of global administrative bodies, in particular by ensuring they meet adequate standards of transparency, participation, reasoned decision, and legality, and by providing effective review of the rules and decision they make".[12] As the Global Administrative Law Project at New York University

[10] This volume sets on a comprehensive definition of International Organisations that includes all types of Organisations (unless otherwise indicated, as in the case of public-private partnerships). For an exhaustive taxonomy of the diverse types of organisations in the domain of global governance See E. Benvenisti, *The Law of Global Governance*, see text at section 1, text n 22 and n 96, chapter 4 n 6 and n 33; P.L. Lindseth, "Supranational Organisations" in I. Hurd, I. Johnstone, J. Katz Cogan (eds.), *Oxford Handbook of International Organisations* (Oxford, Oxford University Press, 2015).

[11] See also S. Cassese, "Relations between International Organizations and National Administrations", in *IISA*, Proceedings, XIXth International Congress of Administrative Sciences, Kluwer 1983. On the foundations of GAL See S. Battini, "L'impatto della globalizzazione sulla pubblica amministrazione e sul diritto amministrativo: quattro percorsi" (2006) *Giornale di diritto amministrativo* 341; S. Benhabib, *Another Cosmopolitanism*: *Hospitality*, *Sovereignity*, *and Democratic Iterations* (Oxford, Oxford University Press, 2006). Benhabib refers to the distinction between international and cosmopolitan norms of justice. The former emerge through treaty obligations to which states and their representatives are signatories. Cosmopolitan norms of justice accrue to individuals as moral and legal persons in a worldwide society.

[12] On Global administrative law See also S. Cassese et al. (eds.), *Global Administrative Law. Cases and Materials* (New York, IRPA – Iilj 2008); S. Cassese, "The Globalization of Law" (2005) *37 New York University Journal of International Law and Politics* 973; S. Battini, *Amministrazioni senza Stato* (Milano 2003); G. Della Cananea, "Beyond the State: The Europeanization and Globalization of Procedural Administrative Law" (2003) 9 *European Public Law* 563; A.C. Aman, "Administrative Law in a Global Era" (2002) 54 *Administrative Law Review* 409, and "Globalization, Democracy, and the Need for a New Administrative Law" (2003) 49 *UCLA Law Review* 1687; G. Dimitropoulos, "Towards a Typology of Administrative Levels and functions in the Global Legal Order" (2011) 23 *European Review of Public Law* 433.

explains,[13] global regulation encompasses a wide range of programs and activities, including development, environmental protection, health and safety, and political, civil, and social rights. Thus, it is safe to say that transparency in rule making; due process in decisions affecting private parties; review mechanisms to ensure legality and the promotion of accountability of IOs are among the key elements of GAL.

It is worth noting that although GAL remains the most frequently used definition (it appears 1077 and 8000 times on Hein Online and Google Scholar, respectively), given its broad nature, other definitions have been coined. A few authors use the definition of global administrative space to describe the space in which administrative functions occur during interplays between officials and institutions on different levels.[14] According to Edith Brown Weiss (2010), this space is kaleidoscopic in character, in that global regulators operating in the same field are linked in complex patterns of competition and cooperation. Sabino Cassese (2003) refers to global administrative space as global legal space or a global legal system. Others have preferred to settle on the definition of "transnational administrative law". From the perspective of Martin Shapiro (2005), transnational administrative law builds on five blocks. First is regulation: a "blossoming regulation moving from parallel national development to transnational arenas". The second – and main – funding block of transnational administrative law is the tension between the democratic control of public policy, including regulatory policy, and the regulation by experts, or technocracy. The European comitology process yields another major building block for imagining transnational administrative law. The fourth-building block consists of the deliberative methods of policy-making (where deliberation is conceived as a strategy used to reach consensus by transcending the traditional interest aggregation model). Ultimately, the fifth building block to transnational administrative law is the replacement of command-and-control regulatory type with an array of alternatives (e.g. "open methods of coordination", "negotiated rulemaking", "benchmarking", "Nudging, Behaviourally informed regulation" and "soft law"). Similar to the idea of GAL is the concept of *cosmocracy* ideated by John Keane (2005).[15] Keane's cosmocracy describes a conglomeration of interlocking and overlapping sub-state, state and suprastate institutions and multi-dimensional processes that interact, and have political and social effects, on a global scale. Differently from Keane, Jonathan Charney's (1993) attempt to theorize a *universal international law* does not take into account actors different from states. Universal international law, in Charney's opinion, would be binding upon states without their consent, not upon entities other than states. GAL has also been described in terms of a mode of governance. As Chap. 2 will explain in greater detail, Grainne De Burca et al. (2013) envisioned GAL as reflecting a broadly shared concern to protect the values of the rule of law

---

[13] See generally www.iilj.org/gal.

[14] See especially N. Krisch, B. Kingsbury, "Introduction: Global Governance and Global Administrative Law in the International Legal Order" (2006) 17 *European Journal of International Law* 13.

[15] On cosmopolitanism, also S. Benhabib *Another Cosmopolitan*, see text n 11.

associated with the democratic nation state. They propose GAL as a bridge between more traditional modes of pluralist global governance and novel ones.

Beyond the various terminologies used to describe GAL, of relevance to the scope of this book is the intensification and increase in material interactions between the EAS and GAL resulting from the exposure to, and overlap between their principles. In their pioneering research on the connections between EAS and GAL Edoardo Chiti and Bernardo Mattarella (2012) admit that the picture is still fragmented. To put it succinctly, Chiti and Mattarella explain that in some areas EU law and global law complement, coordinate and implement each other, while in other areas they ignore or even conflict with each other. Yet, Chiti and Mattarella conclude by defining the interactions between EAS and GAL crucial to understanding present and future patterns of law.

1.4 A Political Perspective: European Rules with Global Significance

Let us move to the political factors that drive the interactions between the EU – a "municipal order of transnational dimensions", as suggested by Advocate General Maduro in the *Kadi* dispute[16] – and other supranational systems of norms. By the 1990s, the European Community had already begun to conclude major international treaties, notably the Land Mines Treaty and the Rome Statute establishing an International Criminal Court. Under contemporary conditions, the array of contractual relations and political dialogues between the EU and its supranational partners are wide in scope. They range from functionally specific terms that address specialized transnational goals, to broad alliances that address general common needs, with many variants in between. In 2013, for instance, the EU dedicated 6.8 billion euros to the goal of strengthening its role in the world. It was at the forefront of the international response to all major humanitarian crises, both natural and made-man (e.g. the armed conflicts in Syria, the Central African Republic and South Sudan, as well as natural disasters as the Philippines' Haiyan Typhoon). During the period from January 2010 to October 2014 the EU high representative for foreign affairs and security policy Catherine Ashton adopted 1022 declarations that referred to specific countries (four declarations a week, on average).[17]

[16] See judgements n. C-402/05 P and C-415/05 P, par. 321. For commentary on this case See J. D'Aspremont, F. Dopagne, "Kadi: The ECJ's Reminder of the Elementary Divide between Legal Orders" (2008) *International Organization Law Review* 1, available at SSRN: www.ssrn.com/abstract=1341982; G. De Burca, "The European Court of Justice and the International Legal Order after *Kadi*" *Jean Monnet* Working Paper 01/09, available at www.jeanmonnetprogram.org.

[17] See S. Lehne, I. Tseminidou, *Where in the world is the EU*? (Brussels, Carnegie Europe, 2015) available here: www.carnegieeurope.eu/2015/04/28/where-in-world-is-eu/i7vr.

The key role of the EU in a number of international *fora* has developed accordingly.[18] To date, the EU is involved in the activities of various global organisations as a full member – as in the cases of the World Trade Organisation (WTO),[19] the Food and Agricultural Organisation of the UN, or the European Bank for Reconstruction and Development –, in an observer status, or a combination thereof – as in the cases of the World Bank (WB), the International Monetary Fund (IMF), the Organization for Economic Co-Operation and Development (OECD), the Organization for Petroleum Exporting Countries and the North Atlantic Treaty Organization, and the Meeting of Parties of the Aarhus Convention.[20] Even when the EU is not a contracting party to a relevant international agreement, its Member States' discretion is constrained by the duty to put their policies in conformity with their obligations as EU members.[21] During the years between 1992 and 2010, for instance, the EU represented the common positions of its Member States in 56 % and 67 % of the conventions and the recommendations adopted, respectively. Not to mention the cases in which participation in the global system does not affect the EU as a whole, but its constituent bodies. Exemplary is the case of the European Central Bank (ECB). The ECB enjoys permanent observer status at the IMF, it is member and shareholder of the Bank for International Settlements, takes part in a number of activities of the OECD, and participates in the G20 Finance Ministers Meetings. Increasingly, the EU imposes its standards to foreign activities with only minor impact on European interests. Examples include the data protection standards and the carbon emissions scheme, applied to third countries and non-EU carriers, respectively.[22] In the field of cyber security, the EU Cyber Security Strategy promotes the engagement with key partners such as India, China and Japan, and close cooperation with the UN, the North Atlantic Treaty Organisation (NATO), the Council of Europe (COE), the Organisation for Security and Cooperation in

---

[18] A full acknowledgement of the EU' participation in global organisations and processes is provided in G. Vesperini, Europe and global law, in C. Cassese (ed.), *Research Handbook on Global Administrative Law* (Cheltenham, Edward Elgar Publishing, 2016).

[19] More specifically on the role of the EU in the WTO and the Codex Alimentarius Commission (with regard to the regulation of food safety matters) See A. Battaglia, "Food Safety: Between European and Global Administration" (2006) 6 *Global Jurist Advances* article 8.

[20] On the relationship between the Aarhus Convention and European law See L. Collins, "Are We There Yet? The Right to Environment in International and European Law" (2007) 2 *The McGill International Journal of Sustainable Development Law and Policy* 119; K. Getliffe, "Proceduralisation and the Aarhus Convention. Does increased participation in the decision-making process lead to more effective EU environmental law?" (2002) 4 *EU Environmental Law Review* 101.

[21] For general discourse on EU as a cosmopolitan democracy and its relationship with other IOs See E.O. Eriksen, "The EU: A Cosmopolitan Vanguard?" (2009) 9 *Global Jurist Advances* article 6. On the concept of "legal transplant" understood as the inclusion of a part of a legal system within another legal system, See A. Watson, *Society and Legal Change* (Edinburgh, Scottish Academic Press, 1977).

[22] See E. Benvenisti, *The Law of Global Governance*, see text at section 1, text n 10 and n 96 and chapter 4 n 6 and n 33, at 73.

Europe (OSCE), the Association of South East Asian Nation (ASEAN), and the Organisation of American States.[23]

This array of relations between the EU and its supranational partners has three major consequences. First is the globalization of certain European rules, which will be discussed shortly. Second, to be investigated in Sect. 1.4.1, are the incentives for EU administration to act in compliance with global rules. The third effect involves EAS, GAL and domestic politics (and it will be analysed in Sect. 1.4.2).

The increase in EU leverage on the world stage is the first effect to be assessed. As anticipated, this has determined the body of principles and rules, which were originally developed to underpin the action of the European public authorities and the national administrations operating as decentralized community agencies, to spread beyond the borders of Europe and to acquire global significance. The EU has championed itself as an agent of democracy promotion since the early 1990s. In the Treaty of Maastricht the EU declared the development and consolidation of democracy as a goal of development cooperation.[24] To this end, the EU established in 2006 the European Instrument for Democracy and Human Rights – a funding programme to strengthen the rule of law and democratic reforms in countries outside the EU. With a financial envelope of over 1.3 million Euros for the period 2014–2020, the programme provides assistance to organisations of civil society, and does not require the consent of national authorities.[25] The principle of democracy was also introduced in all EU external trade and aid agreements. It is no coincidence that a number of principles of good administration are set out in the European Charter of Fundamental Rights as well as in several joint agreements between the EU and other IOs. The 2009 EU/WB framework agreement, for instance, includes provisions on visibility and participation (Article 8), and disclosure of information (Article 10). It also provides rules for consultations of its implementation (Article 11). Further, the agreement states that the affected parties shall endeavour to settle any dispute or complaint amicably (Article 14). In default of amicable settlement, rules for arbitration are provided. Co-financing activities are also particularly instructive. In these kinds of activities the Commission may decide to entrust the implementation of external action to an international organization. The rules on the procedures to be used by the entity to which implementation tasks have been delegated are defined in specific provisions through which the Commission commits to ensure that its partners would apply a minimum set of governance standards. In the Commission staff working documents, SEC (2007) 1519, of 20 November 2007, titled "*The External Dimension of the Single Market Review*", and COM(2006) 629, 24 October 2006, titled "*Commission Legislative and Work Program 2007*", for instance, the Commission mentions the EU as a global rule maker and discusses the

[23] See P. Pawlyak, "Cyber Diplomacy. EU dialogue with third countries" (2015) *European Parliamentary Research Service* available at www.europarl.europa.eu/RegData/etudes/BRIE/2015/564374/EPRS_BRI(2015)564374_EN.pdf.

[24] See art. 130u of the Treaty of Maastricht.

[25] See A. Dobreva, "European Instrument for Democracy and Human Rights" (2015) *European Parliamentary Research Service*.

increasing adoption of EU-inspired regulatory standards across the world. Finally, there are cases in which the export of EU standards is not the outcome of a deliberate policy, but rather it is a mere incidental effect of internal action. In this hypothesis – also known as the "Brussels effect" of EU rules – legal principles of one jurisdiction migrate into another without any imposition from the former, and any will to adopt them from the latter. The Brussels effect has been exemplified in the fields of Antitrust, privacy regulation, health protection, environmental protection and food security.[26]

1.4.1 Incentives for European Administrations to Act in Compliance with Global Law

The second major consequence resulting from the interactions between the EU and other supranational regulators consists of the shared efforts in setting procedures and normative standards for regulatory decision-making. These efforts have created incentives for European administrations (subject to European law) to act in compliance with principles of global significance. Evidence of such matters is provided in official documents and declarations. In its 2002 Annual Report, the WTO affirmed that regional systems of governance are complementary components and steps towards global governance. A few years before, in 1996, the former UN Secretary General Boutros-Ghali had declared that regional organizations and their legal systems might act as surrogates of the UN.[27] Between 2010 and 2014 the EU imposed to 30 states (16 % of those states were members of the UN) some kind of sanction, often decided in accordance with the UN.[28]

Samantha Besson (2009) suggests that the articulation between the international (or global) and the European legal orders is structured in three dimensions. The first articulation is the most evident: it concerns the validity of international norms

---

[26] See, for instance, A. Bradford, "The Brussels Effect" (2012) 107:1 *Northwestern University Law Review* 1.

[27] On the relationship between international law and European law conceptualized as both a constraint for the EU institutions and as an instrument for the advancement of European integration See B. De Witte, "International Law as a Tool for the European Union" (2009) 5 *European Constitutional Law Review* 265. See also M. Koskenniemi (ed.), *International Law Aspects of the European Union* (The Hague, Kluwer Law International, 1998); J.C. Gautron, L. Grard (eds.), *Droit international et droit communautaire, perspectives actuelles* (Paris, Pedone, 2000); A. Peters, "The Position of International Law within the European community Legal Order" (1997) 40 *German Yearbook of International Law*; E. De Smijter, "The European Union as an Actor under International Law" (1999) 19 *Yearbook of European Law*. On the relationship between global governance and regional governance See A.D. Ba, "Contested Spaces. The Politics od Regional and Global Governance", in A.D. Ba, M.J. Hoffmann, *Contending Perspectives on Global Governance. Coherence, Contestation and World Order* (London, New York, Routledge, 2005) 190.

[28] Data available at S. Lehne, I. Tseminidou, *Where in the world is the EU* ? see text n 17 and chapter 2 n 18.

within the EU legal order. This may be granted immediately or after mediation, through incorporation or transformation of international legal norms into EU law. The second dimension regards the rank of international law norms within the EU legal order. As a general principle, explains Besson, international law norms are ranked between EU primary law and general principles of EU law. The third dimension consists of the effect of international law norms within the EU legal order. These former are generally granted a direct effect into the latter. To assume that European administrations act in compliance with principles of global significance only because of subjection to other IOs would be a misconception, though. Incentives to adapt to global governance are also a concrete possibility, as noted by Jan Wouters et al. (2008). The contrary is also possible. Recent research, for instance, has demonstrated that EU institutions show different levels of sensitivity towards WTO compliance and external trade effects.[29]

1.4.2 European Administrative Law, Global Administrative Law, and Domestic Politics

The administrative rules shared between the European and the international level also influence domestic politics. Supranational regimes develop administrative law standards and mechanisms to which national administrations must conform in order to assure their compliance and accountability to the international regime. Obviously, this is not an entirely new phenomenon. Since time immemorial, states have been obliged to observe rules originating outside their domain. However, note Bob Reinalda and Bertjan Veerbek (2004), the increased legalization of international relations has made it more difficult for States, and other international actors, to ignore the policies of IOs such as the EU, the WTO or the WB, to name but a few.

Indeed, adaptation from domestic legal systems to supranational legal rules may be undertaken in different ways – a fascinating topic that has been widely discussed in academia – although is beyond the scope of the present volume. This will therefore only be rapidly acknowledged in the discussion that follows. Supranational norms can apply directly to individuals (e.g. through sanctions, or through empowering them with the right to turn to extra-state authorities to ascertain the compliance of their state to obligations established by international sources) especially when administrative regulatory tasks once deemed to pertain to the national level are assumed by supranational entities (e.g. The World Health Organization's – WHO periodic assessment of global health risks and the consequent issue of warnings). In what Kingsbury, Krisch and Stewart call "distributed administration", domestic regulatory agencies act as part of the global administrative space. This is

[29] See e.g. T. Perisin, "EU Regulatory Policy and World Trade" (2015) 11 *European Constitutional Law Review* 99 .

to say that they make decisions on issues of foreign or global concern.[30] Supranational regulators may also press for horizontal cooperation among states. As a consequence, regulatory acts of one state gain validity in another state. This is, *inter alia*, the case of the WTO and the EU. In the latter case, while this is undoubtedly true with EU Member States, and with countries aspiring to become EU members, it is also true in the case of states that are neither members of the EU nor they are aspiring to become members, and still are convinced of the legitimacy and appropriateness of EU rules.[31] Another type of infusion of supranational regulations into domestic norms coincides with hybrid public-private bodies in which private and governmental actors are present (e.g. the Internet Corporation for Assigned Names and Numbers).

Lastly, and this also serves to introduce the topic of the next section, domestic norms can be modified by the jurisprudence of the supranational judiciary. The Appellate Body (AB) of the WTO, for instance, in the *Shrimps/Turtle* dispute (a case to which this volume will return shortly in this chapter and, again, in Chap. 4) explained that the US, in prescribing laws that have effects on foreign traders, has to provide administrative procedures pursuant to which foreign governments and traders would be able to comment on and challenge the application of such laws before US institutions, either administrative bodies or courts. In substance, the AB required a national government to grant foreign traders and countries a "due process" set of rights. Following the request, the US announced it would revise its procedures and offer foreign governments greater due process rights, including the right to challenge preliminary findings before they become definitive.[32]

1.5 The Cross-Fertilization of European and International Jurisprudence: Judicial Policy-Making

The third crucial element that is driving deep changes in the interactions between the EAS and GAL is closely related to the former two, as both a cause and a consequence. This is the cross-fertilization of the jurisprudence of the handful of courts and arbitration tribunals that currently reside and operate in the international and the European legal spaces. Some 10–15 % of the estimated 2000 global regulatory regimes have courts, tribunals, panels, compliance committees, and inspection or

[30] See B. Kingsbury, N. Krisch, R.B. Stewart, *The Emergence of Global Administrative Law*, see text at section 3, at 21.

[31] See F. Schimmelfennig, "Europeanization beyond Europe" (2015) 10 *Living Reviews in European Governance* 1.

[32] See G. Shaffer, "International Trade-WTO-Quantitative Restrictions_Environmental Protection_ Andangered Species_U.S. Import Ban on Shrimp" (1999) 93 *American Journal of International Law* 513.

assessment panels.[33] Not only are the judicial and quasi-judicial bodies operating at the supranational level becoming more prolific – nearly 90 % of the total output of international courts has been issued over the last two decades[34] – but also they have widely spread their competences, not infrequently outstripping the expectations of the negotiators who had sought to establish them, as the cases of the Appellate Body of the WTO and the International Centre for Settlement of Investment Disputes (ICSID) widely elucidate. During the 46 years of the General Agreement on Tariffs and Trade – GATT – system an average of 12 complaints per year were filed, whereas during the first 8 years of the WTO system over 33 complaints per year were filed in front of the Appellate Body.[35] The ICSID (which is itself a global regulatory regimes, linked with the WB) between 1970 and 1990 registered only 26 cases. In the decade that followed, the number grew to 58. After 2000 ICSID registered 431 cases (209 in the sole year 2014).[36]

Thus, an international legal system populated by a handful of operative courts has rapidly developed into a ramified patchwork where a number of entities, collectively referred to as the "global judiciary" or a "global community of courts", as suggested by Anne-Marie Slaughter (2000, 2003), currently reside, operate and interact. Some scholars have even named the legal regimes constructed and governed by transnational courts, the norms legitimating them and the norms they propound, using the definition of "trans-state legal regimes". They exemplify the idea of trans-national legal regimes by addressing the example of the European Court of Human rights. In their opinion, the Court's regime orders not simply state-to-state relations but multiple patterns of interaction such as those between domestic courts and national political constituencies, as well as those between the EU and individual states.[37] Additional examples come from the environmental arena. No fewer than twelve new non-compliance monitoring bodies have emerged since 1990. Among the most recent are the Kyoto Protocol Compliance System, created in 1997, the 1998 Rotterdam Convention on the Prior Informed Consent Procedure for Certain Hazardous Chemicals and Pesticides in International Trade; the Stockholm Convention on Persistent Organic Pollutants of 2001; the Compliance Committee of the Cartagena Protocol on Biosafety, operating since 2005, and indeed the Aarhus

---

[33] See S. Cassese, *When Legal Orders Collide*: *The Role of Courts* (Global Law Press, Editoria Derecho Global, 2010).

[34] See K.J. Alter, *The New Terrain of International Law*: *Courts, Politics, Rights* (Princeton, Princeton University Press, 2014).

[35] See R.H. Steinberg, "In the Shadow of Law or Power? Consensus-Based Bargaining and Outcomes in the GATT/WTO" (2002) 56 *International Organization* 441; and "Judicial Lawmaking at the WTO: Discursive, Constitutional, and Political Constraints" (2004) 98 *American Journal of International Law* 247.

[36] See International Centre for Settlement of Investment Disputes, Annual report 2014, available at www-wds.worldbank.org/external/default/WDSContentServer/WDSP/IB/2015/01/09/000470435_20150109143952/Rendered/PDF/936120AR0Box380RENCH0ICSID0AR140FRE.pdf.

[37] See L. Friedman Goldstein, C. Ban, The European Human-Rights Regime as a Case Study in the Emergence of Global Governance, in A.D. Ba, M.J. Hoffmann, *Contending Perspectives on Global Governance*, see text n 27, at 154.

Convention on Access to Information, Public Participation in Decision-Making and Access to Justice in Environmental Matters (hereinafter "the Aarhus Convention").[38]

That said, it is beyond doubt that a complete and mature supranational judicial system (at least in the way it is currently understood at the national level) does not exist. There is no hierarchy of powers nor any sort of formal structural relationship among global courts. In fact, concerns exist in academic debate that the absence of a structural framework of the judicial bodies at the supranational level could defer, if not preclude, the uniform application of the rule of law.[39] To dispel such doubts, it is argued that the development of principles of law is not necessarily inhibited by the absence of a formal structure. The interests of legality, this argument goes, could be best served by a less formal hierarchical system, which is adaptable to the constant changes occurring in the global patchwork.[40]

Moving away from the academic debate on the maturity of the supranational judicial system, we will now concentrate on the "horizontal dialogue" among supranational courts. This has developed along three different, although related, dimensions. The first is that of "judicial policy-making", and it will be discussed in the present section. The second dimension concerns the level of cross-citation between different courts and legal systems. Section 1.5.1 will examine it, with a specific focus on its potential to be a source of legal innovation. Section 1.5.2 will then turn to the last dimension of the dialogue among supranational courts, i.e. the involvement of civil society actors in judicial proceedings.

Judicial policy-making is the first dimension of the horizontal dialogue among supranational courts. It is worth highlighting that this is a definition borrowed from American legal doctrine to describe the domestic judiciary making public policy when deciding on cases in which the government is involved. This description implicitly acknowledges the possibility that courts may expand their control to areas beyond the terms of the original agreements that they were established to uphold. In consequence it also applies to supranational judiciary. Judicial policy-making at the supranational level has two major implications. The first, and primary, is that of influencing the legal system in which the judicial body operates. This is particularly evident in the case of the ECJ. As noted by Alex Stone Sweet (2010): "At crucial moments, the Court's case law has shaped market integration, the balance of power among the EU's organs of government, the constitutional boundaries between international, supranational, and national authority, and literally thousands of policy outcomes great and small".

[38] An attempt to classify all international judicial bodies has been made by the Project on International Courts and Tribunals. See www.pict-pcti.org/index.html.

[39] See S. Spelliscy, "The Proliferation of International Tribunals: A Chink in the Armour" (2001–2002) 15 *Columbia Journal of Transnational Law* 143.

[40] See B. Kingsbury, "Is the Proliferation of International Courts and Tribunals a Systemic Problem?" (1999) 31 *New York University Journal of International Law & Policy* 679; S. Cassese, "Administrative Law without the State? The Challenge of Global Regulation" (2005) 37 *New York University Journal of International Law & Politics* 663; E. Benvenisti, "The Interplay Between Actors as a Determinant of the Evolution of Administrative Law in International Institutions" (2004–2005) 68 *Law & Contemporary Problems* 319.

Related to the first, there is a second important implication: through judicial policymaking, supranational courts define the range of interactions between different legal systems. Let us continue, for convenience, with examining the jurisprudence of the ECJ. As a case in point, in a number of cases the Court has outlined the relationship between European law and norms pertaining to other legal systems. In many of its judgments, the ECJ has explicitly recognized the existence of international commitments binding upon the EU. Over time, the Luxembourg judges have recognized that the Communities are bound by the rules of international law, and that these rules may prevail over Community law itself – e.g. the *International Fruit Company* case.[41] In the *Leonid Minim* case,[42] the Court of First Instance rejected the complaint from an Israeli citizen who had his assets frozen by the European Commission, affirming that that UN obligations prevail over the fundamental rights set forth in the EC Treaties and the European Court of Human Rights (ECHR), because of the general supremacy of UN law over Community law. The judges of the ECJ have also accepted general principles of law in cases where no explicit rules were available, as in the *French Semoules* case.[43] More than once, the ECJ has relied on other international treaties for the purpose of interpreting provisions of Community law. In the WTO-related Banana disputes,[44] for instance, the ECJ pointed out that the general principles of Community law are not absolute, but "must be viewed in relation to their social function". In the Court's opinion, principles (or the interpretation thereof) rooted in legal systems outside that of Europe could nevertheless be recognized as part of the latter. However, as further explained by the judges, this assumption does not necessarily mean that such "foreign" principles would be applied *ipso facto*. Rather, their application must result from a case-by-case analysis, following a careful consideration of their applicability within the European domain.

On other occasions, the ECJ has used the existence of inherent European legal "values" to support the uniqueness of the European legal order and to preserve its distinctiveness with regard to that of the international legal order. In *Portugal v. Council*,[45] for example, the ECJ held that it was precluded from taking WTO rules into consideration when examining the validity of EU measures. In another famous judgment, the *Mox Plant* case,[46] the ECJ ruled on its competence to determine

[41] See Joined Cases 21–24/72, Judgment of 12.12.1972, *International Fruit Company NV and Others v Produktschap voor Groenten en Fruit*, 1972.

[42] See Case 362/04, *Leonid Minim v Commission of the European Communities*, 31 January 2007.

[43] See *Conseil D'Etat* Case 62814, 1 March 1968, *Syndicat Général de Fabricants de Semoules de France*.

[44] See Case C-73/97 P, *French Republic v Comafrica Spa & Dole Fresh Fruit Eur. Ltd. & Co.*, 1999; Case C-280/93, *Germany v Council of the EU*, 1994. See also J.P. Trachtman, Bananas, "Direct Effect and Compliance" (1999) 10 *European Journal of International Law* 655. For a general overview of international trade disputes and individual rights See A. Thies, "EU membership of the WTO: International trade disputes and judicial protection of individuals by EU courts" (2013) 2 *Global constitutionalism* 237.

[45] See Case C-149/96, 23 November 1999, *Portuguese Republic v Council of the European Union*.

[46] See Case C-459/03, 30 May 2006, *Commission of the European Communities v Ireland*.

whether, and to what extent, provisions of the UN Convention on the Law of the Sea fall out of its jurisdiction, and whether these provisions may be adjudicated by another dispute settlement body. In substance, the ECJ held that, with regard to issues of Community law, it has exclusive competence to decide whether disputes are within its jurisdiction or not.

Similar to the ECJ, other courts that operate in the supranational arena addressed the interactions of different legal systems. Exemplary is the case known as the "Southern Bluefin Tuna Case", in which the relationship between different global regulatory regimes comes into question.[47] Without need to enter into the merits of the case, it suffices to know that two supranational tribunals, an Arbitral Tribunal and the International Tribunal of the Law of the Sea (ITLOS), were involved. Both had potential jurisdiction in this case, and both are judicial organs established under the provisions of United Nation Convention of the Law of the Sea (UNCLOS). The appropriate tribunal – and thus legal regime – was disputed. Australia and New Zealand claimed that the dispute should be heard by the ITLOS, on the ground that there had been a violation of the UNCLOS. Japan argued that the jurisdiction of ITLOS was limited to disputes closely related to the interpretation of UNCLOS, and could not be extended to controversies arising out of special conventions. Ultimately each tribunal resolved the question of the applicable law differently, though both recognized the existence of a plurality of norms. The ITLOS gave prevalence to the provisions of the Montego Bay Convention, to which the Convention for the Conservation of the Southern Bluefin Tuna is complementary. The UNCLOS Arbitral Tribunal, by contrast, based its decision on the Commission for the Conservation of Southern Bluefin Tuna. It therefore stated that this norm constituted a *lex specialis*, which trumped the competing UNCLOS provisions. It thus denied its own jurisdiction over the dispute, and left it to the parties to negotiate a solution between themselves.

1.5.1 Cross-Citations Between Courts

The second dimension of the horizontal dialogue among supranational judicial bodies concerns the level of cross-citation between different courts and legal systems. Cross-citations are the most direct consequence of the repeated interactions among courts and judicial bodies taking place in the supranational arena. Indeed, courts use other courts' judgments to various ends, including that of affirming that a degree of variability exists in the legal values pertaining to different normative communities. In analysing these cases, some scholars claim that the co-existence of conflicting judgments at the international level will contribute to improving the quality of international law, while others argue that pluralist approaches from supranational courts

---

[47] See B. Carotti, M. Conticelli, "Setting Global Disputes: The Southern Bluefin Tuna Case", in S. Cassese et al. (eds.), *Global Administrative Law. Cases, Materials, Issues*, 3tr edn (Rome-New York, IRPA – IILJ 2012) 145.

are one of the driving forces behind the fragmentation – and thus the weakening – of the international legal order. Given that, it might be emphasized that pluralist judicial strategies, irrespective of the fact that they seldom provide a yardstick for determining which normative value should prevail, can be nonetheless – to borrow the term used by Robert Cover (1983) – "jurisgenerative".[48] To put it explicitly: even conflicts among multiple, overlapping judicial *fora* can sometimes be a source of legal innovation.

In this respect, the dialogue between the ECJ and other international courts can be regarded as an important means for the spread of administrative standards for regulatory decision-making within the supranational arena. The case law is, again, vast. Among the most recent and known judgements is the *Kadi* case, mentioned in Sect. 1.4 of the present chapter, where the ECJ overruled the previous judgment of the Court of First Instance, holding that the EU Regulation implementing the UN Security Council Resolution that had frozen Mr. Kadi's funds on suspicion of financing terrorism did not sufficiently respect certain of his fundamental rights; namely, his right to be heard, his right to property, and his right to an effective legal remedy. In *Kadi* the ECJ also dismissed the relevance of the *Behrami* judgment, in which the European Court of Human rights had reasoned that the commonality in values underpinning the European Convention of Human Rights and the UN Charter provided sufficient reasons for deference on the part of the former to the norms of the latter.

Also widely known is the 2004 *Juno Trader* ruling, in which the ITLOS claimed that, despite the lesser procedural rigour that governs international proceedings vis-à-vis domestic proceedings, all parties of the UN Convention on the Law of the Sea are expected to respect the principle of procedural fairness. Four years earlier, in the *Bosphorus* case, another international tribunal, the European Court of Human Rights, had held that the level of fundamental rights' protection that existed within the European Community, including the available procedures for adequate judicial redress before the ECJ, was equivalent, though not identical, to the relevant international standards. The Strasbourg court refrained from reviewing the European legislation, but declared its own authority to verify, at any time, the consistency of European law with other international standards.

Further, between 1998 and 2002, in the *Shrimp/turtles*, *Asbestos*, *and Sardines cases*, the AB of the WTO formally acknowledged the admissibility of *amicus curiae* (friends-of-the-court) submissions and explained its legal authority to accept such submissions. In particular in the *Shrimp/turtles* dispute, as explained in Sect. 1.4.2, the AB emphasized the importance of affording affected parties the right to be heard prior to the adoption of a decision by a public body. In doing so, it implicitly affirmed the international significance of essential procedural principles such as transparency, participation and judicial review. Interestingly, in the 2005

[48] See also R.B. Siegel, "The Jurisgenerative Role of Social Movements in United States Constitutional Law" *Yale* Working Papers, available at www.law.yale.edu/documents/pdf/The_jurisgenerative_role_of_social_movements.pdf.

award on the *Aguas Argentina* dispute, the Centre for the Settlement of Investment Disputes allowed submissions by third parties, making explicit reference to the AB's practice.[49]

1.5.2 Influence of Common Judicial Approaches on Civil Society Actors

The third, and last, dimension to be considered when assessing the horizontal dialogue among supranational judicial bodies is that of the influence that common judicial approaches have on civil society actors (and also, by reverse, the impact of civil society actors on judicial globalization). This dimension is also one of the most tangible consequences of the innovation brought by the emergence of a global judiciary.

In bygone times, the only available means for individuals to bring a claim within the international legal system was to persuade a government to act on his/her behalf; and even in that case it was not the individual's international right that was being asserted, but the state's own rights. Paradoxically, many of the supranational courts that determined claims were barred to individuals, even though a significant number of their cases arise from actions by, or against, individuals. The starkest example remains that of the *East Timor* case, where the claims of the East Timorese themselves could not be brought to, or directly considered by, the ECJ.[50] It comes as no surprise, then, that writers agreed on the fact that, as Rosalyn Higgins (1995) put it,

---

[49] On the judicial cross-fertilization See A. Del Vecchio, *Giurisdizione internazionale e globalizzazione*, (Milano, Giuffrè 1992); R.P. Alford, "The Proliferation of International Courts and Tribunals: International Adjudication in Ascendance" (2000) 94 *American Society of International Law Proceedings* 160; S.S. Abrahamson, M.J. Fischer, "All the World's a Courtroom: Judging in the New Millennium" (1997) 26 *Hofstra Law Review* 273; P.S. Berman, "The Globalization of Jurisdiction" (2002) 151 *University of Pennsylvania Law Review* 311; T. Burgenthal, "Proliferation of International Courts and Tribunals: Is it Good or Bad" (2001) 14 *Leiden Journal of International Law* 267; J.I. Charney, "The Impact on the International Legal System of the Growth of International Courts and Tribunals" (1999) 31 *New York University Journal of International Law & Politics* 697; T. Treves, "Judicial Lawmaking in an Era of Proliferation of International Courts and Tribunals. Development of Fragmentation of International Law?", in R. Wolfrum, V. Roeben (eds.), *Development of International Law in Treaty Making* (Berlin, Springer, 2005) 587; M.R. Ferrarese, "When National Actors Become Transnational: Transjudicial Dialogue between Democracy and Constitutionalism" (2009) 9 *Global Jurist Frontiers* article 2. E.U. Petersmann, "Justice ad Conflict Resolution: Proliferation, Fragmentation, and Decentralization of Dispute Settlement in International Trade" (2006) 27 *University of Pennsylvania Journal of International Economic Law* 273. Some authors have pointed at the problems raised by the proliferation of judicial bodies at the international level. See Y. Shany, *The Competing Jurisdictions of International Courts and Tribunals* (Oxford, Oxford University Press, 2004); R. Higgins, "A Babel of Judicial Voices? Ruminations from the Bench" (2006) 22 *International and Comparative Law Quarterly* 791. On judicial cross-fertilization in Europe See G. Martinico, F. Fontanelli, "The Hidden Dialogue: When Judicial Competitors Collaborate" (2008) 8 *Global Jurist Advances* article 7.

[50] See East Timor Case (*Portugal v Australia*), Judgement, ICJ Reports 1995, at 90.

"individuals are extremely handicapped in international law from the procedural point of view". The position by which individual could not assert claims directly to international bodies began to change during the twentieth century, in concomitance with the birth of settlement bodies as a means to settle conflicts between states. These bodies included the Central American Court of Justice, the Mixed Arbitral Tribunal in Europe, and the dispute mechanisms settled by the International Labour Organisation (ILO). As things currently stand it is not only international institutions, domestic judges and public administrations that are engaged as active participants in the monitoring and compliance processes. Many litigants, in particular NGOs, corporations and multinationals, have also insisted upon the relevance of the jurisprudence of other tribunals and have repeatedly taken part in the process of review.[51] Not to mention legal professionals. Lawyers in particular have increasingly drawn on the merits of certain decisions when appearing before (or serving on) other judicial bodies. Between 1986 and 1997 the same 14 advocates pleaded the 20 cases in front of the ICJ. The importance of these lawyers is so celebrated (and criticised) that they have long been named "the invisible college".[52]

Individuals (as both moral agents and economic and social actors), corporations and NGOs join supranational judicial review mostly for two reasons. First, to accrue a greater degree of influence and to mobilize support for their demands. Second, complainants from civil society have confidence in global review as a highly effectual way of modifying the national law to their needs and expectations.

The involvement of civil society is pursued in different ways. Private stakeholders are often consulted through individual consultations. Alternatively, the engagement of civil society is secured by fostering its commitment to the local public authorities. From time to time, however, the usage of different, less conventional, forms of interactions occur. The recent *Fuzhou environmental improvement project case*, handled by the Compliance Review Panel of the ADB, offers a suggestive example.[53] As stated in the 2009 report on the case, the requesting parties met several times with the Compliance Review Panel during the assessment of eligibility. They claimed to be negatively affected by the realization of an infrastructure project in the Fuzhou municipality, in the People's Republic of China, which had been granted a loan from the ADB in 2005. Because of the number of participants, and of other practical matters, almost all the meetings between the Review Panel and the requesters were held over Internet. Specifically, they were conducted via teleconferences.

Participation of civil society actors to supranational judicial review processes also effects the cross-fertilization of global courts' jurisprudence. By submitting similar arguments to different courts, civil society actors indirectly help to circulate legal ideas and influence the links between different legal systems. The examples

[51] See A. Reinisch, C. Irgel, "The participation of non-governmental organisations (NGOs) in the WTO dispute settlement system" (2001) 1 *Non-State actors and International Law* 127.

[52] See O. Schachter, "The Invisible College of International Lawyers" (1977) 72 *Northwestern University Scholl of Law Review* 2017.

[53] At present, the process of review is on-going. See the Report on eligibility that has followed the Compliance Review Panel Request No 1/2009.

are many. Take for instance a request the Inspection Panel (IP) of the WB received in 2007 to initiate an investigation on a project for restructuring an electric power generator in Albania.[54] The IP permits individuals who believe that they will be affected detrimentally by a state project to be funded by the WB to ask for an investigation. In the 2007 request, the complainants lamented the negative impact of the project on the local environment and economy. In support of their position, they quoted a 2005 decision from the Compliance Committee of the Aarhus Convention. In that decision, the Compliance Committee had found the Albanian government in non-compliance with the Convention, for a violation of the rules governing public participation and disclosure. In the IP's recommendation to initiate an official investigation, the outcomes of the Compliance Committee review played an important role. The IP, in fact, supported the previous Committee's findings on participation, disclosure and the environmental impact of the project. Another example involves the IP of the WB and the Independent Review Mechanism of the African Development Bank. In May 2007 the two judicial bodies, having received similar requests to launch an investigation into the Bujagali Hydropower Project, agreed to combine their efforts in resolving the complaints. A Memorandum of Understanding was signed to cover the terms of sharing information and the use of specialist consultants between the IP and the Independent Review Mechanism.[55] Previously, due to the International Finance Corporation (IFC) involvement in the financing of the project, another complaint had been lodged with its Compliance Advisory Ombudsman, which carried out its own autonomous investigation.

1.6 Global Civil Society

Thus far the concept of civil society has been called into play three times. Initially as one of the pillars around which revolves the analysis of this book; then again in describing the essential components of EAS and GAL; and once more time in the analysis of the global judiciary. Now is the time to concentrate on the growing involvement of organized and unorganized groupings, collectively referred to as "Global Civil Society" (GCS), in the supranational policy-making. Bearing in mind that the concept of GCS implies a shared understanding of the public sphere which cannot be taken for granted among all countries and states in the world, it can be nonetheless regarded as the fourth crucial means for the spread of common administrative standards for regulatory decision-making within the EAS and the global legal order.

[54] See Request for Inspection No RQ07/03. See generally G. Sgueo, "Proactive Strategies in Global Legality Review" (2010) 1 *Rivista trimestrale di diritto pubblico*.

[55] See the Independent Review Mechanism Eligibility Report for Compliance Review on Compliance Review Request No. RQ2007/1, 24 August 2007, at 20. See also the Compliance Review Report, 20 June 2008.

Chapter 2 will discuss GCS' organizational structures in detail – for this reason only a few preliminary thoughts will now be considered. This section will consider the definition of GCS in legal and sociological reasoning. Sections 1.6.1 and 1.6.2 will therefore turn to considering GCS' foundations, offering an overview of its various articulations and of the play of forces between them. To conclude the examination of GCS, Sect. 1.7 will discuss the counterarguments that challenge the idea that GCS is a meaningful factor to influence the rise of principles of democratic governance between EAS and GAL.

It remains all too common in scientific literature to claim that the idea of a global society is a novel phenomenon. In reality the idea of transnational civil society is not new to philosophical and social thinking. In his 1795 essay "Perpetual Peace: A Philosophical Sketch" Immanuel Kant refers to an ideal world federation of republican states linked together by trading relationships, mentioning the possibility of a universal civil society and of a cosmopolitan right, the *Weltbuergerrecht.* In 1902 Pierre Kazanky (1902) perceived that the activities of international societies were leading to the development of "international social interests". Jurists' reasoning on the possibility that individuals could be actors in the supranational arena goes back even further. In 1532 Francisco de Vitoria considered that indigenous people of South America had some claim to protection under international law, while George Edwards (1792) promoted a "Universal Society" to the purpose of promoting welfare, happiness and peace through the world. In the late nineteenth century, Paul Otlet and Henri LaFontaine founded the principal data repository of international non-governmental organizations: the Union of International Association, contributing to Paul Reinsch's claim (1911) at the onset of the twentieth century: "cosmopolitanism is no longer a castle in the air, but it has been incorporated in numerous associations world-wide".

However, an exact definition (and concept) of GCS has only emerged in legal jargon in the last 50 years, following the perception that civil society could be not only transnational in nature, but also even global. Drawing from the classical notion of *societas civilis*, a community based on consent and therefore peaceful in its operation, GCS has been acknowledged as of increasing significance within political science, social research and, of course, policy-making. Explicit analytical work on transnational civil society actors started during the late 1960s and early 1970s. In 1969 the flagship journal of the German Political Science Association, *Politische Vierteljahresschrift*, published an essay on transnational politics and its main protagonists,[56] followed by the journal *International Organization* that in 1971 published a special issue edited by Robert Keohane and Joseph Nye (1971) on "Transnational Relations and World Politics". Then in 1990 Rein Mullerson (1990) formally advocated for a collective effort to get rid of iron curtains and create a civil society of global stance. Two years later Ronnie Lipschutz (1992) published his landmark article on the emergence of GCS, arguing that its development was a response to the hegemony of the liberal capitalist world order. Echoing Lipschutz,

[56] See T. Risse, "Transnational Actors and World Politics, in W.Ch. Zimmerli, K. Richter, M. Holzinger" (eds.), *Corporate Ethics and Corporate Governance* (Berlin, Springer, 2007).

in 1994 Miguel de Oliveira and Rajesh Tandon (1994) argued that GCS and states are autonomous and interdependent upon each other. In 1995 the Commission on Global Governance stated that the term GCS "covers a multitude of institutions, voluntary associations and networks".[57] In a study published in 2000, Ann Florini argued that transnational civil society (but the same is valid for all its lexical counterparts: for the purposes of this book, definitions as GCS, "world civil society", "transnational civil society", "cross-border civil society", or "international civil society" are used interchangeably) "may be creating the basis for a global polity". A concurring definition was used in the 2000 WB Guidelines, where GCS is defined as "the arena in which people come together to pursue the interests they hold in common (…) because they care enough about something to take collective action".[58] Just recently, in referring to civil society in his 2003 editorial in the New York Times, Patrick Tyler (2003) hailed it as the world's second superpower, following the US. The "exceptional phenomenon" that has appeared on the streets of world cities to protest against the Iraqi War, might not be as profound as the people's revolutions across Eastern Europe in 1989 or in Europe's class struggles of 1848, but – warned Tyler – politicians and leaders were unlikely to ignore it. In the same spirit Time magazine nominated "the protester" person of the year in 2011.[59]

In the last few years, academic research on GCS has flourished. Universities have established new research centres dedicated to this topic, among which stands the Centre for the Study of Global Policy of the London School of Economics and Political Science (LSE). The LSE Centre produces a GCS yearbook for the specific purpose of mapping the contours and trace future developments of GCS. Clearly, academic interest on GCS has not come with common opinions. There are instead a considerable number of different explanations for GCS' existence, leverage and future evolution. Even if words like "global" and "civil society" are now commonplace, what they mean and how they come together are still subject to widely differing interpretations. GCS remains a highly elastic concept. It maintains a complex genealogy of shifting meanings, according to the rhetorical needs of the day. Helmut Anheier et al. (2001) of the above mentioned LSE Centre, for example, identify four different (and alternative) uses of GCS, namely: to define a counterweight to global capitalism (e.g. the protestors in Seattle and Prague or Greenpeace's actions against transnational corporations); to describe the infrastructure that is needed for the spread of democracy and development (e.g. the growth of professional associations, consumer organizations, and interests groups that span many countries); to identify the network of global solidarity provided by actors like Save the Children or Médécins sans Frontières; to refer to the growing connectedness of citizens (exemplified by the authors by reference to Internet chat rooms, networks of peace, environmental or human rights activists, student exchanges, and global media).

[57] See Commission on Global Governance, *Our Global Neighbourhood* (Oxford, Oxford University Press, 1995), at 32.

[58] See World Bank, Consultations with Civil Society Organizations: General Guidelines for World Bank Staff, Washington 2000, at 5.

[59] See K. Andersen, "The Protester" *Time Magazine* (2011) December 14.

More generally, in Kaldor's explanation (2003), GCS is used to map a broad contour, including organizations and institutions operating beyond the territorial bounds of national societies as well as of its received conceptual framework.

Srilatha Batliwala and David Brown (2006) have recently observed that transnational civil society is, first, a *strategy* to make global processes visible and accountable to ordinary citizens who might otherwise be confined to national political arenas; second, a *process* of network building, alliance formation, and advocacy; and, third, a *space* that runs counter to the common-sense geographies of nation, region, and world, all at the same time. And also with the idea of a space, or a "fragmented arena of struggle" as they name it, is concerned the description of transnational civil society used by Keck and Sikkink.[60] Craig Warkentin (2001) articulates the description of GCS by referring to three elements. First is *dynamism* (GCS changes in response to the activities and interests of the actors who use its channels and it inherently adapts to the exigencies of world politics); second is *inclusiveness* (in that GCS is able to capably reflect a broad range of experiences and ideas of the actors who create and employ it); third is *cognizance* (the connections of GCS do not arise accidentally, but are based on particular understandings and specific objectives).

John Keane's analysis of GCS goes further. It gives account of, first, analytic-descriptive usages of the notion, in which key institutions, actors and events are selected and examined in their complex dynamics. Second, it considers strategic political approaches, directly concerned with the political side of GCS. Third, it reports normative ideals, devoted to explain and highlight why a GCS, ethically speaking, is a good thing. Keane considers five features that mark GCS off as historically distinctive. The first is its reference to non-governmental structures and activities. The second and third are the social and civic dimension of GCS, respectively. Fourth is its pluralist (and therefore conflicting) potential. Fifth is, indeed, the global dimension. The author provides for an ideal-type definition, explaining how GCS refers to: "A dynamic non-governmental system of interconnected socio-economic institutions that straddle the whole earth, and that have complex effects that are felt in its four corners. Global civil society is neither a static object nor a fait accompli. It is an unfinished project that consists of sometimes thick, sometimes thinly stretched networks, pyramids and hub-and-spoke clusters of socio-economic institutions and actors who organise themselves across borders, with the deliberate aim of drawing the world together in new ways. These non-governmental institutions and actors tend to pluralise power and to problematize violence; consequently, their peaceful or civil effects that are felt everywhere, here and there, fair and wide, to and from local areas, through wider regions, to the planetary level itself".[61] Even broader is the concept of "international society" proposed by Philip Allott (1992) and James Bohman (2007). In Allott's view international society is not comprised

[60] M.E. Keck, K. Sikkink, *Activists Beyond Borders* see text at section 1, text n 68, chapter 3 n 28, chapter 4 n 29 and chapter 6 n 24, at 33. See also R. Falk, *Global Civil Society: Perspectives, Initiatives, Movements* (Oxford, Oxford Development Studies, 1998).

[61] See J. Keane, *Global Civil Society* see text at section 3 and text n 62.

of States, but arises from the "self-creating" of all human beings. Bohman suggests that transnational democracy should no longer be understood as rule by a singular, territorially identified, *demos*. We should rather talk of *demoi*, or people, that operate across national borders. To complete the picture, it might be useful to remember that authors such as Hedley Bull (1995) resist the notion of an international society made up of individuals. International society, in their opinion, is composed of states. Those states compose a society in the sense that they conceive themselves to be bound by a common set of rules in their relations with one another.

1.6.1 The Global Associational Revolution

Non-state actors are increasingly operating on a supranational rather than just a national stage. John Keane estimates that despite having their main offices in the EU and Switzerland, over one one-third of currently existing NGOs base their offices in all four corners of the earth.[62] Not only are ordinary citizens exercising their right to protest, but a bewildering array of entities, including business companies, multinationals, trade unions, media, religious and social bodies, also play a prominent role in the elaboration of policies and regulations, both in Europe – where they have become the linchpins of the European bureaucracy – and in the global legal sphere. The economic agents lobby for the recognition of common standards in the administrative and regulatory frameworks under which they operate, in order to obtain stable conditions for investments in foreign countries.[63] Social actors, comprising such diverse elements as civic, professional, and advocacy-oriented groups, try to raise awareness and knowledge in the international community by lobbying national and international public institutions for a number of causes including the protection of human rights, the acknowledgement of stronger environmental safeguards, or the reduction of poverty. Organizations of civil society are de facto progressively performing critical functions: to help deliver vital human services, such health and aid to the poor; to empower the disadvantaged and bring unaddressed problems to public attention; or generally to build communities and foster bonds of trust and reciprocity that are necessary for political stability.

---

[62] See J. Keane, *Global Civil Society*? see text at section 3 and text n 61.

[63] On business' direct involvement in processing international law and its problems See N. Klein, *No logo* (New York, Picador 2000) 433; D.M. Trubek, J. Mosher, J.S. Rothstein, "Transnationalism in the Regulation of Labour Relations: International Regimes and Transnational Advocacy Networks" (2000) 25 *Law Social Inquiry* 1187. For more specific focus on collaboration projects between companies and the non-for-profit sector See K. Bastmeijer, J. Verschuuren, "NGO-business collaborations and the law: sustainability, limitations of the law, and the changing relationship between companies and NGOs", in I. Demirag (ed.), *Corporate Social Responsibility, Accountability and Governance. Global Perspectives* (Sheffield, Greenleaf Publishing, 2005) 314; J.P. Doh, H. Teegen, "Non-governmental Organizations as Institutional Actors in International Business: Theory and Implications" (2002) 11 *International Business Review* 665.

So great has their leverage become that non-state actors are considered capable of challenging even the largest governments.[64]

The most prominent role among the panoply of non-state actors operating at the international level is played by NGOs. Described as the tip of the iceberg of the international civil society,[65] NGOs are believed to have widely increased in number over the last 30 years. While this assumption may not be entirely accurate – Thomas Davies' cyclical pattern (2013) is a more appropriate way to measure NGOs and civil society actors evolution and relevance across the last century and half – it nonetheless captures an essential point: NGOs' leverage on the domestic and international stages has increasingly gained momentum. The former Secretary-General of the UN, Kofi Annan, proclaimed the twenty-first century to be the era of NGOs; and scholars reference NGOs' leverage in terms of "global associational revolution".[66] In the opinion of Salamon and Anheiher (1996), the worldwide upsurge of organized private voluntary activities has been as significant to the twentieth and twenty-first centuries as the development of the nation-state system in the preceding two centuries. Susan Strange (1996) compared the growing role of non-state actors (and specifically of NGOs) at all levels of society to modern transition from feudal agriculture to capitalist industry. Antonio Donini (1995) declared that "The Temple of States" – referring to the UN – "would be a rather dull place without NGOs". William de Mars (2005) followed by classifying three dimensions of the NGO bloom. The first and the second are quantitative: NGOs proliferate both geographically and in established issue-areas as human rights or environment. The third dimension is qualitative, i.e. NGOs proliferate by taking the initiative to colonize or create new issues where hitherto they have exerted limited influence. In a similar vein, Sabine Lang (2013) has described the impact of NGOs as organizational formations on modern civil societies with the term "NGOization".

Although precise figures are not available, the number of internationally operating NGOs is estimated at roughly 40,000, and includes two main types of organization. The first are the well-established and known organizations which employ professional staff, dispose of sophisticated fund-raising systems, and represent an astonishing range of different interest. Consider as examples Greenpeace and Friends of the Earth. The former was founded in 1971. By 1985, when the French intelligence blew up the ship Rainbow Warrior in Auckland, Greenpeace had offices in 17 countries, and 1.2 million members around the world. Ten years later the organization reported to have 1330 people working in 43 offices in 30 countries, plus five million supporters located in 158 countries. Equally striking is the example of Friends of the Earth. Founded in 1969, it had already expanded in 25 countries by early 1980s, and 54 by the mid-1990s. The second type of NGO includes small organizations with narrower funds and perspectives. Larger in number compared with the bigger NGOs, these organizations may count on considerable less membership,

[64] See J.T. Matthews, "Power Shift: The Rise of Global Civil Society" (1997) 76 *Foreign Affairs* 50.

[65] See M. Edwards, *NGO Rights and Responsibilities* (London, The Foreign Policy Centre, 2000) and also M. Edwards, *Civil Society* (Cambridge MA, Polity Press, 2004).

[66] See L. Salamon, "The Rise of the Non-Profit Sector" (1994) 4 *Foreign Affairs* 109.

funding opportunities and political leverage. The most comprehensive directory available on this subject, the annual Yearbook published by the Union of International Organizations, reports approximately 1200 new entries every year (intergovernmental organizations are computed in this number, though).

One of the first examples of what is now regarded as NGOs were the associations set up in the seventeenth and eighteenth centuries to promote the abolition of slavery. The year 1863 then saw the establishment of the Red Cross Movement. The Handbook of International Organizations, published in 1929 by the League of Nations, contained entries for 478 international organizations, of which more than nine-tenths were non-governmental. Since then a multitude of NGOs have emerged. Considering that the 1913 Yearbook listed a total of 1083 not-for-profit international organizations, and that in 2013 the number of those is estimated at 66,811 (the most part being NGOs born after 1990), it might be roughly assumed that the not for profit sector grew by 6 percentage points in one century. This is a growth rate confirmed by a sector-by-sector analysis: for example, there are today five times as many civil society organizations working on human rights as there were in the 1950s. Their number, budget and staff grew dramatically in less than one decade, between 1983 and 1993. Environmental transnational environmental organizations, in turn, increased from only two groups in 1953 to 90 in 1993. Their growth is especially evident between the 1970s and the 1990s. Total membership of ten organizations, including Friends of the Earth, the National Wildlife Association and Greenpeace, grew from 4.1 million in 1976 to 8.2 million in 1990.

GCS consistently impacts on national and international markets, as well as on domestic economical and social systems. Civil society organizations mobilize thousands of workers and volunteers. Back in 1991 the Johns Hopkins Comparative Non-profit Sector Project showed that the number of full-time equivalent employment in international non-governmental organizations for France, Germany, Japan, the Netherlands, Spain, and the United Kingdom alone amounted to over 100,000. In the 42 countries analysed by the Johns Hopkins Project in 2010, non-profits employed nearly 56 million full-time workers or an average of 5.6 % of the economically active population of these countries. This, noted the participants to the project, exceeded the workforce of many sizeable industries in the surveyed countries, such as utilities, construction, transport and communications.

Also in 1991 the John Hopkins Project indicated that volunteers of Non-profits represented an additional 1.2 million full-time jobs in these countries. Recent estimates calculate, in a typical year, nearly one billion people across the globe volunteering their time through public, non-profit, or for-profit organizations (approximately 36 %), or directly for friends or neighbours (64 %).[67] In OECD countries an estimated 31 % of the adult population volunteers, either directly or through organizations, compared to less than 20 % in middle and low-income countries. In terms of geographic region, over half (51 %) of the estimated volunteers turn out

[67] See M. Salamon, S.W. Sokolowski, M.A, Haddock, "Measuring the Economic Value of Volunteer Work Globally: concepts, Estimates, and a Roadmap to the Future" (2011) 82 *Analysis of Public and Cooperative Economics* 217. For further details See International Labor Organization, Manual on the Measurement of Volunteer Work, available at www.ccss.jhu.edu.

to be located in Asia. North America and Western Europe have 11 % and 10.2 % of the world's volunteers, respectively. Africa is next in line with 7.8 % of the estimated global volunteers, followed by Eastern Europe (7.4 %), South America (5.8 %), and the Middle East (6.6 %). If "Volunteerland" existed as a country where all the world's volunteers lived, it would have the second largest adult population in the world, behind only China. Its workforce (as of 2005) would be valued 1348 trillion dollars. Enough to make "Volunteerland" the seventh largest workforce in the world, behind the US, Japan, Germany, China, the UK, and France, but ahead of Canada, Spain, and Italy.

1.6.2 Labelling Civil Society Actors

Since conceptual thinking about non-state actors poses numerous challenges, academic discussion on their role in the supranational legal sphere is extremely wide. One prominent strand of the academic literature focuses on the contribution given to international law by civil society, and particularly NGOs.[68] The range of topics of interest to scholars includes the variation of purposes, sizes and functions of non-state actors (a topic that Chap. 4 of this volume will expound further),[69] and the recognition of legal personality to non-state actors. Not least, the academic debate

[68] On the contribution of NGOs to the formation of the international legal order See M.E. Keck, K. Sikkink, *Activists Beyond Borders* see text at section 1, text n 60, chapter 3 n 28, chapter 4 n 29 and chapter 6 n 24; R. Krut, *Globalization and Civil Society: NGO Influence in International Decision Making* (Geneva, UNRISD, 1997); D. Held, *Democracy and the Global Legal Order* (Stanford, Polity Press, 1995); M. Shaw, *Global Society and International Relations* (Cambridge, Polity Press, 1995); R. Falk, *On Humane Governance: Toward a New Global Politics* (Cambridge, Polity Press, 1995); H.J. Steiner, P. Alston, *International Human Rights in Context* (Oxford, Oxford University Press, 2000); H. Anheier et al., *Global Civil Society*, see text at section 6.1, text n 81 and see chapter 2 n 27; D. Eberly, *The Rise of Global Civil Society. Building Communities and Nations from the Bottom Up* (New York - London, Encounter Books, 2008); K. Martens, "NGOs in the UN System: Examining Formal and Informal Mechanisms of Interaction" (2004) 11 *International Law Journal of Civil Society* 11; H. Cullen, K. Morrow, "International civil society in international law: The growth of NGO participation" (2001) 1 *Non-State Actors and International Law* 7; R.D. Martenstz, *Reconstructing World Politics* see text at section 6.1; S. Charnovitz, "Two Centuries of Participation: NGOs and International governance"(1996–1997) 18 *Michigan Journal of International Law* 183; and, also, S. Charnovitz, "WTO Cosmopolitics" (2002) 34 *New York University Journal of International Law and Politics* 299; P. Ghils, "International Civil Society: International Non-governmental Organizations in the International System" (1992) 44 *The International Journal of Science in Society* 417; D. Tarlock, "The Role of Non-Governmental Organizations in the Development of International Environmental Law" (1993) 68 *Chicago-Kent Law Review* 61.

[69] See B. Kingsbury, "First Amendment Liberalism as Global Legal Architecture: Ascriptive Groups and the Problems of the Liberal NGO Model of International Civil Society" (2002) 3 *Chicago Journal of International Law* 183; M.J. Peterson, "Transnational Activity, International Society, and world Politics" (1992) 21 *Millennium* 371; K. Raustiala, "The Participatory Revolution in International Environmental Law" (1997) 21 *Harvard Environmental Law Review* 537; G.A. Christenson, "World Civil Society and the International Rule of Law" (1997) 19 *Human Rights Quarterly* 724; S.E. Eizenstat, "Non-governmental Organizations as the Fifth Estate" (2004) 5 *Seton Hall Journal of Diplomacy and International Relations* 15.

is particularly concerned with the issue of terminology to define civil society actors. A debate that, due to its inconsistencies, has resulted in the usage of different classifications to label and distinguish the actors representing private interests towards the public power. When and how exactly the terminology problem made its way into scholarly debate is controversial. However, Andrea Bianchi notes that, despite the increasing use of "non-state actors" as a term of art, no systematization gives satisfactory account of the role played by those actors in the supranational arena.[70]

The EU is an example of the described controversy.[71] In EU legislation civil society actors are currently referred to (or have been referred to in the recent past) as "private, non-profit institutions serving households", "NGOs", "non-profit associations", "voluntary associations/organisations", or more generally as the "non-profit sector", "third system" or even "social economy". Specific definitions are also in use. The European Court of Auditors, for instance, considers the term "non-state actors" as the most appropriate to define organisations of civil society. In the Eurostat database, cooperatives and mutual societies are grouped with for-profit companies, as they are labelled "market producers". The EU Joint Transparency Register (JTR) run by the European Parliament and the Commission allows six categories of organisations to register, including "NGOs", "think-tanks, research and academic institutions". Whilst in the JTR these categories are separated from "professional consultancies/law firms/self-employed consultants" and "in-house lobbyists and trade/professional associations", they are associated with the category "Organisations representing local/regional and municipal authorities, other public and mixed entities". The European Commission's internal financial information and accounting system includes the possibility to label legal entities as "not-for-profit organisations" (NFPOs) and as NGOs. In 2013, ABAC registered 8275 NFPOs and 2005 NGOs. However, the status of NFPO (or FPO, as the case may be) is determined on an objective criterion: the legal form of the entity, whereas an NGO's status depends on the self-declaration of the concerned entity and the judgement of the authorising officer responsible. Considering that this volume aims at examining a phenomenon in which a variety of non-state actors, individuals included, are comprised, it is perhaps unnecessary to enter the scholarly debate over the taxonomies of GCS' presence in the supranational legal sphere in depth. In what follows, the most recurring definitions and classifications used to describe non-state actors operating at the supranational level – i.e. aims, structure, membership, geographical reach of activity or methods and means of action – will be dealt with in setting the scope for the basics of the analysis that will follow. First, a quick caveat before proceeding. In the following pages only the terminology used to describe single non-state actors will be considered. Labels used for collective bodies will not be included. These will be introduced and explicated when necessary, as in Chap. 3 for

[70] See K. Martens, "Mission Impossible? Defining Nongovernmental Organizations" (2002) 13 *International Journal of Voluntary & Non-profit Organizations* 271.

[71] See G. Sgueo, "Financial Accountability of Civil Society Organisations. Improving Cooperation with EU Institutions" (2015) *European Parliament*.

Quasi-autonomous Non-Governmental Organisation (QUANGOs) and Government Organized non Governmental Organization (GONGOs).

A preliminary distinction between the term "NGO" and the term "non-state actor" is needed. The difference between the two terms draws from the non-profit character and the presence of a basic organizational structure of the former with respect to the latter.[72] As a matter of fact, according to Seema Sapra (2009), the term non-state actor is a residual catch-all category that may include all private non-governmental or societal actors and can accommodate the diversity deriving from differences in size, duration, rang and scope of activities. With this in mind, the present volume will prevalently use the term non-state actor and, residually, the term NGO. The former is more appropriate to capture the complexity of GCS' networks and coalitions; the latter will be used with specific reference to NGOs' involvement in such networks. Speaking of which, it might be useful to remember that the very label NGO has many alternative and sometimes overlapping terms in use. Bertam Pickard (1956) criticized its semantic negation, noting that it excludes certain organizations and precludes to any continuance of the pragmatic relationship with IOs (in his case the UN). Agreeing on Pickard, and assuming that a semantic negation neglects the most significant part of NGOs, Lador-Lederer (1963) has proposed "International Autonomous Entities". But the wordplay has not caught on. Also "civil society organization" (CSO) in the recent past gained popularity as an alternative to NGO. In the parlance of many scholars, CSO applies to organizations with natural persons as members, as well as to associations in which legal persons are organized. CSO is adopted in the field of aid effectiveness, where a broad conception of non-governmental organizations prevails. Also "TNGO", a term emerged during the 1970s, due to the increase of environmental and economic issues in the global community, was used to describe "Transnational NGOs". TNGO included non-governmental organizations not confined to only one country, but existing in two or more countries. However, the term is no longer used. By contrast, TSMO, which refers to "Transnational Social Movement Organization", is an acronym still in use. The list of the definitions no longer used is completed by "private international organizations".[73] A line of reasoning among commentators that recognize the long-time usage of the NGO acronym includes those that, instead of suggesting its change, suggest a change in its meaning: from Non-Governmental Organizations to "Necessary to Governance Organizations".[74]

Among the acronyms still in use INGO (International Non-Governmental Organizations) – a definition coined by the UN Economic and Social Council (ECOSOC) and currently used by the Yearbook of International Organizations – describes those "organizations that are not established by inter-governmental agreement",[75] "including organizations which accept members designated by government authorities, provided that such membership does not interfere with the

---

[72] See A. Bianchi, *Non State Actors in International Law* (Burlington, Ashgate, 2009).

[73] See L. Cromwell White, *The Structure of Private International Organizations* (Philadelphia, Pa., George S. Ferguson company, 1933).

[74] See K. Martens, *Mission Impossible*? see text n 70.

[75] See ECOSOC Resolution 288 (X) the 27th February 1950.

free expression of views of the organizations".[76] INGOs are usually distinguished between those that place advocacy at the centre of their objectives (e.g. Amnesty International) and those focused on service provision, as in the case of the Internet Corporation for Assigned Names and Numbers. While the two former categories have not a dedicated acronym, Religious INGOS are also labelled as RINGOs. Instead, INGOs advocating for youth interests are named INGYOs (a definition that is especially used in the European context). BINGO, in turn, describes, alternatively, "Big International NGOs" or "Business-friendly international NGO" (in the latter case also BONGO is sporadically used, as "Business-Organized NGOs"). Thomas Davies reports that before 1889 only few BINGOs (understood in the latter sense) existed.[77] They significantly increased in number from 1889 onward, beginning with the International Commission of Agriculture. Of particular interest are two inter-related definitions: Northern Non-Governmental Organization (NNGO) and Southern Non-Governmental Organization (SNGO). The former is used to describe large, English-language speaking, based in industrialized countries NGOs; whereas SNGO is the label to describe the NGOs mainly operating in developing countries. The separation between NNGOs and SNGOs will be the object of further discussion in Chap. 5, when the problem of IC's accountability will be addressed. Finally, associated with GCS is the definition of TNCs, transnational corporations. The UN described TNCs in 1988 as "the most important actors in the world economy", given that the biggest among them had sales exceeding the aggregate outputs of most countries.[78] To examine TNCs thoroughly would require a separate volume. It is nonetheless useful to recall, as Davies does in his volume on the history of transnational civil society,[79] that the rise of TNCs has had a significant impact on both IOs and NGOs, albeit for different reasons. Because of the dramatic development TNCs experienced after 1960s they become targets of IOs' action, alongside governments and NGOs. Since then many scholars have considered TNCs fully-fledged members of Paul Wapner's "world civic politics" (1995), i.e. part of the panoply of actors that curtail state action and influence IOs' governance. But TNCs are target of advocacy themselves. Since 1970 a growing number of NGOs have formed to promote corporate social responsibility by corporations based in their countries. One of the pioneering cases of mobilization against a TNC is the 1970 "Baby Killer" campaign against Nestlé's marketing of breast milk substitutes in developing countries. Jarol Manheim (2001) has documented 34 corporate campaigns launched by non-labour groups between 1989 and 1999, including the 1989 worldwide campaign against Nike sweatshops in Asia and other relevant environmental campaigns.

---

[76] See ECOSOC Resolution 1296 (XLV) of 25th June 1968.

[77] See T. Davies, *NGOs, A New History of Transnational Civil Society* see text at section 6.2, see n 79 and see chapter 4 n 28, at 52.

[78] See United Nation Centre on Transnational Corporations, Transnational Corporations in World Development: Trends and Prospects, New York 1988, at 24.

[79] See T. Davies, *NGOs, A New History of Transnational Civil Society* see text at section 6.2, text n 77 and chapter 4 n 28, at 150.

1.7 Three Counter-Arguments to Global Civil Society. Accountability and Efficiency

This book argues that the number, extent and widespread presence of social movements, not-for-profits organizations, and more generally of the various articulations of GCS, make them indisputably relevant in policy-making at both national and supranational levels. More specifically, this volume claims that the expanding co-operation between this "transboundary" operating civil society, the EU, and other IOs, is likely to: provide a window into transnational regulatory corporatism, and thus help a core of common procedural values to spread within the supranational decision-making processes; benefit the integration between the EAS and GAL, both in the policy formulation and in the implementation of rules; and, ultimately, reshape governance into a web in which national and supranational organisms, the public and the private sphere are all united "under a single logic of rule".[80] The validity of this hypothesis, however, might be challenged with three distinct, if often inter-related, counterarguments. *First* is the accountability problem. *Second* is the issue of efficiency. *Third* is the broader problem of the democratic deficit. In what follows the first two issues will be given only concise account, leaving to Chap. 5 the task of its analysis; whereas Sects. 1.7.1 and 1.7.2 of the current chapter will expound the problem of democratic deficit.

Let us start with the problem of GCS accountability. Non-state actors' finances, agenda, and governance, the critical argument runs, are not legitimate themselves. Neither a representative nor an electoral process makes them accountable. At its heart, the only source of legitimacy of GCS actors is the factual and diffuse acceptance of their presence and active role in the supranational arena. Hence, the problems they potentially raise: how can accountability be provided to IOs by bodies that are not accountable for themselves? The clearest argument for understanding the critique on the illegitimacy of GCS's advocacy has been made with the so-called "theory of the second bite of the apple", ideated by John Bolton in 2000. Bolton (2000) described NGOs' detachment from governments troubling for democracies because "it provides a second opportunity for intrastate advocates to reargue their positions, thus advantaging them over their opponents who are unwilling or unable to reargue their cases in international fora". Drawing from that view, Anderson and Rieff expressed further concern about non-state actors in the supranational arena.[81] Differently from the domestic domain where non-state actors "*play the role of single-minded advocates*", they argued, in the international realm non-state actors aspire to quite different roles, including both representativeness and standing between GCS and various IOs. This ambiguity of role, according to Marina Ottaway (2001), has pushed the concept of corporate representation to a new extreme. NGOs and other non-state actors claim to have the right to speak for people that have not

[80] See M. Hardt, A. Negri, *Empire* (Cambridge MA, Harvard University Press, 2000).

[81] See K. Anderson, D. Rieff, "Global Civil Society: A Sceptical View" in H. Anheier, M. Glausius, M. Kaldor, *Global Civil Society* see text at section 6.1, text n 68 and chapter 2 n 27, at 26.

been consulted in any meaningful way. This denotes, in Ottaway's opinion, a sort of "global corporativism". An ambiguity of roles, someone note, that IOs are not necessarily (or sufficiently) engaged in fighting back. "No global systems of social insurance or redistribution exist to offset the resulting losses suffered by the disregarded", affirms Richard Stewart (2014) in illustrating what he names "the problem of disregard" of weak private interests. The ECOSOC 1996 guidelines, for instance, postulate that only NGOs having a "democratic adopted constitution" are allowed to be accredited consultative relations. Yet, the ECOSOC's accreditation committee has never enforced this requirement, as it is proved by the dramatic increase of the number of NGOs with consultative status at the ECOSOC (from 41 in 1948 to about 3500 in 2012).[82] Many of these NGOs, however, are accredited in spite of not conforming to this requirement. Menno Kamminga (2007) calculates that only a handful of more than 2700 NGOs accredited with the ECOSOC can be said to be truly democratic A second example is in the Explanatory Memorandum of the Principles on the Status of NGOs in Europe of the COE. Here it is stated that NGOs are sovereign about matters of internal structure.[83] The Principles thus do not require NGOs' internal democracy to the scope of participating in the COE. Also in the Memorandum, the submission from NGOs of an annual report on their accounts and activities is described as a "good practice". A third example is reported in Carlo Ruzza's analysis (2007) of the participation of the organised civil society in the EU. The European Commission, explains Ruzza, has repeatedly argued that, at least in principle, consultation with representative bodies such as trade unions have to be considered more important than consultation with non-representative bodies. This distinction, however, has turned out to be unsustainable in practice. In fact, the representativeness of civil society organisations is not easy to be checked. Consequently, the criterion of representativeness has been used instrumentally to justify a preference for certain organisations with respect to others. A fourth, and final, example is illustrated in Beate Kohler-Koch's and Christine Quittkat's research (2013) on participatory democracy in Europe. They mention the case of the Civil Society Contact Group, an umbrella organization whose claim is to represent the "value and right based NGOs", as explicatory of the difficulty in separating NGOs that focus on common goods from associations that focus on the interest of their members. The Civil Society Contact Group includes among its members the patient associations organized within the EPHA Platform (the European Public Health Alliance) and the Roma and Sinti associations represented in the Social Platform. As a result, note Kohler-Koch and Quittkat, the groups' self-interests are inextricably mingled with the enforcement of universal right as the right to health or social equality.

A second challenge that merits closer scrutiny pertains to the practical implications of non-state actors' contribution to supranational decision-making.

---

[82] See United Nations, ECOSOC, Basic Facts about ECOSOC Status, New York 2012, available here www.csonet.org/index.php?menu=17.

[83] See Council of Europe, Fundamental Principles on the Status of Non-governmental Organisations in Europe and Explanatory Memorandum, 2002, paragraphs 33 and 45, available here www.coe.int/t/dghl/standardsetting/cdcj/ONG/Fundamental%20Principles%20E.pdf.

Regardless of the possible benefits for the "democratization" of the supranational legal order, critics submit that a major opening to private parties' interests may distort or delay the decisional workflow. The problem is not merely rhetorical. The massive and direct participation of stakeholders in decision-making processes held at the supranational level is often perceived as counterproductive, rather than beneficial for the effectiveness of international decision-making. A problem that Michel Crozier et al. (1975) named "democratic overload", and exemplified with the negative effects that, in their opinion, the excessive demands from social group formerly excluded from participation caused to decision-making. In contrast, it is argued that a smaller number of participants, working with no influence from the outside, could guarantee, first, faster decisions and, second, would reduce the much-complained-of organizational high costs. The issue of fastness may be exemplified borrowing from Hugo Heclo's study (1978) on pressure groups. Heclo uses a powerful metaphor to illustrate the risks of increasing interdependence of Washington politics from lobbyists. He evokes a scene from "Play Time", the famous movie from Jacques Tati. The scene focuses on a Parisian roundabout. The roundabout is so dense with traffic that no one can get in or out; instead, the drivers drive in endless circles while socialising with each other. The profound influence of civil society actors on IOs' policy-making, Heclo thinks, ends up in adding new layers of complexity to the exercise of public power. Basically, critics of civil society's participation in supranational decision-making use the same argument. They maintain that the more civil society is involved into IOs' decision-making implies the less common grounds for agreement are found, at the cost of fastness. Speaking of which: the second issue is actually that of costs. Transparent negotiations cost in terms of loss of creativity and freedom of negotiators to say things that they would not think or say in public.[84] Transparency may also raise conformist pressures, strengthening the incentives for public posturing, and even increase the risks for negotiation breakdowns.[85] Confidentiality is often essential in matters of security or law enforcement. The WHO, for instance, decided to follow the practice of not disclosing the identities of the experts that is enlisted to address the H1N1 pandemic in order to insulate them from outside pressures.[86] In Moravsik's provocative comment (2004) some IOs like the WTO might be even thought of as institutional complements to the US "fast track" – and, in the case of the EU, even a substitute for it – in that they empower national executives to override powerful particularistic interests in the name of the

[84] See J. Mansbridge, "A "Selection Model" of Political Representation" (2009) 17 *Journal of Political Philosophy* 369.

[85] See generally J. De fine Licht, D. Naurin, P. Esaiasson, M. Gilljam, "Does Transparency Generate Legitimacy? An Experimental Study of Procedure Acceptance of Open- and Closed-Door Decision-Making" (2011) *QoG* Working Paper Series 8.

[86] See generally World Health Organization, Implementation of the International Health Regulations, Report of the Review Committee on the Functioning of the International Health Regulations (2005) in Relation to Pandemic (H1N1) 2009, A64/10, available at www.apps.who.int/gb/ebwha/pdf_files/WHA64/A64_10-en.pdf.

national (or median) interest. This might clarify why, as noted by Steve Charnovitz,[87] governments rely on civil society actors almost exclusively when is the moment of creating IOs or when they have to handle new issues with existing IOs. When they feel they are no longer dependent of civil society's assistance, however, they pull back. The fact, explains Haas (1976), is that IOs operate in a turbulent environment: they must respond to new problems thrown up by the quickening pace of globalization. This means that they have to be dynamic and adaptive, or they will become irrelevant. Rapid adaptation, however, is in evident tension with reliance on democratic consensus. As clarified by John McGinnis (2012), "the central political problem of our time is how to adapt our vulnerable democracy to the acceleration of the information age". Advancing in Haas' footsteps, Lorenzo Casini and Benedict Kingsbury (2009) remind us of the examples of the WB and the WTO as meaningful representations of rapid adaptation by IOs. The WB has introduced structures dedicated to delivering rapid response to emergencies.[88] These include: the possibility of retroactive authorization of finance provided before legal agreements could be put in place; grants awarded to NGOs instead of states where "weak-capacity environments" demand it; and also on-going supervisory controls against fraud and corruption in the place of *ex ante* controls. Differently from the WB, the WTO does not have detailed procedures for emergencies. The outcomes, however, are similar. During the SARS crisis the WTO Director General operated through recommendations and measures that, perhaps, were beyond the explicit mandate of the institution. Casini and Kingsbury agree upon the impossibility to block administrative action of IOs when circumstances require urgent action. "Entitlements to a lengthy hearing and appeal" – they write – "may "ossify" procedures and dissuade an underfunded and overstretched agency from acting at all".

Limitations to the number of civil society representatives sitting at the table may come also in moments when no particular urgency is needed. As research on "institutional selectivity" indicates, invitations to sit at the table of negotiations are most likely extended to those civil society representatives whose message is in broad accordance with the public agenda. Contentious or radical positions, by contrast, are less likely to be invited.[89] In such cases, submit critical voices, civil society actors' inclusion in IOs' decision-making processes only serves the purpose of enhancing legitimacy.

[87] See S. Charnovitz, *WTO Cosmopolitics* see text n 68, at 270.

[88] See WB Operational Policy 8.00 on Rapid Response to Crises and Emergencies (March 2007), available at www.web.worldbank.org/WBSITE/EXTERNAL/PROJECTS/EXTPOLICIES/EXTOPMANUAL/0,contentMDK:21238942~menuPK:4564185~pagePK:64709096~piPK:64709108~theSitePK:502184,00.html.

[89] See J.M. Brinkerhoff, D.W. Brinkeroff, "Government-Nonprofit Relations in Comparative Perspective. Evolution, Themes and New Directions" (2012) 22 *Public Administration and Development* 3.

1.7.1 Indirect Democracy at the Supranational Level

Third, and most significant, while theories on legal globalization have been quite successful in shedding light on the assumption that increased IOs' legitimacy would prelude to an engaged and committed global democratic public sphere, these theoretical accounts suffer from a lack of empirical evidence.

On the theoretical level, academic debate has explained how perceptions of democracy are changing at the supranational level. Democratic participation is no longer seen as bounded by the confines of states. Rather, it has taken on a global character. Stakeholders are consulted by IOs both indirectly (through indirect representation of their interests) and directly (through procedural mechanisms resembling the typical structure of an administrative process of law). Yet, scholars argue, despite its far-reaching implementation of participatory models, IOs remain *loci* where private interests receive poor or inadequate attention. It is one thing to argue that IOs provide arenas in which the activities of GCS' actors are allowed to flourish. It is quite a different thing to conclude that, because of this, GCS has had a significant impact on IOs' policies. To put it simply: access does not guarantee impact, i.e. the mechanisms of participation and review that are taken for granted in domestic administrative action at the supranational level may lack substance.

A first set of concerns regard indirect representation. Three modern revolutions (British, American, and French) imposed the principle that all legitimate authority is based on the consent of those over whom it is exercised. Hence the weakness of indirect representation: this lies in the shift from the representative to the executive experience. Jeremy Rabkin (2005) notes that while national bureaucracies are embedded in democratic states and are electorally accountable to the people, even in large, disparate and contentious communities, supranational technocratic institutions are, in comparison, illegitimate and ineffective, since they generally precede electorally accountable governments. "Internationalization" – concurs Ralf Dahrendorf (1999) – "almost inevitably means a loss of democracy". Even those who take a relatively strong position in favour of the transposition of democratic values at the supranational level recognize that the gap between political procedures designed to work at the national level, and the development of social relations that occur at a transnational level is a central problem to globalization. They end up arguing that the remoteness of most IOs from democratic publics makes unlikely to provide sufficient legitimacy through long and complex chains of delegation. In these circumstances, it is generally argued, supranational democracy provides no straightforward analogue to national democracies.

The supposed incapability of the supranational legal order to be truly democratic has been referred to by various terms, including "bureaucratic distance", the well-known "democratic deficit", the "deficit of mutual awareness" between civil society and public authorities,[90] and the "vertical incongruence" implying that supranational

[90] See N. Lebessis, J. Paterson, *Developing New Modes of Governance* (European Commission, Forward Studies Unit, 2000).

regulators increasingly impinge on the life chances of national populations, without being accountable to them.[91] The EU notorious democratic deficit (the redressing of which was the primary purpose for calling a constitutional convention in late 2000s) is an obvious example. As Michael Zurn (1998) ironically pointed out already 20 years ago: "if the EU were to apply for membership in the EU, it would not qualify because of the inadequate democratic content of its constitution". Many efforts have been made to the end of eliminating the democratic deficit. In an often-celebrated speech before the European Parliament on March 1994, Vaclav Havel expressed doubt that European citizens could understand a complex organisation such as the EU. The European project's most important task, concluded Havel, was to be "more accessible to all". In January 1999, the European Commission published a first electronic register of groups to be involved in public consultations. In 2005 the register – by then known as CONNECS (Consultation, the European Commission and Civil Society) – included nearly 1000 civil society organisations. Between 2009 and 2014 stakeholders' views were sought through more than 500 open consultations published on the "Your Voice in Europe" website. Legal modifications to the framing of civil society have kept occurring. The Lisbon Treaty confirms: "the functioning of the Union is founded on representative democracy". Further, EU institutions are urged to "maintain an open and regular dialogue with representative associations and civil society", and the EU Commission "shall carry out broad consultations with parties concerned to ensure that the Union's actions are coherent and transparent". Thus in 2012 the Commission reviewed its consultation policy, and the citizens' initiative – a participatory bottom-up instrument – entered into force. These efforts notwithstanding, the EU is still believed by many to be a place suffering from a deficit in democracy.[92] A place where the European Parliament represents more than 500 million persons across 28 states, and has a right to co-determination in the Council's legislation, but cannot exercise political control over the Council; and the Commission cannot be held directly accountable by the European Parliament, the Council, and even less by citizens. The same definition of democratic deficit has been used more broadly with reference to other IOs. Most notably, with the WTO at the 1999 Ministerial Conference (when the lack of transparency, accountability and citizens' inclusiveness in international policy-making was acknowledged a major political issue) and with the WB and the IMF (where developed countries, who makes up 15 % of the world population, account for over 60 % of the voting strength).[93] In Norris' explanation (2011), democratic deficit is a concept that can be applied to "any object where the perceived democratic performance fails to meet public expectations, whether concerning a specific

[91] See H. Kriesi, Daniel Bochsler, Jörg Matthes, Sandra Lavenex, Marc Bühlmann, Frank Esser (eds.), *Democracy in the Age of Globalization and Mediatization* (London-New York, Palgrave, 2013).

[92] See EU Commission, Communication on EU Regulatory Fitness of December 2012 ("REFIT Communication 2012").

[93] See G. Helleiner, "Markets, Politics and Globalisation" (2001) 2 *Journal of Human Development* 1.

public sector agency or institution, (…) or the agencies of global governance and multilateral organizations". Legal doctrine has gone as far as to assume that democratic deficit is a natural condition in IOs. Exemplary is the research conducted by Andrew Moravcsik and Martin Shapiro. Moravcsik (2002) pragmatically suggests that it would be wrong to judge IOs according to the same criteria as for national governments. Assuming that IOs have a limited and delegated mandate, adds Moravcsik, they should specialize on technocratic issues: i.e. those issues that tend to involve less political participation. The last few years, however, have showed a different reality. IOs have increasingly engaged in the exercise of regulatory powers that directly affect citizens. Martin Shapiro's concerns regard the likely involvement from transnational regimes of what he names "the standard logic of cartels". As the author explains, the need to establish some sort of non-electoral legitimacy, and the complexity of transnational regulatory issues, create a natural push toward technocratic governance by IOs.[94] Technocracy endows IOs' agents with wide discretion, discretion that breeds concerns of unaccountability, recklessness, and even corruption.

According to the idea of indirect representation, political actors are charged with the responsibility of acting in the people's interest, but are also acknowledged the possession of duties of trusteeship. In his telling work on politics, Ankersmit (1996) draws a distinction between aesthetic and mimetic representation. *Mimetic representation*, or "representation as a mirror of society", finds its expression in calls for direct democracy. However, this is suggested to be a concept that "dishonours" democracy because it extradites it to the desires of a collective political libido. *Aesthetic representation*, on the contrary, acknowledges the possession of duties of trusteeship in political actors, but also recognizes that they have a power of creativity in managing social conflict. Ankersmit concludes that the fact that supranational regulatory-makers have an acknowledged power of creativity in developing public policies and managing social conflict means that, in the face of changing circumstances, the results of consultation may not be fully transposed into the final decisions, or may not be correctly implemented.

1.7.2 Direct Democracy at the Supranational Level

Second in line are direct (or procedural) representation's drawbacks that develop from scarcity in transparency and openness of IOs' decision-making processes. An acute problem at the national levels, the deficit of openness and transparency in supranational regulators is even more critical. The complex nature of international politics, in fact, makes it difficult to identify the causal chain that links rule-makers with rule-takers. A complexity accrued by a recent trend in supranational regulation – i.e. "informal international law-making" – described by Jan Wouters et al. (2012) as

[94] See M. Shapiro, ""*Deliberative*", "*Independent*" *Technocracy V. Democratic Politics*" see text at section 6.1, at 349.

"cross-border cooperation between public authorities, with or without the participation of private actors and/or IOs".[95] While IOs tend to disagree – they either consider themselves to be bound to only what they explicitly consented to, or they regard themselves as mere coordinators of domestic agencies, and thus suggest that are domestic regulators those who should offer account for implementing their guidelines [96] – there is a consensus among scholars that IOs suffer from a severe deficit in direct democracy.[97] Robert Dahl (1999) maintains that IOs are inherently unable to support direct democratic deliberation and decision-making by virtue of their large-scale distance from the electorate. Since IOs characteristically lack what domestic institutions gain from elections or interest group accountability – argue David Held and Mathias Archibugi (2004) – then "systematizing the provision of global public goods requires not just building on existing forms of multilateral institutions, but also extending and developing them in order to address questions of transparency, accountability and democracy". No matter how formally democratic and inclusive IOs may be, adds Larry Siedentop (2000), the distance and lack of intermediating social and cultural institutions encourage the trend towards little meaningful public deliberation.

There are three main arguments related with the drawbacks of direct democracy: transparency; the definitions of the actors involved in participation; and the variability of approaches. For one thing, transparency in IOs is thwarted by the negotiations held behind closed-doors and shielded from public scrutiny. States resist to major opening in transparency out of the wish to keep control over the outcome of decisions. The Permanent Five veto holders at the UN Security Council, for instance, are long time opponents of a more transparent decision-making.[98] The most recent example is the draft resolution titled "Enhancing the accountability, transparency and effectiveness of the Security Council" presented in 2012 by the "Small5" (the group of small states at UN) and ultimately rejected by the General Assembly.[99] Civil society actors' influence on IOs' decision-making remains a matter of discretion for states who find it opportune to support interests in a selective, ad-hoc manner, as in the case of the WTO. The norm-setting process within the WTO involves all member states and is mainly an informal, behind-the-scenes process of negotiation and consultation. In consequence, the process of deliberation remains largely

---

[95] See J. Pauwelyn, R.A. Wessel, J. Wouters (eds.), *Informal International Lawmaking* (Oxford, Oxford University Press, 2012).

[96] See E. Benvenisti, The Law of Global Governance, see text at section 1, text n 10 and n 22, and see chapter 4 n 6 and n 33, at 87. See also UN Secretary General, Delivering Justice: Programme of Action to Strengthen the Rule of Law at the National and International Levels, doc A/66/749, 2012, available here: www.unrol.org/doc.aspx?d=3141.

[97] Exceptions include A. Moravcsik, *Is there a "Democratic Deficit" in World Politics*? see text at section 7.2, at 346. With specific regard to the European democratic deficit See F.W. Scharpf, *Governing in Europe: Effective or Democratic*? (Oxford, Oxford University Press, 1999).

[98] See D.M. Malone, "The Security Council in the Post-Cold War Era: A Study in the Creative Interpretation of the U.N. Charter" (2003) 35 *New York University Journal of International Law & Policy* 487.

[99] See UN Doc. A/66L.42/Rev. 1.

opaque to civil society. Every time that public interest groups called on the WTO to be transparent, WTO national representatives responded that trade negotiations would have been difficult to finalize if scrutinized during the bargaining process. Only occasionally NGOs representing diverse interests might use this opacity to present their views and gather information, as noted by Jeffrey Dunoff (1998).

IOs have tried to respond to criticism on decision-making secrecy by providing wider public access to internal documents. Examples are many. Anne Peters and Andrea Bianchi (2013) have labelled such efforts the "transparency turn" in global governance. The turn concerns both the transparency for governance (requirements imposed by international law on states) and the transparency demand of the supranational regulators themselves. The *Codex Alimentarius* Commission adopts standards on food safety through a decisional process that includes significant information to concerned stakeholders and participation by non-state actors. In 2010 the WB issued a "World Bank Policy on Access to Information".[100] The new policies drastically reformed the institution's policy on transparency. Following years of criticism of its opaque operations, the WB decided to shift to presumption of disclosure of the majority of its documents. The ADB in 2011 reviewed its transparency policy, and limited information to seven categories that are not automatically released to the public. In the EU Transparency Regulation of 2001 (followed in 2008 by an, albeit voluntary, JTR for civil society organizations interacting with Parliament or the Commission) a number of transparency requirements were laid down.[101] Yet, as Peters and Bianchi admit, transparency measures can still be circumvented. This is to say that the legal and political actors might hold conclave behind the façade of the public meeting, and keep secret files apart from those that are public. In so doing, the entire effort to be transparent would be rendered ineffective, or even counterproductive. Not to mention the fact that, as David Stasavage (2004) points out, open-door bargaining in IOs might "encourage representatives to posture by adopting overly aggressive bargaining positions that increase the risks of breakdown in negotiations".

Further increasing the complexity of the involvement of GCS in IOs' decision-making, is the absence of clear definitions of the actors involved. It is often uncertain which "group" of individuals is being addressed by the IOs' rules concerned with participatory rights. Should only NGOs, and more generally organized groupings to be considered eligible for participatory rights? Or, perhaps, single individuals sharing a common interest should be included as well? Although the answers are variable, depending on IO's regulatory framework, more often than not the right to be consulted within the global decision-making processes is a right that de facto only organized groups – and precisely NGOs – are entitled to exercise.

As a further consequence, IOs' approaches towards inclusion of stakeholders within its decision-making processes are variable, being generally "moderate" – that is, approaches that do not tend to incorporate hard procedural rights into

[100] See Policy of 1 July 2010, available at www.documents.worldbank.org.

[101] See Regulation No. 1049/2001 of the European Parliament and the Council of 30 May 2001 Regarding Public Access to Documents (OJ 2001 No. L145/43, 31 May 2001).

definitions – due to the extreme diversification of the interests potentially eligible for consultation. In the EU, where people are invited to express their opinions through online referenda held at regular intervals, the topics subject to referenda are often low in salience or very complex, meaning that people's voting will reflect little real deliberation. The WTO does not provide a structure deliberately tailored to respond to the inclusion of the interests of civil society within its rule-making activities. This choice, however, is followed by the decentralization of consultative functions – and the related responsibilities – at the domestic level. Elsewhere, as in the case of the World Bank Group (WBG), the global sphere complements the results of domestic consultative procedures with further procedures and structures operating at the global level. In other cases still, the *locus standi* of the private actors is both national (although in respect of the standards set at the supranational level) and global. This happens, for instance, in the network established under the auspices of the Aarhus Convention.[102]

The most direct consequence of these shortcomings is that while the efforts made by civil society representatives into increasing IOs' transparency and openness might well result in changes relevant to the legitimacy of specific decision-making processes (and perhaps even for the legitimacy of single IOs' regulatory frameworks), it might not be as significant for influencing the formation of a global system of governance in which principles and values of administrative fashion are shared. The suggestion that GCS active role in the supranational legal space is fostering the harmonious growth of EAS and GAL may thus be opposed. If, as critical voices maintain, the discourse over the risks and the costs behind the greater involvement of stakeholders in supranational policy-making proves to be exact, it might then be suggested that the presence of civil society at the supranational level reflects, and perhaps encourages, the fragmentation – and thus the weakening – of the supranational legal order. In such a fragmented international legal regime we should recognize that the various legal systems are governed by principles and rules that have little or nothing in common.

1.8 The Volume Outline

This volume attempts to explore this last controversy. In order to fully illustrate it, and to understand whether, and to what extent the presence of GCS in the supranational legal space brings the EAS and GAL closer, this book is divided into seven chapters.

To begin with, Chap. 2 briefly acknowledges how the concept of networks is important in qualifying structured linkages of interests and people and explores seven factors behind the emergence of civil society networks. Chapters 3 and 4 provide a conceptual framework through which the phenomenon of civil society

[102] The three models of consultations are examined in G. Sgueo, "Decentralization, Integration and Transposition" (2010) 1 *Three Models of Consultation in the Global Legal Order* 253.

participation in the supranational decision-making may be identified and analysed. The discussion is organized around two themes. To begin with, in Chap. 3 the activity of GCS through coalitions and networks is delineated in some of its recurrent characteristics. Sequentially, in Chap. 4 focus is directed towards the contribution of civil society's networks to bolstering principles of administrative governance at the European and the global levels. Two main argumentative strategies will be used to substantiate the analysis: a description of networks' chief characteristics; and a focus on networks' activities (mediation, rulemaking and implementation).

Are networks of GCS legitimate to influence the relationship between EAS and GAL? Chapter 5 turns to the problems related to the involvement of transnational civil society's networks within the supranational decision-making processes. The framework for examining these problems is based around three fundamental questions: do the networks of civil society actors provide a solution to the accountability issue? Is the IOs' legitimacy rate improved by the cooperation with civil society networks? Are these networks impacting IOs' effectiveness? Chapter 5 eventually aims to warn against a common mistake in scholarly debate about globalization. This is the diffuse tendency to describe GCS as a direct effect of political, economical, and legal globalization. While it is undoubtedly true that the formation of a civil society of global dimension draws from the integration of economies, societies, and cultures through a global network of communication and trade, the opposite is also true. On the face of it, Chap. 5 discusses the capacity of international civil society networks – in some of its varied forms and hues – to impact on IOs' accountability, legitimacy, and effectiveness.

Building on the analysis set forth in Chaps. 4 and 5, Chaps. 6 and 7 develop a theoretical framework for reflections on the role of international civil society in shaping closer connections between the EAS and GAL. Doing so, however, will require moving beyond the simplistic and polarizing views of globalization and democratization. Hence, in Chap. 6 a preliminary distinction between the contribution given by single non-state actors and by cross-border civil society's networks to the evolution of the supranational legal order is presented. The analysis rests on a claim of similarity between the impact of single non-state actors and civil society networks on the elaboration of principles of administrative law in the supranational legal space. It is argued that only the latter potentially contribute to the meaningful interaction between the EAS and GAL. In order to elucidate this potential, two additional distinctions are introduced. First, the theoretical notion and the practical outcomes of the global civil society networks' contribution to the shaping of supranational governance are conceptually divorced. The second distinction is more topical. It addresses two forms of convergence between administrative systems, namely attractiveness and imposition. The narrative on EAS/GAL convergence through international civil society networks, Chap. 6 cautiously suggests, encompasses both these forms of convergence. It might be experienced as much as works of administrative attractiveness as works of administrative imposition, and should be therefore classified as a third type of convergence.

To conclude, Chap. 7 details the potential of civil society's network to develop and enlarge in the future, and envisages a number of tensions that may raise doubts about network's desirability as drivers of harmonized principles of participatory democracy at the European and global levels. The analysis is grounded on a comparison of structural and functional elements pertaining to networks of civil society actors. It is suggested that an evolutionary process in supranational civil society's networking is already under way, at the end of which new organizational forms, or meta-networks, are likely to emerge. The paradigm of meta-networks demonstrates how transnational civil society is increasingly organized in formal sets of connections to support its activities, and how a closer integration between principles of administrative fashion pertaining to different supranational legal systems have developed through networks' activities. Yet this assumption remains uncharted by official statistics and only superficially explored in its counter-effects. The findings of this volume indicate that networking in civil society shows a number of tensions. Chapter 7 fulfils the task of portraying such tensions. The most evident is related to networks' functioning. Holding civil society groups together in a coalition is a difficult task. This is especially apparent when networks grow bigger and, as a consequence, the likeliness of controversial positions among its members increases. A second tension may occur between different coalitions in competition. A third tension may occur when particular IOs refuse to co-operate with a coalition on the basis of rules or standards formerly approved by a different IO, assuming their uniqueness or the presence of important differences. Lastly, a fourth tension relates to the loss of creativity and experimentation that might occur when the same standards and practices are massively recycled from different coalitions. Indeed, these tensions introduce new areas of concern, which are also discussed in the conclusion of this volume. These concerns include the "impact factor" of civil society's networks, i.e. the effective relevance of such networks on the evolution of democratic governance at the supranational level, and the further consequences that this may have on the array of relationship between supranational regimes of administrative law.

1.8.1 The Empirical Evidence. Part I: Europe

The arguments presented in the remainder of this chapter will be illustrated by reference to selected case studies. This empirical account is not only meant to highlight the actual presence of supranational networks of civil society actors. Cutting across these case studies is also a way to set broader questions concerning GCS. The empirical account presented in this volume, then, serves four main purposes: to map a number of relevant networks of non-state actors and to generate sufficient understanding of their origins, strategies and limits; to provide a foundation for the claim that these networks are increasingly situated in the supranational arena and its rapidly changing configuration; to capture how interactions between civil society networks and IOs provoke integration dynamics and institutional change; and to show that, overall, networks of civil society actors are a central component for the diffusion of regulatory rules and procedures between the EAS and GAL.

The following description will first provide an outline of seven cases pertaining to the European arena. Nine cases from the extra-European legal arena will be introduced afterwards. In addition to the main case studies, a few minor examples are also presented. The whole of data that has been harvested is summarized in a synoptic table, annexed to the volume. The table categorizes the networks described in this volume under a series of broad (and inevitably somewhat overlapping) factors, and specifically its activities, the range of action (European or global), and the number and quality of its components. The table also serves the scope of identifying the similarities and pinpointing the differences among organized networks of non-state actors.

The first case is provided by the "Pan-European ECO forum" (hereinafter, the ECO forum). The *ECO forum* coalition was established in concomitance to the 1993 "Environment for Europe" Ministerial Conference under the name of "Pan-European NGO Coalition". The coalition has coordinated civil society's participation and involvement in the political process set out in the final declaration of the Conference, also known as "EFE process", ever since. The current name was adopted in 1998, during the negotiations for the ratification of the Aarhus Convention, signed in Aarhus in 1998. The government representatives decided that non-governmental interested parties should be given the opportunity to express their opinion and ideas. The invitation to participate in the negotiations was then extended to all the NGOs concerned with environmental issues. In order to be more influential, the NGOs that adhered to the invitation melted into the ECO Forum. At present, the *Forum* is in charge of coordinating the civil society interests with the Meeting of the Parties (MOP) of the Aarhus Convention.[103]

The second case is also involved with environmental matters. This is the European Environmental Bureau (EEB),[104] the first European network created in defence of environmental interests. Established in 1974, the EEB claims to be the Europe's largest federation of environmental organisations, with 140 member organisations who, as the EEB's website states, "are guided by the voices of 15 million European citizens". The EEB is involved in a vast array of activities, labelled in five big areas: "biodiversity & nature", "climate & energy", "governance & tools", "industry & health", and "sustainability". For the sake of ease, this book considers the EEB among the European cases. In actuality, over the years the network has become an official interlocutor of both European and global institutions. The EEB policy officers are in dialogue with the European Commission, Parliament and Council, as well as with the relevant departments of the UN (Department of Economic and Social Affairs – UNDESA, United Nations Environment Programme – UNEP) and OECD.

Third is the "Consultative Platform", which collaborates with the European Food Safety Authority (EFSA). The Consultative Platform was established in 2004 by the EFSA Management Board (MB) pursuing Article 36 of the Regulation n. 178/2002, which disposes on the EFSA's duty to establish and to promote a network

[103] See generally www.eco-forum.org.

[104] See generally www.eeb.org.

of organizations operating in the field of food security.[105] The aim of such networking is to facilitate scientific cooperation, to exchange information, and to implement future projects. The Consultative Platform undertakes the main task of improving the relationships between interested parties and the EFSA.

The European Energy and Transport Forum (hereinafter "The Transport Forum"),[106] which is the fourth case, is similar to the Consultative Forum. The Transport Forum was established with the Commission Decision 2001/456/EC, based on the conclusions of the Transport Council of 20 September 2000, which called upon the Commission to set up a transport forum to replace the Energy Consultative Committee, set up in 1996 (the mandate of which expired few months later, in February 2001). A total of 34 members sit in the Transport Forum. Chosen by the Commission, with a 2 year-renewable mandate, the members of the Transport Forum represent all sectors involved in energy and transport policy. Namely: nine operators (energy producers and land, sea and air freight carriers, manufacturing industry); five representatives of networks and infrastructures (gas, electricity, rail, road, ports, airports, air traffic control); seven users and consumers (including demand management); six representative of trade unions; five from environmental organisations and organisations responsible for safety, particularly in the field of transport; and, finally, two representatives from the academic world or from think tanks.

Fifth is the Euclid Network, a network that connects around 300 organizations of various kinds from 24 countries from across Europe, including large international charities, social enterprises, cooperatives, and small grass-roots initiatives, to facilitate peer-learning, pan-European partnerships, and influence processes, and make the sector as a whole stronger and more innovative at the core of civil society in Europe and worldwide. The Euclid Network also runs projects across Europe to develop civil society leaders.[107]

The sixth example has already been introduced. This is ALTER-EU, a coalition of about 200 European civil society groups, trade unions, academics and public affairs firms concerned with the increasing influence exerted by corporate lobbyists on the political agenda in Europe, the resulting loss of democracy in EU decision-making and the postponement, weakening, or blockage even, of urgently needed progress on social, environmental and consumer-protection reforms.[108]

Seventh, and final, is the Alternative Trade Mandate (ATM).[109] ATM is an alliance that was born in October 2011. It is composed of more than 50 organizations from civil society (including development and farmers' groups, Fair Trade activists, aid agencies, trade unionists, migrant workers, environmentalists, women's, human rights, faith and consumer groups) as well as of networks of activists from Germany,

---

[105] See generally www.efsa.europa.eu.

[106] See generally www.europa.eu/legislation_summaries/energy/european_energy_policy/l27044_en.htm.

[107] See generally www.euclidnetwork.eu.

[108] See generally www.alter-eu.org.

[109] See generally www.alternativetrademandate.org.

France, Spain, Austria, Belgium, Italy, Ireland, Netherlands, UK and Bulgaria. As the name of the coalition suggests, ATM members are devoted to developing a European trade policy that is more inclusive, respectful of human rights and ecologically sustainable.

1.8.2 The Empirical Evidence. Part II: the Global Arena

The empirical evidence from the global arena includes, as a first case, the "NGO Forum", described at the outsets of this chapter. The mission of this Asian-led network of civil society organizations is to enhance the capacity of civil society to negotiate with the ADB.[110] The objectives of the NGO Forum include public awareness raising activities; the development of a cohesive framework supported by other public interest groups to develop strategies on issues related to the ADB's activities; the influence on the ADB to adopt poverty reduction-focused and grassroots-based policies for sustainable development; and, finally, the assistance towards local communities through networks aimed at fighting for equitable, social, and environmental justice, democratic governance, and safeguards in the ADB's projects.

Second is the "Conference of International Non-Governmental Organisations" (CINGO), which provides a venue where NGOs awarded participatory status by the COE may have their initiatives considered.[111] The CINGO was created in 2005, and it is now recognized as an institution of the COE. In view of this, it constitutes a fundamental pillar in the COE "Quadrilogue" with the Committee of Ministers, the Parliamentary Assembly, and the Congress of Local and Regional Authorities. Among the tasks that are fulfilled by the CINGO, two deserve further attention. First, the CINGO ensures that the participatory status of single NGOs functions correctly. In so doing, the *forum* helps to affirm the political role of civil society at the COE. Second, and more relevantly, the CINGO decides on policy lines and defines and adopts action programs.

Third is the "Consultative Committee of the Universal Postal Union" (CCUPU), established by the Universal Postal Union (UPU) Congress on September 16, 2004. The CCUPU is composed of NGOs representing customers, delivery service providers, workers' organizations, suppliers of goods and services to the postal sector, and other organizations that have an interest in international postal services including direct marketers, private operators, international mailers, and printers. Its main task is to provide a framework for effective dialogue between these postal industry stakeholders and Members of the UPU. The CCUPU is also responsible for analysing the documents and reports of the main UPU bodies, preparing reports, and formulating recommendations in support of the work of the UPU decision-making bodies.[112]

---

[110] See generally www.forum-adb.org.

[111] See generally www.coe.int/T/NGO/default_en.asp.

[112] See generally www.upu.int/consultative_committee/en/index.shtml.

Fourth is the Climate Action Network (CAN), a global network of over 900 NGOs in more than 100 countries, working to promote government and individual action to limit human-induced climate change to ecologically sustainable levels. Its many purposes include: exchanging information and expertise between network members, stimulating joint actions, and attending governmental meetings on environmental issues. CAN members work to achieve these goals through information exchange and the coordinated development of NGO strategy on international, regional, and national climate issues.[113]

Fifth is the BetterAid network, created in 2007 to advocate the Organization for Economic Development and Cooperation Development Assistance Committee (OECD DAC) on development cooperation and aid effectiveness. At the beginning BetterAid included over 700 development organizations from civil society.[114] Interestingly, this network has gone through various iterations since 2007, becoming a consultative body for the OECD DAC, then splitting into two different, although related, coalitions, and finally merging into a broader network of civil society actors.

Sixth is the Conference of NGOs in Consultative Relationships with the United Nations (CONGO).[115] Established in 1948, CONGO's declared mission is to facilitate through various means the development of a dynamic and informed worldwide NGO community able to influence policies and actions at all levels of the UN. Among its objectives is the improvement of NGOs accessibility and presence at all levels of the UN, the engagement of member NGOs to construct better working relationship, and the advocacy on principles and goals shared with the UN. But CONGO also serves as an organ of communication and co-operation. The meetings of CONGO's sub-committees can be important in influencing political strategy both within and outside the UN.

A seventh case is that of the UNCAC Coalition, a global network of over 350 civil society organisations spanning 100 countries, committed to promoting the ratification, implementation and monitoring of the UN Convention against Corruption (UNCAC).[116] The UNCAC Coalition was established in August 2006, and since then it has engaged in joint action around common positions on the UNCAC, it facilitates the exchange of information among members, and it supports national civil society efforts to promote the UNCAC.

Eighth is the case of the Global Call to Action Against Poverty (GCAP).[117] Formed in 2004, the GCAP is an alliance composed of more than 100 national coalitions and over 300 supporting organizations (trade unions, community groups, faith groups, women and youth organisations, NGOs and other campaigners) from six continents, working together across more than 100 national platforms. Other organisations and groups work in partnership with the GCAP, either globally or as

---

[113] See generally www.climatenetwork.org/.

[114] See generally www.betteraid.org/en/about-us.html.

[115] See generally www.ngocongo.org.

[116] See generally www.uncaccoalition.org/en/.

[117] See generally www.whiteband.org/en.

part of national coalitions, supporting and collaborating in the fight against poverty. The GCAP, in fact, claims to be "the world's largest civil society movement calling for an end to poverty and inequality". The GCAP adds to existing campaigning on poverty by forming diverse, inclusive national platforms that are able to open up civil society space and advocate more effectively than individual organisations would be able to do on their own.

The last case is among the most broad-based civil society networks currently in operation: CIVICUS. This alliance emerged in 1991 on the initiative of a range of civil society leaders from all over the world. The aim was to form a global alliance of individuals and organizations that might strengthen civil society institution. CIVICUS advocates to stimulate dialogue among civil society organizations and across the non-profit, business and public sectors. How successful it has been is debated. CIVICUS reports continuous growth, with 150 organisational and individual in full membership, and 1120 members (both organisations and individuals) who provide solidarity in its work. Critics argue that the principal achievement of this network has been the publishing on data on civil society at the global level.

1.8.3 The Empirical Evidence. Part III: Minor Examples

In addition to the main case studies, a few minor examples will be occasionally used. These include the "Informal Council", the "NGO Advisory Body", and the "Consultative Board on the Future of the WTO", all set up by WTO Director Generals between 2001 and 2003 with the scope of studying and clarifying the institutional challenges faced by the WTO, communicate the concerns of civil society, and recommend how the WTO could meet these concerns.[118]

Seven other cases will also provide minor examples within the volume. First, The European Peacebuilding Liaison Office (EPLO), the platform of European NGOs, networks of NGOs, and think tanks active in the field of peace-building, created with the aim of promoting sustainable peace building policies among decision-makers in the EU.[119]

Second, the Human Rights and Democracy Network (HRDN), an informal grouping of NGOs operating at EU level in the broader areas of human rights, democracy and conflict prevention (the network aims to influence EU and member state human rights policies and the programming of their funding instruments to promote democracy, human rights, and sustainable peace).[120]

Third is the "Global Climate Coalition", which represented between 1989 and 2002 the group of businesses opposing immediate action to reduce greenhouse gas emissions. The group – to which mostly US businesses adhered – formed in response

[118] See WTO Press Release n. 236/2001 "More Appoints Advisory Panel on WTO Affairs", July 5, 2001.

[119] See generally www.eplo.org.

[120] See generally www.act4europe.org/code/en/about.asp?Page=41.

to several reports from the Intergovernmental Panel on Climate Change (IPCC). Members began to abandon the Coalition in 1997. In the year 2000, the rate of corporate members leaving accelerated after they became the target of a national divestiture campaign. The Coalition was "deactivated" in 2002.

Fourth is the "NGO monitor".[121] Founded in 2002, a few months after the UN World Conference Against Racism in Durban, NGO Monitor commits to generate and distribute critical analysis and reports on the output of the international NGO community for the benefit of government policy makers, journalists, philanthropic organizations and the general public. The main scope of this coalition is to increase the accountability of its NGOs members.

Similar to NGO Monitor is the fifth minor example referred to in this volume. This is the "Humanitarian Accountability Partnership" (HAP).[122] Established in 2003, HAP is a partnership of humanitarian and development organizations dedicated to ensuring greater accountability to people affected by crises through the promotion of standards on quality and accountability. HAP also certifies organizations against those Standards.

The sixth, and final, minor example referred to in this volume is the World Third Network (WTN). The WTN's international secretariat is located in Malaysia, with offices in Europe, Latina American and Africa. Composed of civil society organisations and individuals, the WTN advocates for topics as development, developing countries and North-South affairs.[123]

References

Allott, P. 1992. Reconstituting humanity – New international law. *European Journal of International Law* 3: 219.
Anheier, H., M. Glasius, and M. Kaldor. 2001. *Global civil society*. Oxford: Oxford University Press.
Ankersmit, F.R. 1996. *Aesthetic politics: Political philosophy beyond fact and value*. Stanford: Stanford University Press.
Avant, D.D., M. Finnemore, and S.K. Sell. 2010. *Who governs the globe?* Cambridge: Cambridge University Press.
Batliwala, S., and D. Brown (eds.). 2006. *Transnational civil society. An introduction*. Bloomfield: Kumarian Press.
Benvenisti, E. 2014. *The law of global governance*. The Hague: Martinus Nijhoff.
Berman, P. 2007. A pluralist approach to international law. *Yale Journal of International Law* 32: 301.
Besson, S. 2009. European legal pluralism after Kadi. *European Constitutional Law Review* 5: 237.
Bohman, J. 2007. *Democracy across borders. From Demos to Demoi*. Cambridge: MIT Press.
Bolton, J. 2000. Should we take global governance seriously? *Chicago Journal of International Law* 1: 217.

[121] See generally www.ngo-monitor.org.

[122] See generally www.hapinternational.org.

[123] See generally www.twn.my/.

Brown Weiss, E. 2010. On being accountable in a kaleidoscopic world. *American Society of International Law Proceedings* 104: 477.
Bull, H. 1995. *The anarchical society: A study of order in world politics*. New York: Columbia University Press.
Casini, L., and B. Kingsbury. 2009. Global administrative law dimensions of international organizations law. *IILJ* Working Paper 9.
Cassese, S. 2003. *Lo Spazio Giuridico Globale*. Laterza: Roma-Bari.
Cassese, S. 2009. *Il diritto globale*. Torino: Einaudi.
Charney, J.I. 1993. Universal international law. *American Journal of International Law* 87: 529.
Chiti, E., and B. Mattarella. 2012. *Global administrative law and EU administrative law. Relationships, legal issues and comparison*. Berlin: Springer.
Chryssochoou, D.N. 2009. The European Synarchy: New discourses on sovereignty. *Göttingen Journal of International Law* 1: 115.
Cover, R.M. 1983. The Supreme Court, 1982 Term-Foreword: Nomos and narrative. *Harvard Law Review* 97: 4.
Crozier, M., S. Huntington, and J. Watanuki. 1975. *The crisis of democracy: Report on the governability of democracies to the Trilateral Commission*. New York: New York University Press.
Dahl, R. 1999. Can international organizations be democratic? A skeptic's view. In *Democracy's edges*, ed. I. Shapiro and C. Hacker-Cordon. Cambridge: Cambridge University Press.
Dahrendorf, R. 1999. The third way and liberty: An authoritarian streak in Europe's new center. *Foreign Affairs* 16.
Davies, T. 2013. *NGOs, a new history of transnational civil society*. Oxford: Oxford University Press.
De Burca, G., R.O. Keohane, C. Sabel. 2013. New modes of pluralist global governance. *IILJ* Working Paper 1.
De Mars, W.E. 2005. *NGOs and transnational networks. Wild cards in world politics*. London: Pluto Press.
De Oliveira, M.D., and R. Tandon (eds.). 1994. *Citizens strengthening global civil society*. Civicus.
Donini, A. 1995. The bureaucracy and the free spirits: Stagnation and innovation in the relationship between the UN and NGOs. *Third World Quarterly* 16: 421.
Dunoff, J.L. 1998. The misguided debate over NGO participation at the WTO. *Journal of International Economic Law* 1: 433.
Edwards, G. 1792. *Form and foundation, views and laws, proposed for the consideration of members of an universal society*. London.
Haas, E.B. 1976. Turbulent fields and the theory of regional integration. *International Organization* 30: 173.
Hall, R.B., and T.J. Biersteker (eds.). 2002. *The emergence of private authority in global governance*. Cambridge: Cambridge University Press.
Heclo, H. 1978. Issue networks and the executive establishment. In *The new American political system*, ed. A. King. Washington, DC: American Enterprise Institute.
Held, D., and K. Koenig-Archibugi. 2004. Introduction. *Government and Opposition* 39: 125.
Higgins, R. 1995. *Problems and process: International law and how we use it*. Oxford: Oxford University Press.
Kaldor, M. 2003. The idea of global civil society. *International Affairs* 79: 583.
Kamminga, M.T. 2007. What makes an NGO "Legitimate" in the eyes of states? In *The involvement of NGOs in international governance and policy: Sources of legitimacy*, ed. A. Vedder. Leiden: Martinus Nijhoff Publishers.
Kazansky, P. 1902. Théorie de l'administration international. *Revue Generale de Droit International Publique* 9: 353.
Keane, J. 2005. *Global civil society?* Cambridge: Cambridge University Press.
Keck, M.E., and K. Sikkink. 1998. *Activists beyond borders: Advocacy networks in international politics*. Ithaca: Cornell University Press.

Kegley, C., and E. Wittkopf (eds.). 1995. *The global agenda: Issues and perspectives*. New York: McGraw-Hill.
Keohane, R.O., and J.S. Nye (eds.). 1971. *Transnational relations and world politics*. Cambridge: Harvard University Press.
Keohane, R.O., and J.S. Nye. 1977. *Power and interdependence: World politics in transition*. Boston: Little Brown.
Kingsbury, B., N. Krisch, and R.B. Stewart. 2005. The emergence of global administrative law. *Law and Contemporary Problems* 68: 15.
Kissinger, H. 2014. *World order. Reflections on the character of nations and the course of history*. London: Penguin.
Kohler-Koch, B., and C. Quittkat. 2013. *De-mystification of participatory democracy: EU governance and civil society*. Oxford: Oxford University Press.
Krasner, S. (ed.). 1983. *International regimes*. Ithaca: Cornell University Press.
Lador-Lederer, J. 1963. *International non-governmental organizations and economic entities: A study in autonomous organization and Ius Gentium*. Leyden: A.W. Sythoff.
Lang, S. 2013. *NGOs, civil society and the public sphere*. Cambridge: Cambridge University Press.
Lipschutz, R. 1992. Reconstructing world politics, the emergence of global civil society. *Millenium: Journal of International Studies* 21: 399.
Manheim, J. 2001. *The death of thousand cuts: Corporate campaigns and the attack on the corporation*. Mahwah: Lawrence Erlbaum.
Marzower, M. 2013. *Governing the world. The history of an idea, 1815 to the present*. New York: Penguin.
McGinnis, J.O. 2012. *Accelerating democracy: Transforming government through technology*. Princeton: Princeton University Press.
Moravcsik, A. 2002. In defense of the "Democratic Deficit", reassessing legitimacy in the European Union. *Journal of Media and communication Studies* 40: 603.
Moravcsik, A. 2004. Is there a "Democratic Deficit" in world politics? A framework for analysis. *Government and Opposition* 39: 336.
Mullerson, R. 1990. Right to survival as right to life of humanity. *Denver Journal of International Law and Policy* 19: 1.
Norris, P. (ed.). 2011. *Democratic deficit: Critical citizens revisited*. Cambridge: Cambridge University Press.
Ottaway, M. 2001. Corporatism goes global: International organizations, nongovernmental organization networks, and transnational business. *Global Governance* 7: 3.
Peters, A., and A. Bianchi (eds.). 2013. *Transparency in international law*. Cambridge: Cambridge University Press.
Pickard, B. 1956. *The greater United Nations*. New York: Carnegie Endowment.
Rabkin, J. 2005. *Law without nations? Why constitutional government requires sovereign states*. Princeton: Princeton University Press.
Reinalda, B., and B. Verbeek. 2004. *Decision making within international organizations*. Abingdon: Routledge.
Reinsch, P.S. 1911. *Public international unions: Their work and organization: A study in international administrative law*. Boston: Ginn and Company.
Ruggie, J.G. 2004. Reconstructing the global public domain – Issues, actors, and practices. *European Journal of International Relations* 10: 499.
Ruzza, C. 2007. Advocacy coalitions and the participation of organised civil society in the European Union. In *Governance and civil society in the European union: Exploring policy issues*, ed. V. Della Sala and C. Ruzza. Manchester: Manchester University Press.
Salamon, L., and H. Anheier. 1996. *The emerging non-profit sector*. Manchester: Manchester University Press.
Sapra, S. 2009. The WTO system of trade governance: The stale NGO debate and the appropriate role for non-state actors. *Oregon Review of International Law* 11: 71.

Scholte, J.A. 2014. Reinventing global democracy. *European Journal of International Relations* 20: 4.
Shapiro, M. 2001. The institutionalization of European administrative space. In *The institutionalization of Europe*, ed. A. Stone Sweet, W. Sandholtz, and N. Fligstein. Oxford: Oxford University Press.
Shapiro, M. 2005. "Deliberative", "Independent" Technocracy V. democratic politics: Will the globe echo the E.U.? *Law and Contemporary Problems* 68: 341.
Siedentop, L. 2000. *Democracy in Europe*. London: Penguin.
Slaughter, A.M. 2000. Judicial globalization. *Virginia Journal of International Law* 40: 1103.
Slaughter, A.M. 2003. A global community of courts. *Harvard International Law Journal* 44: 191.
Slaughter, A.M. 2004. *A new world order*. Princeton: Princeton University Press.
Stavasage, D. 2004. Open-door or closed door? Transparency in domestic and international bargaining. *International Organization* 58: 667.
Stewart, R.B. 2014. Remedying disregard in global regulatory governance: Accountability, participation, and responsiveness. *The American Journal of International Law* 108: 211.
Stone Sweet, A. 2010. The European Court of Justice and the judicialization of EU governance, living reviews in European governance. *Living Reviews in European Governance* 2: 5.
Strange, S. 1996. *The retreat of the state: The diffusion of power in the world economy*. Cambridge: Cambridge University Press.
Tyler, P.E. 2003. Threats and responses: A new power in the streets. *New York Times*, February 17.
Wapner, P. 1995. Politics beyond the state. *World Politics* 47: 311.
Warkentin, C. 2001. *Reshaping world politics. NGOs, the internet, and global civil society*. Lanham: Rowman & Littlefield.
Wouters, J., A. Nollkaemper, and E. De Wet (eds.). 2008. *The Europeanisation of international law. The status of international law in the EU and its member states*. The Hague: TMC Asser Press.
Wouters, J., J. Pauwelyn and R.A. Wessel (eds.). 2012. *Informal international law making*. Oxford: Oxford University Press.
Zurn, M. 1998. Democratic governance beyond the nation state?. *Institut für Interkulturelle und Internationale Studien Arbeitspapier* n. 12.

Chapter 2
The Emergence of Civil Society Networks

2.1 Civil Society Networks

In Chap. 1, GCS was presented as a potential driving force behind the rise of common administrative standards for regulatory decision-making within the EAS and the global legal regimes. Chapters 2 and 3 further explore the nature of this participation in supranational decision-making, in particular the role of supranational networks of civil society. NGOs and other non-state actors may in fact cooperate through networks constructed by reference to their common interests and needs. Indeed, the terms "network" and "networking" are already widely used in a variety of disciplines, ranging from political, social, and legal studies. The works of Castells, Keck and Sikkink, and Slaughter, mentioned in Chap. 1, cover just a small portion of the academic literature on networks. Conceptually, networks offer a viable solution to qualify many structured linkages of interests and people. This ranges from civil society itself – described by Martin Shaw in terms of a network "of institutions through which groups in society in general represent themselves, both to each other and to the state"[1] – to governance partnerships, within which governments retain various strategic roles, communities of practice or hubs of knowledge. Significantly, in 1981 the Yearbook of International Organizations introduced a new category of organizations – those with "non-formal, unconventional or unusual structures" – in an effort to classify composed transnational networks. Increased focus on this topic, however, has not produced scholarly agreement on the understanding and descriptions of networks. Consider as an example, the radical changes that the notion of (issue) network has experienced over the last 40 years. In a seminal work published in 1978, the American political scientist Hugo Heclo theorised that a connection exists between the terms "issue" and network.[2] Heclo's aim was

[1] See M. Shaw, *Global Society and International Relations*, see chapter 1 n 68, at 647.

[2] See H. Heclo, *Issue Networks and the Executive Establishment*, see chapter 1 at section 7.1.

G. Sgueo, *Beyond Networks - Interlocutory Coalitions, the European and Global Legal Orders*, Studies in European Economic Law and Regulation 8,
DOI 10.1007/978-3-319-28875-8_2

to problematise, and indeed criticise, a new form of political organisation that had risen in Washington D.C., during the administration of Jimmy Carter. According to Heclo, NGOs – or "issue-activists" as he termed them – were forming loose alliances in which they defined political affairs by sharing information about them. A worrisome phenomenon, noted Heclo, because it was bound to alienate the broader public from public affairs, and eventually weaken American democracy. Today, the common understanding of issue networks is positive. These denote forms of organisation that are compatible (or may even be instance of) liberal democracy.

Returning to Keck and Sikkink, there are essentially three types of structured linkages: those with essentially instrumental goals (e.g. transnational corporations or banks); those motivated primarily by shared causal ideas (e.g. scientific groups); and those motivated primarily by shared principles (which fit the description of transnational advocacy networks). Similar to the latter account is that of Wolfgang Reinicke (2001), who speaks of "global public policy networks" in which businesses, NGOs and other civil society actors, as well as governmental agencies and IOs are comprised. Paul Craig identifies three typologies of networks, and distinguishes them according to their role. These are "enforcement networks", which are designed to render enforcement more efficacious across international boundaries; the "information networks", which are aimed at the exchange of information between governmental agencies; finally, the "harmonization networks", which are created to foster closer uniformity in regulatory standards.[3] Other scholars have expanded the concept of networks. Walter Powell (1990), for instance, defines networks as a third mode of economic organization, distinguishing them from hierarchies (because "networks are lighter on their feet") as well as from markets (because "networks are part for the exchange of commodities whose value is not easily measured"). Grainne de Burca, Robert Keohane and Charles Sabel concur.[4] In their description of three modes of pluralist global governance, networks are located between the second and the third modes. The first mode of governance actually involves the creation of comprehensive and integrated international regimes. It is therefore characterized in terms of a principal-agent model: the nation-states are considered the principals, whereas the agents consist of the international regimes created by nation states. The WB, the Bretton Woods Monetary Regime, and the WTO are worthy ideals of this mode of governance. The second mode of governance illustrated by de Burca, Keohane and Sabel features a departure from hierarchy as a structured principle of IOs, replaced by the spread of forms of networked information exchange. Thus, in mode two, it is the network of connecting entities, rather than the entities themselves, that represent the expression of governance. Examples of mode two can be found in regime complexes (described by Raustiala and Victor as "partially overlapping and non-hierarchical institutions governing a particular issue area") and GAL. The former are also a substantial part of mode

[3] See P. Craig, "Global networks and shared administration", in S. Cassese et al. (ed.), *Research Handbook on Global Administrative Law* (Cheltenham, Edward Elgar, 2016).

[4] See G. de Burca, R.O. Keohane, C. Sabel, *New Modes of Pluralist Global Governance*, see chapter 1 at section 3 and chapter 3 n 15.

three of governance, further described in terms of "Experimentalist Governance". This, in the words of the authors, consists of a "a set of practices involving open participation by a variety of entities (public or private), lack of formal hierarchy within governance arrangements, and extensive deliberation throughout the process of decision making and implementation". Illustrations of experimentalist governance include the Inter-American Tropical Tuna Commission, the UN Convention of the Rights of Persons with Disabilities, and the Montreal Protocol on Substances Depleting the Ozone Layer. With these capacities, networks have proven useful also for describing endeavours as diverse as international business, transnational organized crime, and international terrorism. Finally, many other scholars have understood networks mainly as dynamic, open, and voluntary loose associational structures.[5] In particular David Singh Grewal (2008) and Jeffrey Juris subscribe to this notion. According to Grewal networks are "interconnected groups of people linked to one another in way that makes them capable of beneficial cooperation, which can take various forms, including the exchange of goods and ideas". In the opinion of Jeffrey Juris (2008), activists follow a "cultural logic of networking" when they generate concrete networking practices. Juris' logic of networking includes "(1) the building of horizontal ties and connections among diverse autonomous elements, (2) the free and open circulation of information, (3) collaboration through decentralised coordination and consensus-based decision making".

This volume uses these propositions as a point of departure. However in an effort to avoid confusion or overlapping with similar definitions used to describe civil society actors' groups and associations that often differ dramatically in the context of their organization or goals, the term "network" will not be used to describe civil society groupings. Those will be referred to as "interlocutory coalitions" (IC). Obviously, the word "coalition" is not brand new. Carlo Ruzza (2006), for instance, theorised the "movement advocacy coalitions" – i.e., institutionalised social movements organisations active at the EU level and involved into stable or semi stable coalitions with sectors of left-liberal parties. But in this volume, the definition of IC is used only in the context of a single organizational model of network. The ICs as theorized in this book are situated in the between of the pluralist and globalist schools of thought described by William de Mars in classifying scientific literature on civil society actors (and specifically on NGOs).[6] The pluralist approach describes the approach from civil society to world politics in terms of a cumulative impact;

---

[5] See, for instance, H. Compston, *Policy Networks and Policy Change: Putting Policy Network Theory to the Test* (London, 2009); G. H. McCarthy, P. Miller, P. Skidmore (eds.), *Network Logic: Who Governs in an Interconnected World?* (2004) available at www.demos.co.uk/catalogue/networks; T. Borzel, "Organizing Babylon – On the Different Conceptions of Policy Networks" (1998) 76 *Public Administration* 253; K.G. Provan, H.B. Milward, "Do Networks Really Work? A Framework For Evaluating Public-Sector Organizational Networks" (2001) 61 *Public Administration Review* 4; A. Aviram, "Regulation by Networks" (2003) *Brigham Young University Law Review* 1179; C. Heckscher, "Organizations, Movements, and Networks" (2005–2006) 50 *New York Law School Law Review* 313. See also the 2002 UN Development Program, which has counted 20,000 international networks of NGOs.

[6] See W.E. de Mars, *NGOs and Transnational Networks*, see chapter 1 at section 6.2, at 37.

whereas in the globalist approach civil society is regarded as a way to implement and enforce global norms. In describing the ICs, this book builds upon pluralism in recognizing the importance of societal partners and networking as a tactic for GCS' actors. But it also draws from globalism, in that it focuses on the influence that GCS exerts on norms and IOs at the global level.

2.1.1 The Factors Behind the Emergence of Supranational Civil Society Networks: Global Issues

Before proceeding with a detailed account of the composition and activities of the ICs (Chap. 3), the present chapter will explore the factors that drive their rise. There are many and diverse factors that drive the emergence of coalitions of civil society actors, both in a direct and indirect manner. Seven factors are key: (1) the global nature of problems dealt by civil society (2) the diffusion of technology; (3) the globalisation of media; (4) the dramatic increase of transportation of goods and people around the world; (5) an increasingly globalised higher education; (6) the recent evolution of fundraising; (7) and, finally, but decisively, the benefits for both non-state actors and IOs that result from joining into a network.

The first factor influencing the birth of supranational coalitions of civil society actors was touched upon, albeit indirectly, in Chap. 1 in the preliminary description of GCS and assessment of the weight of civil society actors at the supranational level. This is the dramatic increase in problems of global rather than just local dimensions, such as environmental protection, labour rights, women's rights, and human rights. Some of today's most pressing problems, observes Robert Howse (2008), are problems that can only be solved by the coordinated exercise of sovereignty. This is why issues of global dimensions have produced transnational activities and cooperation. Civil society's activists increasingly liaise with colleagues from different organizations, located in places far away from their offices, but with the same goals towards a specific issue. An incredible number of websites and self-promoted initiatives from all around the world have spread, and continue to spread, via the web to explain how global issues are developing, to suggest solutions, to call for action and to demand for collaboration with governments and IOs.

Take the case of tropical deforestation, one of the major global issues to have occupied international debate in the last decades. The term "tropical deforestation" entered in the environmental debate only in the early 1970s. Prior to that, neither international conferences, nor academic debate mentioned this issue. The situation changed when ozone and climate change brought awareness into public debate, and gave new urgency to environmental concerns like deforestation. In 1974 the WWF considered the protection of tropical rainforests as the most important nature conservation objective of the decade. Shortly after, US President Carter declared tropical rainforests a global issue, which were followed by stronger conservation efforts by the Reagan Administration. By the end of the 1980s, deforestation had become the epitome of third world environmental problems: and a global issue had emerged. Similarly, the issue of violence against women did not receive international recognition until the early 1980s, and only became an object of UN activity from 1985 onwards. However, by the 1990s, having global standing, the issue was considered amongst the most important international women's issues. It received significant institutional support and was advocated in increasing numbers by civil society actors, both domestically and internationally. As early as 2000, the UN Entity for Gender Equality and the Empowerment of Women (UN Women) estimated that over 60 initiatives to tackle the gender gap (including violence against women) were on-going around the world. In the EU alone, in addition to the principles enshrined in the Treaties, gender equality is addressed in 15 European Directives adopted between 1975 and 2010, as well as a great number of the EU's strategic documents (e.g. the EU 2020 Strategy). The increased global recognition of issues such as labour rights, international terrorism, and global diseases resemble the pattern of emergence described for tropical deforestation and violence against women.

The globalization of governance issues makes an interesting point about the power of GCS. As long as matters of governance (e.g. security) concern only international public actors, civil society actors are at comparative disadvantage. But as soon as global issues begin to dominate the international agenda, civil society actors active in their respective fields gradually succeed in making their voices heard at the international level. This happens because states are considered unable to deal effectively with transnational problems, while civil society offers an alternative that may bypass state institutions altogether. Perhaps demonstrating this point, in 1995 Archibugi and Held (1995) proposed reforms to the UN General Assembly, where people, rather than nation-states, should be represented. In the authors' opinion the "People's Assembly" would represent individuals on the basis of "one person, one vote" and, most importantly, would only consider global issues.

Supranational regulators are aware of the tight bounds that make issues around the world connected and interdependent, and therefore of global concern. An illustration of this awareness is the section of the UN website dedicated to "Global Issues". This section offers an overview of some of the global issues that engage the efforts of the UN. These include safeguarding peace, protecting human rights, establishing the framework for international justice and promoting economic and social progress, the organisation of Olympic Games, the fight to climate change, international terrorism and AIDS. Other examples come from the World Economic Forum and the Union of International Associations. Since 2006 the World Economic Forum has published "Global Risks", a report highlighting global risks that can be systemic in nature, and are capable of causing breakdowns of entire systems and not merely their component parts.[7] In such reports, the assessed risks are considered global in nature insofar they have the potential to cause significant negative impact across entire countries and industries. The risks are grouped under five classifications – economic, environmental, geopolitical, societal and technological – and

[7] See Global Risk 2014, available at www3.weforum.org/docs/WEF_GlobalRisks_Report_2014.pdf

measured in terms of their likelihood and potential impact. In turn, from 1976 to 1995, the Union of International Associations, a well-known institute devoted to research on international associations and organizations, published an "Encyclopaedia of World Problems and Human Potential". This is the result of an ambitious effort to collect and present information on the problems facing humanity, as well as the challenges posed by such problem.

2.1.2 The Diffusion of Technology

A second, and decisive, factor driving the emergence of networks of civil society actors at the supranational level relates to the diffusion of technology. The widespread use of technology has decreased the costs of trans-boundary communications, including the costs of phone calls, postal services and faxes, providing means for non-state actors to communicate with greater frequency. The use of Internet has allowed NGOs to coordinate global campaigns to an extent that would have been impossible even as recently as 20 years ago. New forms of organization via the Internet have enabled the recruitment of previously inactive citizens into social participation and civic action. As a result of global communication systems, proximity now appears unimportant for social interaction, as well as for political and economic organization. As Marshall McLuhan (1962) theorized in the 1960s with the idea of the "Global Village", the advancement in the fields of science and technology have contributed to the shrink of the world into a village.

To understand the relevance of technology to non-state actors one might consider the Report on Global Trends in the Not-For-Profit Sector.[8] According to the report, in the US 73 % of the non-profits have technology budgets in place. In New Zealand the number is 69 %, while in Australia 68 %, and in Canada and UK 64 %. In Germany, The Netherlands and France the technology budgets in place in non-profits are, respectively, 61 %, 44 %, and 34 %. The 2009 John Hopkins Non-profit Listening Post Project similarly found that the majority (88 %) of non-profit actors surveyed reported that technology is integrated into many (if not all) aspects of their organization; that (86 %) their organization used technologies "sophisticated" or "moderately sophisticated"; that (96 %) had an organizational website and were connected to the Internet (97 %).[9]

Needless to say, early commentators have regarded the spread of new technologies in civil society's activism with enthusiasm. Back in 1841, François-René de Chateaubriand wrote that technological advances could be expected to bring about an international society. Few years before this, in 1827, Jean Charles Léonard de

[8] See Global Trends in the Non-Profit Sector, Report 2012, available at www.grantthornton.co.nz/Assets/documents/pubSeminars/GTI-Not-for-Profit-Sector-Industry-Report.pdf

[9] See S.L. Geller, A.J. Abramson, E. de Leon, *The Nonprofit Technology Gap. Myth or Reality?*, Johns Hopkins University – Center for Civil Society Studies, available at ccss.jhu.edu/wp-content/uploads/downloads/2011/09/LP_Communique20_2010.pdf.

Sismondi (1827) in the *Revue Encyclopédique* celebrated the acceleration of communications that brought the disappearance of distances and sped up the circulation of thought. In addition, the organizers of the international congresses of the early and mid-nineteenth century used to celebrate such progresses in technology. In 1999, Scott Kirstner (1999) from Wired magazine in the article "Nonprofit Motive" reported "The new breed of Silicon Valley Philanthropists would make Mother Teresa crunch the numbers". The article echoed the excitement that surrounded the spread of the upcoming global-scale use of the Internet. Those arguing that technologies, and particularly the Internet, were transforming civil society's activism came from the upper echelons of politics, journalism, public policy, and social sciences. The web, argued the enthusiasts, would provide a low-cost and adaptable "platform" where civil society activists could rapidly acquire information, engage in peer-to-peer conversations, share their knowledge, and therefore maximize the results of their efforts. Flowery dot-org fantasies suggested that an epochal shift was about to be realized. At the national level, the Internet seemed to have the capacity to open up the world to users even in shut-in places, and could erode dictatorships. In a famous 1997 judgment, the US Supreme Court emphasized the potential of Internet, arguing that "through the use of chat rooms, any person with a phone line can become a town crier with a voice that resonates farther than it could from any soapbox".[10] At the supranational level the promise was even greater. The Internet, it was suggested, would enable civil society actors to operate on a global scale, profoundly impacting on the spread of democratic values in trans-national policy-making.

Undoubtedly, the proliferation of the Internet on a planetary scale has contributed to some of the largest advancements in democracy, social activism and advocacy. The increased availability of high-speed connections, the expansion of mobile-based services, media-rich, real-time data sharing, and voice-data communications have enhanced the potential of civil society. In the age of "global collaboration", information is disseminated online, awareness and engagement are fostered through social networks, and advocacy relies on a heavy usage of web-related tools. Early examples include the use of slide show in 1900s by the Congo Reform Movement to campaign for human rights[11]; and the 1990s International Campaign to Ban Landmines was almost entirely a web-based endeavour (ironically, due to the fact that coordination of actions and exchange of views and information between the participants to the campaign had been entirely done through the web, when in 1997 the campaigners were awarded the Nobel Peace Prize, they were forced to create a bank account in order to be transferred the money). Also during the 1989 Chinese Revolution, Chinese activists avoided the tight controls on telecommunications systems set up by the Chinese government by using fax machines. Another example is the 2007 mobilization against the military junta in Myanmar. The first demonstrations were filmed with video cell phones and immediately uploaded on

[10] See Reno v. ACLU, U.S. 521 (1997).

[11] See S. Sliwinski, "The Childhood of Human Rights: Kodak on the Congo" (2006) 5 *Journal of Visual Culture* 333.

YouTube. These videos soon went viral and made their way to the front line around the world. By the time the dictatorship closed down all Internet providers and cut off mobile phones operators, the brutality of the regime had been globally exposed.

Meanwhile, online political organizations and petitions platforms have attracted millions of members, raised tens of millions of dollars, and campaigned for a vast array of issues. Examples include the US based left-leaning group MoveOn.org and Change.org, introduced in Chap. 1 of this volume, the world's large petitions platform with 70 million users in 196 countries. Also discussed in Chap. 1 is the case of Avaaz, an online community involved in campaigning, signing petitions, funding direct actions, emailing, calling and lobbying governments in 15 languages, served by a core team on six continents and thousands of volunteers. Avaaz became internationally recognized after the Bali Climate Change Conference in 2007, which was credited by the Canadian delegation as changing their position on climate change.[12] Finally, smaller initiatives include iPetitions and Petitions Online.

Other consequences of the massive use of technology will be discussed in Sects. 2.3 and 2.6. However as a brief introduction here, we can say that the massive use of technology has encouraged the rise of a range of web-based media outlets thanks to which information has become widely accessible to the world population; and, in the second place, it has promoted networked fundraising strategies from no profits around the world. In terms of the former, globally spread and accessible information indirectly strengthens the process of formation of partnerships between civil society actors. Knowledge and information are in fact essential to the activities of civil society's networks. Technology is also important in developing networked fundraising strategies. Being part of a network with strong technological assets, in fact, potentially duplicates the opportunities to receive donations. For most non-profits, email marketing and websites are now the primary and the most important marketing platforms, while the relevance of mediums such as SMS's and paid advertising have decreased significantly over the last 10 years. That is not all. A large majority of non-profits are now actively allocating budgets towards technology, so that they can improve their visibility to donors, generate awareness about their causes and improve their fundraising abilities.

Despite this, the current state of technology available to non-state actors does not resemble the revolution celebrated by the fanatics of a digital democracy. At the supranational level, the vulgate of a widespread, democratic, decentralized and virtual network of non-state actors capable of promoting global values is little more than fable. Supranational activism has not yet given birth to the non-hierarchical and self-organizing meshwork sketched by Wendy Harcourt (2003), nor has it generated the virtual communities described by Howard Rheingold (1993) as "caretakers of electronic public space". At the domestic level trends relating to avenues for political engagement other than political parties are equally concerning. Consider the following. Of 49 democracies surveyed by the World Forum for Democracy in 2013, 40 saw turnout decline in elections to national Parliaments between 1980–

[12] See the official report of the event from Avaaz available at www.avaaz.org/en/bali_report_back/

1984 and 2007–2013.[13] The World Forum for Democracy reports that on average turnout declined by 10 percentage points across these 49 countries. Further, The World Values Survey explains that those who reported having a "great deal" or "quite a lot" of confidence in political parties dropped from 49 % in 1990 to 27 % in 2006. Between 1990 and the late 2000s, decreases were also reported in matters such as the willingness of individuals to engage in activities such as signing a petition or attending a demonstration. Those who reported that they might, or have already, signed a petition, dropped by 20 percentage points, from 76 % to just over half, at 56 %. Over the same period of time, those who said they had or might participate in a political demonstration dropped from 62 % to 51 %.[14] Furthermore, in spite of the dramatic expansion of the Internet, important differences in the access to the Net remain between white, educated, Western citizens and those defined as "disadvantaged groups" (the poor, the elderly, the undereducated, and those in rural areas, not to mention those living in Countries where the access to the Internet is controlled by the government).

The contrast described above between the benefits provided by technologies to civil society activists and organization, and its limits (in terms of digital-divide and insufficient engagement from individuals) can be taken to mean two different things. On the positive side, it is crucial to the birth of civil society's networks. Given that technology is a vector for supranational activism, effective networks would not exist without the role it plays in communication, logistics and strategies. They attract the type of citizens that Lance Bennett (2008) would describe as "actualizing citizens" – people that are distrustful of traditional forms of authority and are inclined to adopt more privatized responses to changing social circumstances – and would oppose to "dutiful citizens" – to whom involvement in civic life is an obligation to be fulfilled through conventional activities, such as voting. On the negative side, technologies reveal the restrictions of networks and more generally of GCS, because they have not fulfilled the promise to make GCS even more global. In this sense, having come to terms with the limits of modern technologies, future developments of civil society coalitions may well be depended on a broader set of factors. Chief among them, as will be discussed in the following sections, are globalized media and transportations, the diffusion of knowledge, as well as economic and practical reasons.

[13] See A. Clarke, "Exploiting the web as a tool of democracy: new ways forward in the study and practice of digital democracy" (2013) *World Forum for Democracy Issues Paper*, available at www.coe.int/t/dg4/cultureheritage/news/wfd/study_en.pdf

[14] See World Values Survey, 2014, available at www.worldvaluessurvey.org/wvs.jsp

2.1.3 Globalized Media

Technological advancement has not only shattered social boundaries and transformed the activism and organizational models of GCS. It has also impacted the landscape of mass media. Because of this, the media can be considered the third factor that is (indirectly) driving the tendency to a networked civil society. Media is the only source that is easily accessible by all walks of people through various electronic appliances (i.e., TV, Radio, Internet, News Papers, tablets and mobile phones). Nayan Chanda (2007) offers a powerful example to illustrate this: back in 1453, it took 40 days for the Pope to learn that Constantinopolis had fallen to the Turks. In 2011, the destruction of the Twin Towers of the World Trade Center in New York was broadcasted on television, in real time, all over the globe.

Historically governments have always succeeded in monopolizing information or in effectively preventing trans-border communication. It was with the emergence of international news agencies in the nineteenth century, such as Reuters, that a global system of news codification emerged and, accordingly, state control of informational flows begun to erode. Until the 1990s, however, mainstream media systems in most countries remained relatively national in scope. It has only been since the second half of the 1990s that communication media have become increasingly global, extending their reach beyond the nation-state to conquer audiences worldwide. The production, distribution and consumption of an increasing number of media products now take place in a transnational context.[15]

Of all the changes in the media environment that have occurred since 2000, the growth of digital media is arguably the biggest. Blogs, citizen's journalism, and participatory journalism are among the most appealing new features of the informational landscape. As of 2013, the blog search engine Technorati had tracked more than 133 million blogs.[16] More than 346 million people globally read blogs published in 81 languages, and 900,000 blog posts are generated in an average 24 h period. Dissemination of information through digital and participatory channels has partly replaced what bloggers derisively term the "elite media". People have access to information and are given the opportunity to contribute to the formation of collective knowledge. "Electronic means", explain Weiss and Gordenker (1996) in addressing the emerging scene of world public opinion making, "have literally made it possible to ignore borders and to create the kinds of communities based on common values and objectives that were once almost the exclusive prerogative of nationalism". To the point that, adds Benkler (2006), in the information economy the primary raw materials have become the information, the knowledge and the culture. In this new scenario, that Benkler calls the "networked information economy", the roles of "sender" and "receiver" are far less clearly divided than in the

[15] This is called the "third age of political communication" by J.G. Blumler, D. Kavanagh, "The Third Age of Political Communication. Influences and Features" (1999) 16 *Political Communication*.

[16] See the 2013 Technorati Report, available at www.technorati.com/wp-content/uploads/2013/06/tm2013DIR2.pdf.

traditional media landscape. In addition to empowering the formerly voiceless, the new media have given consumers of political information a broader menu to choose from, contributing to a more competitive marketplace of political ideas. Yet, the more the availability of information has spread, the more a need for a filter that can mediate and organize the informational flow is needed. Networks are also created out of this necessity.

2.1.4 Globalized Transportations of Goods and People

The dramatic increase in travel and transportation of goods and people around the globe should be mentioned as being a fourth powerful factor in shaping and facilitating the rise and influence of the ICs. Objectively, distances in the current world are shorter than ever before, and positively affect both goods and people. In the case of goods, the latest data available from the Global Transportation Forum reports a 2,4 % growth in world export volume in 2013, same pace as 2012; a 5 % growth in world container traffic; and a 1,4 % increase in airfreight tonne-km, a reversed trend from 2012 contraction. But globalization of mobility is especially evident with the mass movement of people. With modern transport, no two cities in the world are any more than about a day's travel apart. And costs are lower, too. In 1997 the Air Transport Association reported that the constant dollar yield of airline tickets 2 years earlier, in 1995, was one half of what it was in 1966, while the number of international passengers increased more than four times in the same period.

The decline in airfares, together with the convenience of modern transport, has shifted international travel beyond the exclusive privilege of the wealthy. Around the world it is estimated that 200 million people currently live and work outside of their country of origin. According to the 2008–2009 Global Information Technology Report an overall of 200 million people live and work outside of their country of origin.[17] This is reportedly a phenomenon on the increase. The OECD countries alone host some 75 million migrants (persons having adopted a residence outside of the country where they were born). The availability of talented knowledge workers in coming years is not expected to grow as fast as the global demand for their skills. In such a situation, mobility (understood as both physical, e.g. through temporary or permanent migrations, and virtual, e.g. information networks or virtual teams across networks) is key for narrowing the existing gap between supply and demand.

In the present situation, fast-growing countries attract the most migrant workers in sectors such as construction or domestic services. In many cases, however, such movements are compounded by significant in-flows of highly skilled foreign workers ("expats") providing services as consultants or managers in local or international businesses, and sometimes in government (a country such as Qatar, for

[17] See V. Ivaturi, B. Lanvin, H. Mohan, "Global Mobility of Talents: What Will Make People Move, Stay or Leave in 2015 and Beyond?" *Global Information Technology Report 2008–2009*, available at www.insead.edu/v1/gitr/wef/main/fullreport/

example, has a population of about one million, of whom only 20 % were born in Qatar). Migrations of workers affect both economics and societies. Companies located in countries less equipped with the ability to produce enough scientists and engineers (such as China, Spain, Italy, or smaller European economies) are likely to continue paying a premium to attract necessary talent, while pressuring their respective governments to adopt measures to attract a greater presence of foreign workers. In turn, attracting the necessary numbers of skilled workers require governments to address social and cultural factors at the root of their systems. Improvements to domestic educational systems might be an example of this.

The globalization of transportation and global mobility has impacted upon GCS and its organizations in numerous ways – although two stand out as the most significant. The first regards physical mobility. The reality that travelling costs have significantly reduced over the last 10 years has had direct effect on non-state actors mobility. The Union of International Organization Yearbook reports that in 2012, 392,588 official meetings were held in 167 Countries and 1,374 cities. Carnegie Europe reports that between 2010 and 2014 the President of the European Council and the President of the European Commission had cumulatively 339 official visits (including participation in multilateral summits and bilateral visits). The EU has about 140 delegations, second only to the network of the three biggest EU member states: France, Germany and UK.[18] The second major consequence of global mobility for GCS is virtual. Many of the leaders of civil society movements have been educated abroad, and have gained work experience around the world. Building from this background, their visions of advocacy and lobbying are based upon massive networking efforts carried out on a global scale.

2.1.5 The Globalization of Education and Knowledge

A fifth catalyst of a networked GCS is globalized knowledge. This "faculty club culture", as Peter Berger and Samuel Huntington (2002) have called it, the "cultural internationalism", to borrow the definition from Akira Irye (1997), or the "pluralistic security communities", as Karl Deutsch (1957) described collective identification processes, nurtures its beliefs chiefly through the educational systems. The quantitative and qualitative growth of cross-border partnerships among public and private universities and think tanks has become the epicentre of a vigorous scientific debate over globalization and civil society. The number of examples is vast. Chapter 1 introduced the case of the Global Alliance for Liberal Arts, a network of 16 universities from Europe to Asia, committed to joint teaching programs, the development of collaborative research and offering opportunities for staff and students to move between them. Other cases include the Worldwide University Network, an organization that uses the combined resources of its members, 17 research institutions spanning 5 continents, to achieve collective international objectives and to

[18] See S. Lehne, I. Tseminidou, *Where in the world is the EU?*, see chapter 1 n 17 and n 28.

stretch international ambitions[19]; the University Global Partnership Network, a multilateral network of 5 universities from Europe, US and South America, collaborating in research, learning and teaching to "benefit global society"[20]; the Global Research Council, a virtual organization, comprised of the heads of science and engineering funding agencies from around the world, and dedicated to promoting the sharing of data and best practices for high-quality collaboration among funding agencies worldwide[21]; and, finally, eLabEurope, an European think tank that in 2015 launched "The Good Lobby" – a project aimed at creating a platform to connect professionals across different disciplines to support civil society organisations in need of professional services.[22]

Thousands of conferences, research projects, and teaching programmes gather an increasingly developed network of students and scholars from all over the world. New modes of transportation and communication have facilitated mobility among students, scholars, and knowledge itself. Mobility, in turn, has allowed students (at least elite students) to move fluidly across institutions, while open access has made it possible for non-elite students to seek higher education *en masse*. In the inaugural Online College Students report, released in 2012 by Learning House, 80 % of surveyed students said they enrolled in fully online programs at institution within 100 miles from where they live. In 2014, only 54 % said the same.[23] This is largely driven by graduate students, 48 % of whom said they prefer to study at an institution more than 100 miles away from home. Moreover, 72 % of surveyed students declared that their primary motivation for studying online were related to their careers. In 2014 the Harvard Business Review confirmed this assumption.[24] The survey on the top 100 CEOs in the world explicated that 61 % of those have been college educated outside their country. In many respects, college graduates have become the principal drivers of economic development for nations. These "communities of thought" share their expertise and information to design and build infrastructure, to establish healthcare and education systems, to create jobs across all sectors of the economy, and to make agriculture sustainable. Scholarly exchanges form common patterns of understanding of public policies and connect politically allied countries to build technical expertise and system capacity.

Accordingly, higher education is undergoing a rapid transformation propelled by a confluence of factors. Those include fluctuating enrolments and funding resources associated with global economic booms and busts and increasing demands for applied science, technical expertise, and innovation. Neoliberal views of university believe that strategies of internationalization will render the institution place-less, that new forms of digital learning will make physical campuses obsolete; that virtual media will enable students to download lectures wherever they may be, even if

[19] See generally www.wun.ac.uk

[20] See generally www.ugpn.org

[21] See generally www.globalresearchcouncil.org

[22] See generally www.elabeurope.eu/thegoodlobby

[23] The report is available here www.learninghouse.com/ocs2013-report/

[24] See www.hbr.org/2013/01/the-best-performing-ceos-in-the-world/ar/1

they have no intention of completing a course. In neoliberal views of universities private investments supplement – or supersede – public funding as higher education and corporate industry become "synergized". All these changes, it is predicted, will make "the global university" of the future more cost-effective and serviceable in a competitive knowledge economy.[25]

How does a globalized higher education – and a consequently globalized knowledge – influence the growth of GCS' networks? In two ways. The first was just discussed. The globalization of knowledge creates the conditions for a growing number of interactions between students, scholars, universities, think tanks and other centres of cultural activity. The globalization of knowledge is also important in shaping the identity of future civil society leaders – leaders who are increasingly educated in the same universities, and who have been taught to share the same set of values and vision of the world – values and vision that they will most likely promote throughout their professional lives. Such leaders-activists are not celebrities in the sense we commonly understand celebrity. According to Andrew Webster (2009) "these people are faceless, even odourless in some sense, at least in the context of the media". Yet global activists-leaders compensate this facelessness by being a precious resource for both GCS and the ICs. They gain specialist knowledge of their subject; and they gain skills in presenting their cause to the public and to the media. Considerable examples are those provided by Nyaradzayi Gumbonzvanda, Board Chair and Chair of the Executive Committee at CIVICUS; Wael Hmaidan, director of CAN since April 2012; Cyril Ritchie, President of CONGO between 2010 and 2014; Stephen Barnett, Director of the Euclid Network; and Rayyan Hassan, Executive Director of the NGO Forum. All of them, albeit in different ways, are perfect illustrations of contemporary leaders in a globalized world. First, they all attended elite universities – Wael Hmaidan graduated with an executive MBA from INSEAD, Stephen Barnett attended the College of Europe, where he graduated in European Studies – or are somewhat linked with academia: Rayyan Hassan, for example, before joining the NGO Forum was senior lecturer at the East West University in Bangladesh. Second, they gained considerable experience in advocacy for GCS at the international level. Cyril Ritchie, for instance, served in a number of management roles. To name but a few: he was Vice President of the Union of International Associations, President of the International Civil Society Forum in Doha, and from 2000 to 2008 President of the CINGO Grouping "Civil society and democracy in Europe". Ritchie currently serves as the President of the Federation of International NGOs in Geneva, and as member of the Steering committee of the UBUNTU World Campaign for in-depth Reform of International Institutions, based in Barcelona. Alongside her position at CIVICUS, Nyaradzayi Gumbonzvanda leads the World YWCA (another global organisation whose core mission is to enhance women leadership). Previously, she served on Boards of Action Aid International. As well as working GCS' activists, current leaders of civil society also matured as entrepreneurs (Hmaidan for example founded IndyACT, an

[25] See Universities 2030: Learning from the Past to Anticipate the Future, available at www.globalhighered.files.wordpress.com/2014/04/universities-2030-final-for-posting.pdf

organization that started in Lebanon in 2007 and now is spread all over the Arab World and Europe), or consultants for international organizations. It is the case of Barnet, who worked with local and regional authorities, EU institutions and stakeholders in various contexts, including the Europe 2020 Strategy and the "European Semester" for policy coordination across EU Member States. And it is again the case of Gumbonzvanda, who served for 10 years with the UN, both UNICEF in Zimbabwe and Liberia and subsequently with UNIFEM, now UN Women, as Regional Director for East and Horn of Africa. The list of examples could extend much further. Kumi Naidoo, who perhaps needs no introduction, before becoming international executive director at Greenpeace, served 10 years as secretary general at CIVICUS. He also leads the Global Call for Climate Action, a network that is bringing together environmental, aid, religious and human rights groups, labour unions, scientists and others to advocate on climate negotiations. Jacqueline Hale, currently member of the governing board of the HRDN, is a graduate from the University of Cambridge, worked in the United Nations and the European Parliament, as well as for no-profits as Open Society Institute, while she currently serves as head of the advocacy of Save the Children in Brussels. The Nobel Peace Prize is a further example. Since 1974 it has often been awarded to individuals closely associated with an NGO cause. Among the civil society leaders who were acknowledged the Nobel Prize for Peace there is Sean MacBride, the President of the International Peace Bureau, Andrei Sakharov, who campaigned for human rights in the Soviet Union in 1975, Mother Teresa of Calcutta, Lech Walesa, and the Guatemalan campaigner for indigenous peoples' rights: Rigoberta Menhu Tum.

2.1.6 Networked Fundraising

Fundraising is another factor driving the emergence of networks of GCS. Not incidentally, a discussion of resources initiates most scholarly work on interest group coalitions. Scholars maintain that networks serve as an economical and efficient means to form more powerful advocacy blocs. Obviously, no civil society actor can continue to exist for long without the generosity of donors. Fundraising is at the foundation of any not-for-profit activity. On the one hand, the increased number and visibility at the international level of GCS' actors has augmented the accessibility to donations (both from the private and the public sector). Even without precise and comprehensive figures, and considering that non-profits around the world faced a major funding crunch during 2009–2010 due to the global economic slowdown, available data suggests a significant economic scale of not-for-profit fundraising activities. According to OECD estimations, NGOs operating at the international level currently disburse more that the UN, and channel almost two-thirds of the EU's relief aid.[26] The London School of Economics in 2001 estimated that NGOs had collected in 1 year 7 billion dollars in development funds and 2 billion dollars

[26] See OECD, Geographical Distribution of Financial Aid to Developing Countries, Paris 1997.

in funds from US foundations.[27] Even more expansively, according to the 2003 UN Handbook of Nonprofits Institutions, the civil society sector is estimated to account on average for 5 % of the Gross Domestic Product (GDP) in the majority of Western democracies (exceeding 7 % in Canada and US). This means that the GDP contribution of the non-profit sector exceeds or is on a par with the GDP contribution of many industries in these same countries, such as utilities and financial intermediation. Moreover, it is believed that charitable giving will increase in the years to come for a number of reasons, including the progressive growth in the global population of the "ultra-high-net-worth individuals" (10.2 % growth in 2010, according to the World Wealth Report); the ageing world population that, according to experts forecasts, may donate more to charities (the World Giving Index estimates that only 24 % of 15–24 years old make charitable donations, while 33 % of those in the age group of 50 or more engage in charity); and, as previously discussed in Sect. 2.2, technology is also encouraging greater awareness towards humanitarian causes. Non-profits such as Kiva, an online organisation that allows people to lend money via the Internet to microfinance institutions in developing countries, enables donors to assist to underprivileged entrepreneurs with little access to credit. The net result is that individual donors are able to collectively make a difference to the enterprise of their choice.

On the other hand, this increased accessibility to funds and the positive forecasts have not corresponded with an equitable and overspread distribution of the grants and donations available globally. On the contrary, it is well acknowledged that chronic under-funding and understaffing affect many NGOs through their lifespan. Exemplary is the case of non-profits that rely heavily on government grants and contracts, which have been the most affected by the recent economic recession. In the US, more than 40 states have reduced spending on services such as health care, education, and care for the elderly and disabled since 2010. The Blackbaud Index of Charitable Giving (representing 1468 organisations, with 2.2 billion dollars in charitable income) also showed a decline in charitable giving throughout 2010.[28] The OECD reported how revenues for many non-profit organizations decreased dramatically after 2009, as in the case of the International Federation of Red Cross, whose net voluntary contributions declined of 50 % between 2008 and 2009. Recovery is expected, but at a slow rate. Giving US reports that in 2013 Americans donated 335 billion dollars to charitable causes. For the first time in 7 years, charitable giving is going back to the pre-recession levels. Not to mention the fact that many non-profit organizations face opposition from governments with regard to foreign funds. The International Centre for Non-Profit Law reports six countries that have passed laws in the past 2 years affecting NGOs that receive foreign funds, and a dozen more countries that plan to do so. The "Closing Space" report from the Carnegie Endowment for International Peace lists 50 countries that place some

[27] See H. Anheier, M. Glasius, M. Kaldor, *Global Civil Society,* see chapter 1 at section 6.1, chapter 1 n 68 and n 81.

[28] See Blackbaud Report 2012 available at www.blackbaud.com/files/resources/downloads/2012.CharitableGivingReport.pdf

restrictions on overseas funding of NGOs.[29] Restrictions may be motivated by security reasons (as in the case of India, Russia or Egypt) or transparency reasons, as in the case of US. To address this problem in 2011 the UN appointed Maina Kiai as a Special Rapporteur on the Rights to Freedom of Peaceful Assembly and of Association.

More often than not, smaller civil society organizations are unable to update their websites because initial grants funded the building of the site, but not its maintenance. There is often a high turnover of volunteer staff, which can lead to the abandonment of certain projects considered beyond the capability of the organization. Smaller organizations may not rely on personnel who master the English or the French languages. Newcomers to transnational advocacy may lack the resources to send delegates to conferences and other networking opportunities. In sum, many organizations find it a constant struggle to raise enough funds not only to keep their advocacy projects running, but also to improve and widen their reach.

Networking may be thus explained, on the plus side, in the light of the drive for growth embedded in NGOs' increased entrepreneurship and expanded operating expenditures or, on the minus side, as a pragmatic solution for NGOs to enhance their limited budget to effectively fulfil their social goals.[30] By accessing a network, smaller actors seek to overcome their lack of experience to write funding proposals and, also, to escape certain criteria such as "financial accountability" that may preclude their participation. Not to mention attempts to fight the unwillingness of donors to evaluate start-up grants (the ones that are the most needed by small organizations). As clearly explained by the 2012 Report on Global Trends in the Not-For-Profit Sector, not only are online marketing strategies now perceived as critical by many non-profits for fundraising, marketing and generating awareness for their cause, but also and particularly the funding crunch that happened during the recession has motivated many non-profits around the globe to start forming alliances to create a common pool of funds and combine their various programmes under one umbrella. One may look at EU grants as an example. EU funds are notoriously awarded to organised networks of civil society actors rather than to single NGOs. In 2015, for instance, 16 out of the 24 operating grants of the LIFE programme where awarded to ICs, including the CAN and the EEB.[31]

---

[29] The report is available at www.carnegieendowment.org/2014/02/20/closing-space-democracy-and-human-rights-support-under-fire/h1by

[30] See D.C. Hammack, D. Young, *Nonprofit Organizations in a Market Economy. Understanding New Roles, Issues and Trends* (San Francisco, Jossey Bass, 1993); C. Cicoria, "European Competition Law and Nonprofit Organizations: A Law and Economics Analysis" (2006) 6 *Global Jurist Topics* article 3.

[31] See European Commission, European Environmental NGOs – LIFE operating grants 2015, 2015.

2.1.7 Networks' Benefits

Finally, the growing prominence of the ICs may be explained by the substantial benefits that are associated with networks' membership. Benefits associated with civil society networks are manifold. First, by routinizing practices, interactions, and exchange among its participants, networks enhance the possibilities for them to focus on projects while leaving the administrative functions to a centralised body, and to engage in debate and negotiation with IOs. Second, they increase the opportunities to access relevant information at reduced costs, and to exchange expertise and best possible practices. Becoming members of a network, in other words, provides opportunity for civil society actors that are geographically dispersed, and would be otherwise politically mute, to access IOs' activities, at no additional cost (or, at least, without the costs of re-locating activities from their place of origin to some other city or state). Third, networks offer their members the opportunity to increase their global visibility. Finally, networks enhance the credibility of their members through the adoption of formal procedures to select participants and to certify their accountability. Scholars have also listed additional benefits for civil society actors entering into a network. Claudia Liebler and Marisa Ferri, for instance, mention increased access to information, increased efficiency, and increased visibility. They also list solidarity and support, risk mitigation, reduced isolation, and enhanced credibility.[32]

The benefits are, however, mutual. Through the synergies with the ICs, the IOs aim at *first* increasing their democratic legitimacy in the face of growing political challenges; *second* and equally important, IOs aim at adopting more appropriate regulations by relying on genuine grassroots support; and, *third*, they aim at being perceived as accountable in the development of laws and policies. As supranational coalitions of civil society actors emerged from the fundamental needs of IOs to maximize their problem-solving capacity, a utilitarian stance may suggest that IOs find it easier to negotiate with a single coalition instead of managing multiple negotiations with a multitude of NGOs. The preference for EU-level organisations expressed by the European Commission in the civil dialogue is an example of this. This preference for a "centralised, neo-corporatist model of state civil-society relations", in the description of Carlo Ruzza, reveals the will to leave the task of aggregating preferences to civil society itself.[33]

For all the above reasons, the ICs – whether they are composed solely of NGOs or also of other non-state actors – are welcomed by IOs as a momentous shift in supranational rule-making, proving how interstate relations have transformed into

---

[32] C. Liebler, M. Ferri, *NGO Networks, Building Capacity in a Changing World*, Study supported by Bureau for Democracy, Conflict, and Humanitarian Assistance Office of Private and Voluntary Cooperation 2004 (available at www.kenia.usaid.gov) list eight different benefits for NGOs in a network. These include increased access to information, increased efficiency, solidarity and support, increased visibility, risk mitigation, reduced isolation, and credibility.

[33] See C. Ruzza, *Advocacy coalitions and the participation of organised civil society in the European Union* see text at section 1, at 64.

composite and multi-levelled systems of governance. At the same time, such coalitions are increasingly considered ideal mechanisms by NGOs and other non-state actors for developing large-scale strategies to stronger advocate their requests towards IOs.

It should also be considered that the ICs – or, generally, networks – do not only convey benefits. As Middendorf and Busch (1997) have explained, mechanisms for public participation can be distorted and appear to represent a broad constituency, and yet in fact be highly unrepresentative. Thus, the effective participation of their members and, above all, the actual influence on IOs' rule-making activities represents the main risk of the ICs. Whether this approach may be warranted, the ICs may turn out to be only expensive *fora* for deliberative communication whose actual influence over the formation of IOs' policies is actually scarce, or even ineffective. In addition to the issue of effectiveness, coalitions of civil society actors generate two additional classes of concerns. The first class of concern relates to its functioning. Holding NGOs and other civil society's groupings together in a coalition constitutes a complicated enterprise, especially when such coalitions grow bigger and, in consequence, the likeliness of controversial positions increases. Second, but not least, concerns are related to possible competition among the ICs, or the loss in creativity that comes from the constant replication of the same advocacy strategy from different coalitions. The more problematic aspects of civil society's networks will be touched on later, in the conclusions of this volume.

References

Archibugi, D., and D. Held (eds.). 1995. *Cosmopolitan democracy: An agenda for a new world order*. Cambridge: Polity Press.

Benkler, Y. 2006. *The wealth of networks: How social production transforms markets and freedom*. New Haven: Yale University Press.

Bennett, L.W. (ed.). 2008. *Civic life online: Learning how digital media can engage youth*. Cambridge, MA: Cambridge University Press.

Berger, P.L., and S.P. Huntington (eds.). 2002. *Many globalizations: Cultural diversity in the contemporary world*. Oxford: Oxford University Press.

Chanda, N. 2007. *Bound together. How traders, preachers, adventurers, and warriors shaped globalisation*. New Haven: Yale University Press.

De Sismondi J.C.L., "L'Amérique" (1827) *Revue Encyclopédique* 22.

Deutsch, K.W. 1957. *Political community and the North Atlantic area*. Princeton: Princeton University Press.

Harcourt, W. 2003. The impact of transnational discourses on local community organizing. *Development* 46: 74.

Howse, R. 2008. The end of the globalization debate: A review essay. *Harvard Law Review* 121: 1528–1554.

Irye, A. 1997. *Cultural internationalism and world order*. Baltimore: Johns Hopkins University Press.

Juris, J.S. 2008. *Networking futures: The movements against corporate globalization*. Durham: Duke University Press.

Kirstner, S. 1999. Non profit motive. *Wired Magazine* 7, 7 September.

McLuhan, M. 1962. *The Gutenberg Galaxy: The making of typographic man*. Toronto: University of Toronto Press.

Middendorf, G., and L. Busch. 1997. Inquiry for the public good: Democratic participation in agricultural research. *Agriculture and Human Values* 14: 45.

Powell, W.W. 1990. Neither market nor hierarchy: Network forms of organization. *Research in Organizational Behavior* 12: 295.

Reinicke, W. 2001. *Walking the talk: Global public policy in action, global public policies and programs*. Washington, DC: World Bank, World Bank Publications.

Rheingold, H. 1993. *The virtual community: Homesteading on the electronic frontier*. Boston: MIT Press.

Ruzza, C. 2006. European institutions and the policy discourse of organized civil society. In *Civil society and legitimate European governance*, ed. S. Smismans. Cheltenham: Edward Edgar.

Singh Grewal, D. 2008. *Network power. The social dynamics of globalization*. New Haven: Yale University Press.

Webster, A. 2009. Discussion at the Annenberg School of Journalism.

Weiss, T.G., and L. Gordenker (eds.). 1996. *NGOs the UN, and global governance*. Boulder: Lynne Rienner.

Chapter 3
The Interlocutory Coalitions: Composition, Governance and Supranational Stance

3.1 The Composition of Interlocutory Coalitions

This chapter outlines key characteristics of the ICs, including their composition, the rules for accession, the juridical status, and the rules governing their functioning. The description will be presented in schematic form by way of differentiation from other typologies of networks and/or groupings of civil society actors. The activities of the ICs will be described in Chap. 4.

The ICs are prevalently, but non-exclusively, composed of NGOs. As a general rule, individuals are not admitted as members. When conceded to be members of a coalition, individuals either play a secondary role with respect to other members, or serve to the coalitions' tasks out of commitment to a collective interest rather than in person. Only in rare occasions, individuals enjoy the same rights of collective members. One of those exceptions is Alter-EU. This coalition admits academics to be members and to serve in their personal capacity, instead of, say, representing the university or research centre where they are professionally located. Consider the synoptic table annexed to this volume. The entirety of the ICs exemplified in the table includes NGOs as members. In ten cases – accounting for 47 % of the total – civil society actors other than NGOs are also included. Of those, however, only in few cases single individuals are entitled to the IC's membership (most notably in the cases of CIVICUS and ALTER-EU); while in 14 ICs NGOs compose the majority (from 51 % onwards) of the members. In the following cases, the only members are NGOs: CAN, CINGO, CONGO, Consultative Platform, EEB, EPLO, NGO Advisory Body, NGO Forum, ECO Forum. This suggests that the term "individual" may include the ICs, in that it refers to both single human beings (natural persons) and persons that form groups due to common interests (legal persons). By contrast, the ICs differentiate from individuals in that its membership may indeed cover private individuals, but it tends to consider them minor players in the pursuit of its activities.

G. Sgueo, *Beyond Networks - Interlocutory Coalitions, the European and Global Legal Orders*, Studies in European Economic Law and Regulation 8,
DOI 10.1007/978-3-319-28875-8_3

3.2 Interlocutory Coalitions and Social Movements

In view of the composition, the ICs can be distinguished from the "social movements" (SM) – theorized by Alain Touraine and Sydney Tarrow – and from social networks. The current section will introduce the differences between the ICs and the SMs, while the next section will discuss the differences between the ICs and social networks.

There are three major differences between SMs and the ICs. A first, critical, distinction relies on membership. SMs are informal networks in which a more heterogeneous number of actors are involved, ranging from individuals, groups of people who act together to achieve specific goals, and only to a minor extent, NGOs. Not coincidentally, the SM theory started to appear in late 1960s and 1970s to explain new waves of political activism, such as student protests and feminism. The People's Global Action, launched in Geneva in 1998 (the hallmarks of this movement included a rejection of global trade and capitalism and the adoption of forms of direct action and civil disobedience)[1] or, more recently, the massive protests against the invasion of Iraq by the United States in 2003, are all cases used in the SM theory.

How SMs and the ICs approach issues is a second distinguishing factor between the pair. SMs mostly rise and fall through cycles of protest. In this sense, the definition of Anheier, Glasius and Kaldor reported in Chap. 1 of this volume is pertinent: SMs can be seen as a counterweight to global capitalism. As taught by the examples of the Seattle movement, the Spanish *Indignados*, Occupy Wall Street and the protests that occurred in Greece during the 2002–2003, both the mobilization of resources and the strategies to link these resources originated from a protest against a specific target. Building upon this assumption, SM scholars suggest that modern societies are "movement societies", i.e. societies where protests are an integral part of everyday politics.[2] Sidney Tarrow further reminds that boycotts, non-violent resistance, strikes, mass petitioning, barricades or other collective actions are frequently diffused and emulated from one SM to another. Similarly, the ICs are engaged in resource-mobilization and strategy-elaboration. As with the SMs, the ICs help bring the values of civil society and the voice of the citizen to the forefront. However, its approach to target issues, originates from a different focus – advocacy rather than protest – and works to different outcomes.

[1] See www.agp.org. See also S. Tarrow, *Power in Movements: Social Movements and Contentious Politics* (Cambridge, 1998); "Transnational Politics: Contentions and Institutions in International Politics" (2001) 4 *Annual Review of Political Science* 1. See generally H. Kohn, "Pan-Movements" (1935) 11 *Encyclopaedia of the Social Sciences* New York; R. Kolins Givan, K.M. Roberts, S.A. Soule (eds.), *The Diffusion of Social Movements. Actors, Mechanisms, and Political Effects* (Cambridge, Cambridge University Press, 2010).

[2] See D. Fuchs, *The Normalization of the Unconventional: Forms of Political Action and New Social Movements* (Berlin, 1990); D. Meyer, S. Tarrow (eds.), *The Social Movement Society* (Oxford, Rowman & Littlefield Publishers, 1998); E. Avril, J.N. Neem (eds.), *Democracy, Participation and Contestation* (Abingdon, Routledge, 2015).

A third difference exists between SMs and the ICs. While the former is a fluid structure that changes over time, has blurred borders, and can take on a range of organizational forms, the ICs can be significantly – albeit not exclusively – described by addressing its formal organization. In other words, the ICs consider a formal organizational structure as to the end of pursuing its activities and spreading its core-values. SMs, by contrast, are missing a similar organizational structure. They ignore political parties, do not recognise leadership and often reject formal organisation.[3] Even when some sort of organization is present – e.g. Global Trade Watch organized the 1999 "Battle of Seattle" for a year prior to the meeting, and so have been all the protests at multilateral economic institutions' meetings – this is not formally structured. The SM literature refers to such organized structures as Social Movement Organizations (SMO).[4]

The cases of CINGO and the Transport Forum move the discussion out of theory and into the tangible. In the CINGO a pyramidal structure is present. It is comprised of a plenary assembly that meets twice a year during the ordinary sessions of the Parliamentary Assembly and which all members are invited to attend. The CINGO-Assembly is chaired by its President-in-office whom is elected every 3 years. Central to the organizational structure of CINGO is a permanent body: the Standing Committee. This is a collective body that includes the members of the Bureau of the Conference, the Chairs and Vice-Chairs of the Committees and the Transversal Groups, the Chairs of Expert Councils, and in a consultative capacity, the outgoing President of the INGO Conference for 3 years and the Honorary Presidents of the INGO Conference. Next in order, and essential for the operations of CINGO, is the Bureau. This is made up of nine members who are delegates from NGOs belonging to the network and who sit on the Bureau in a personal capacity. Finally, three committees are in charge for specific topics of interest of the CINGO. Namely: Democracy, Global Cohesion and Social Challenge; Education and Culture; Human Rights. Differently from CINGO the Transport Forum relies on a mixed structure. The members of the Forum, i.e. a President and four Vice-Presidents elected among its members, a Bureau in which all the former sit, and a variable number of focus-oriented working parties compose the structure of this coalition. Another part of the Transport Forum's structure consists of the administrative structure of the Commission. Article 7 of the Commission Decision No. 2001/546/EC, in fact, states that "the Commission shall provide secretariat services for the Forum, the Bureau and the working parties". The administrative assistance from the IO to an IC – is not infrequent.

---

[3] See M. Castels, *Networks of Outrage and Hope. Social Movements in the Internet Age* (Cambridge, Polity Press, 2012), at 4.

[4] See C. Warkentin, *Reshaping World Politics*, see chapter 1 at section 6.1, at 21.

3.3 Interlocutory Coalitions and Social Networks

There are several similarities between Social Networks and the ICs. First is the relevance that technologies and media communication have had in the birth and development of the pair; and, second, is that in neither forum, power structures involve the command of a superior over a subordinate. But despite these commonalities, they differ in one key aspect: their purposes. Differently from Social Networks, the ICs have a purpose and a mission that goes beyond mere sociability. In this sense, the ICs resemble a "community", at least according to the description offered by Singh Grewal (not to be confused with the communities described by John Peterson, to which Sect. 3.12 of this chapter will return).

The underlying idea behind Social Networks analysis is that "ties" connect sets of actors, depicted as "notes". Three are the common characteristics to identify social networks. First is the size (the number of nodes, or participants, a network possesses). Second is the typology of the tie (reciprocal or one-way, and strong or weak). Third is the proportion of ties present in a network out of all possible ties, which is defined in terms of network density. In this sense, the ICs are described as social networks, in that they also have different sizes, of different typologies (even though always reciprocal), and of diverse density.

Another common (broader) description of Social Networks is that everyone on the Web can potentially take part in discussions and initiate topics, an area previously monopolized by mass media and other professional communicators. As reflected by the concept known as "*produsage*", production and usage in Social Networks form a joint process in which contents are changed dynamically by means of interactivity, multiple user groups and thematic shifts. In many respects, this is also the case of the ICs. As explained in Chap. 2, networks of civil society actors are supported by the tremendous acceleration in processes of interaction and the exchange of information, brought about by the spread of technologies and the ubiquity of media communications. Communicative strategies of Social Networks and the ICs also have similarities. Both promote a "bottom-up" form of opinion making (as opposed to former top-down influences). In the case of Social Networks this is due especially to low access barriers and the aid of a new, participatory journalism. Consider the case of the "*scenes*". In the words of Haunss and Leach (2007), a scene is defined as "a network of people who identify as part of a group and share certain belief system or set of convictions, that is also necessarily centred around a certain location or set of locations where that group is known to congregate". The ICs rely less on low access barriers and more on the use of various discussion forums to advocate towards IOs.

The differences between the ICs and Social Networks include, as explained before, the fact that only the former rely on the same values. The ICs are similar to the communities described by Singh Grewal: "a close-knit group of people who share a great deal – values, language, and, usually, some specific geographic location".[5] Hence, while membership in an IC is predicated upon the acceptance of such values (and sometimes also rules) as a precondition for access, Social Networks do not impose such limitations. However, and crucially, the fact that members adhere to ICs because they share a common set of values does not necessarily imply that they do not engage into antagonistic relations. The opposite is actually true. While Social Networks are mainly based on collaboration among their members, the opposite is true with ICs: they are based on antagonism. ICs are founded to the end of favouring cooperation among competing actors: these are requested to mediate (as Chap. 3 will examine in more depth) in order to overcome their differences and eventually find satisfactorily compromises.

3.4 Interlocutory Coalitions and Trans-governmental Committees

A second critical distinction can be made between the ICs and trans-governmental committees/networks. In the abstract, the ICs and trans-governmental committees have two common features. First, in both cases participants to the coalitions/committees aim at achieving the same advantages – that is the knowledge of other members' lines of action and the possibility to coordinate their action consequentially (moreover, the ICs may receive a significant share of their income from the IO to whom they cooperate). Second, both types of networks are based on agreements among their participants rather than established by an international treaty. In spite of these commonalities, trans-governmental committees, differently from the ICs, are entirely composed of national civil servants. Moreover, trans-governmental committees/networks have a "twilight existence", to use the words of Oscar Schachter (1971). In other words, they are almost non-existent in legal terms, since they consist of meetings and informal contacts between national regulators. ICs instead show a higher degree of formalisation, as shown in Sect. 3.9 onwards.

The European "comitology" committees offer the earliest and most developed example of trans-governmental committees. There are also interesting case studies of trans-governmental networks of sub-national actors (such as independent regulatory authorities) that meet and interact with their counterparts from other nations. Comitology committees are made up of national specialized civil servants and chaired by a *functionnaire* of the Commission, working to prepare legislation and oversee rule-making.[6] Networks of the second type in some sectors (such as data protection) have come to replace or have been layered on top of traditional comitology procedures. There are a few more examples in the international arena. The "Military Staff Committee", for instance, operates as a consultative body of the UN Security Council in all questions regarding military actions for the maintenance of

[5] See D. Singh Grewal, *Network Power*, see chapter 2 at section 1, at 21.

[6] See generally C. Joerges, E. Vods (ed.), *E.U. Committees: Social Regulation, Law and Politics* (Oxford-Portland, Hart Publishing, 1999).

peace and security. The "*Codex Commission*" operates as a subsidiary body of the *Codex Alimentarius* Commission. The "International Competition Network", founded in 2001, includes 117 competition agencies from 103 domestic jurisdictions. This network organizes training programs, publishes best practices, and develops policies that local agencies are encouraged to adopt. The Financial Action Task Force is composed of regulatory officials from 30 states and two regional organisations. This network develops and promotes policies against money laundering and terrorist financing to be adopted by states as well as by supranational regulators like the EU.[7] Finally, other examples are those of the "Basel Committee on Banking Supervision", the many regional committees collaborating with the WHO, the "G8" and "G20" meetings.[8]

3.5 Interlocutory Coalitions and QUANGOs

Finally, the composition of the ICs distinguishes them from the committees/groups in which civil servants and individuals without hierarchical relations with their governments are brought together to examine, discuss, and eventually reach agreement on the content of specific provisions. While there is no definitive agreement on the definition of these mixed committees, a recurrent one is that of QUANGO used to emphasize a closer proximity to civil society with respect to public powers.

The "International Organization for Standardization" (ISO), for instance, is not purely an NGO, since its membership is by nation, and each nation is represented by what the ISO Council determines to be the "most broadly representative" standardization body of a nation. That body might itself be a nongovernmental

[7] See, for instance, G. Sgueo, *Counter-terrorism financing in the EU budget* (2015) European Parliament.

[8] See M. Savino, "The role of Transnational Committees in the European and Global Orders" (2006) 6 *Global Jurist Advances* article 5, and *I comitati dell'Unione europea. La collegialità negli ordinamenti composite* (Milano, Giuffrè, 2005). On the contribution of trans-governmental committees to the shaping of global governance See A.M. Slaughter, "The Accountability of Government Networks" (2000–2001) 8 *Indiana Journal of Global Legal Studies* 347; and "Global Government Networks, Global Information Agencies, and Disaggregated Democracy" (2002–2003) 24 *Michigan Journal of International Law* 1041. See also K. Raustiala, "The Architecture of International cooperation: Transgovernmental Networks and the Future of International Law" (2002–2003) 43 *Virginia Journal of International Law* 1; F. Bignami, "Transgovernmental Networks vs. Democracy: The Case of the European Information Privacy Network" (2004–2005) 26 *Michigan Journal of International Law* 807. For more specific analysis on trans-governmental networks in economic regulation See S. Picciotto, "Networks in International Economic Integration: Fragmented States and the Dilemmas of Neo-Liberalism" (1996–1997) 17 *Northwestern Journal of International Law & Business* 1014. On G8 meetings See R.D. Putnam, N. Bayne, *Hanging Together: The Seven-power Summits* (Cambridge MA, Harvard University Press, 1984); M. Conticelli, "The G8 and "The Others"" (2006) 6 *Global Jurist Advances* article 2. On G20 meetings (in comparison to G8 meetings) See R. Goldbach, T. Hasche, J. Muller, S. Schuder, "Global Governance of the World Financial Crisis?" (2010) 2 *Göttingen Journal of International Law* 11.

organization (for example, the US is represented in ISO by the American National Standards Institute, which is independent of the federal government). Another example is the "G-20 Group", a permanent group composed of civil servants and private stakeholders that cooperate with the World Trade Organization in the assumption of decisions regarding agriculture. Similar in name, but different in composition and scope, is the "Civil G-20".[9] This is a meeting for policy dialogue between the political leaders of G20 countries and representatives of civil society organizations working on the issues related to the agenda of G20 Summit. The goal of this QUANGO is to facilitate exchange of ideas and opinions about the agenda of the G20 Summit and discuss pertinent issues that are of relevance to civil society. Also in the WTO framework, in the "Sub-Committee on Cotton" created during the Doha Round the Committee members were African NGOs, NGOs from developed countries, and African member states. The alliance collaborated with other groups, both composed of governmental officials and NGOs.[10] The United Cities and Local Governments is a QUANGO composed of NGOs and subnational governments. The organization harks back to 1913 and today has members in more than 100 countries.[11] The "Inter-Agency Standing Committee", created in 1992 as the central humanitarian policy-making body in the UN system and composed of heads of UN agencies, representatives of the Red Cross and other NGOs *consortia*; the "European National Human Rights Institutions"[12]; and the "global public-policy" networks,[13] provide additional interesting examples. Further, the UN Conference on Environment and Development gathered together official national delegates from countries around the world, scientists, and a vast number of NGOs; while the "International Union for Conservation of Nature", widely known as "World Conservation Union", include a variegated membership of 82 states, 111 governmental agencies, and over 800 NGOs.[14]

European examples include the Civil Society Contact Group set up in 1999 by the EU Commission Trade Directorate, and, second, the Permanent Stakeholder's Group established within the framework of the European Network and Information Security Agency. The former included representatives of human rights, social, environment, and development NGOs as well as consumers' organizations, trade unions, and the EU Economic and Social Committee. Article 8 of Regulation (EC) No 460/2004 of the European Parliament and the Council establishes the latter. The Regulation creates the "European Network and Information Security Agency". According to Article 8 of the Regulation, the Executive Director of the Agency has

[9] See generally www.g20civil.com

[10] See for further details E. Lynn Heinisch, "West Africa Versus the United States on Cotton Subsidies: How, Why and What Next?" (2006) 44 *Journal of Modern African Studies* 251.

[11] See www.uclg.org

[12] See G. de Beco, "Networks of European National Human Rights Institutions" (2008) 14 *European Law Journal* 860.

[13] See W.H. Reinicke, F. Deng, *Critical Choices. The United Nations, Networks, and the Future of Global Governance* (Ottawa, International Development Research Centre, 2000).

[14] See www.iucn.org.

the duty to create a Permanent Stakeholders' Group composed of experts representing the relevant stakeholders, such as information and communication technologies industry, consumer groups and academic experts in network and information security. However, not only does the Executive Director chairs the Permanent Stakeholders Group, but members of the European Commission are also entitled to be present in its meetings and to participate in its workings. Both these cases are exemplary of the "Open Method of Coordination" (OMC), a model of governance where different institutions and actors on the same of different levels do not stand in clear hierarchical relationship, but they rather operate alongside each other, in the quest for best possible solutions. In the description of Charles Sabel and Jonathan Zeitlin (2006), the EU OMC's process does not require policy harmonization, but rather seeks to promote learning by establishing common objectives, developing comparable metrics for assessing progress, and setting benchmarks for good performance. Because of this structure, explain Sabel and Zeitlin, the OMC are more flexible and adaptive than centralized hierarchies. Remarkably, Sabel (together with De Burca and Keohane)[15] considered the OMC as a failed attempt in experimentalist governance. Although the resemblance of the models is striking, as the authors explain, the outcomes of the OMC have diverged significantly, depending largely on the actors' disposition to allow others into the decision-making processes. The "Tuesday Group" is also concerned with European issues. Although created as a national-level initiative, Congresswoman Nancy Pelosi extended (with an amendment) its scope to the International Financial Institutions Act. The Tuesday Group was initially composed of representatives of US government agencies and big NGOs such as Greenpeace or Friends of the Earth. Eventually, participation was opened to any interested NGO.

By contrast, it is worth emphasizing that the mere presence of IOs' representatives in meetings does not necessarily imply that the coalition can be defined in terms of a QUANGO. Take the case of the Transport Forum. It is established that "Representatives of interested Commission services can take part in the meetings of the Forum, the Bureau and the working parties".[16] As in the case of the Consultative Platform – where EFSA's staff members are entitled to participate, to the only extent of providing technical support to the workings of the Platform – IOs' participants are only invited as observer. They are not entitled to vote, nor they are legitimated to express official dissent to the decisions taken by the IC. This is confirmed by the use of the acronym GONGO in the place of QUANGO, to pinpoint the case in which, regardless of its legal nature, the organization has been created, and it is controlled or even manipulated, by a government. It is actually the case of the Hugo Chavez's Bolivarian Circles or, according to CIVICUS, of the four fifths of registered NGOs in China. Recipient governments also create GONGOs to receive foreign grants, and by donor governments to conduct sensitive operations.

[15] See G. de Burca, R.O. Keohane, C. Sabel, *New Modes of Pluralist Global Governance*, see chapter 1 at section 3 and chapter 2 n 4.

[16] See Article 7 of Regulation 2001/546/EC.

In residual cases, networks originally structured as the ICs may become QUANGOs, even transitionally. The BetterAid coalition is the most illustrative example. BetterAid grew out of the necessity to advocate towards the OECD DAC on topics such aid effectiveness. Only NGOs and civil society actors composed the original composition of this coalition. However, soon after its creation, BetterAid created an advisory group on civil society and aid effectiveness to operate within the OECD DAC structure. BetterAid temporarily lost the character of an IC when it gathered civil society and states representatives and reported to the working party on aid effectiveness constituted within the DAC structure. However, when in October 2008 the OECD-based advisory group ceased to exist, BetterAid remained operational.

3.6 Politics and Activism

A technical and a political component are present in each coalition. The technical component may include scientists, academics, jurists, economists, or more generally experts in specific matters. These "knowledge-based", or "epistemic" in the words of Peter Haas (1992)[17] communities provide a technical expertise that is essential to the private as well as to the public sector. In the definition provided by Haas, these communities are networks among professionals with an authoritative claim to policy-relevant knowledge. It was thanks to epistemic communities that an ideologically hostile Reagan administration became convinced about the connections between chlorofluorocarbons and the ozone layer. Epistemic communities, clarifies Haas, "are both politically empowered through their claims to exercise authoritative knowledge and motivated by shared causal and principled beliefs". It is well known that corporations have long sought to integrate this epistemic community (and its authority)[18] into their structures in order to enhance the legitimacy of its standards and certification mechanisms. In consequence, the scale and density of exchange within communities of scientists and academics has grown significantly, and they begun to operate under the aegis of international administrative bodies (e.g. the UN agencies). Former WB Chief Economist Joe Stiglitz (2000) welcomed the launch of the Global Development Network[19] – a research institute

[17] See also P.M. Haas, "Do Regimes Matter? Epistemic Communities and Mediterranean Pollution Control" (1999) 34 *International Organizations* 377 and, also, P.M. Haas, *Saving the Mediterranean*, (New York, Columbia University Press, 1990). References on epistemic communities can be also found in P.H. Sand, "Lessons Learned in Global Environmental Governance" (1991) 18 *BC Environmental Affair Law Review* 213.

[18] On the concept of "epistemic authority" See T.J. Sinclair, "A private Authority Perspective on Global Governance", in A.D. Ba, M.J. Hoffmann see chapter 1 n 27, at 179; S. Wheatley, "Democratic Governance Beyond the State: The Legitimacy of Non-State Actors as Standard Setters", in A. Peters, L. Koechlin, T. Forster, G Fenner Zinkernagel (eds.), *Non-state Actors as Standard Setters* (Cambridge, Cambridge University Press, 2009), at 216.

[19] See generally www.gdnet.org

promoted by the WB and aimed at synthetizing economic knowledge into best practices that are then advocated towards governments – as the proof that think tanks "have become important agents to introduce and adapt new policy initiatives". Diane Stone (2004) reports the cases of the Open Society Institutes, the Evian Group, and the International Simultaneous Policy Organization.[20] The first serves as a medium of Western ideas in transition; the second orbits around the WTO and include corporates, academics and government leaders aligned in a normative project to instil in the public the virtues of an open world economy; the third advocates the harmonization of legislation between countries on topics such as global warming, financial market regulation, environmental destruction, war, and social injustice.[21] Isabelle Bruno, Emmanuel Didier (2013) reports the case of "*statactivism*" – a term formed by the contraction of statistics and activism – to designate those statistical practices utilised by activists to criticise figures and numbers used by public authorities. The Global Footprint Network offers an interesting example of such statactivism. This consists of an accounting tool used to measure the human impact on environment globally.[22]

Experts play an important role also in the EU regulatory apparatus. They assist the EU Commission and EU Agencies in multiple functions ranging from policy-making to monitoring and implementation. This condition is not without its critics. The "citadel of expertise", as Alex de Waal decries (1997),[23] would create an aura of technocratic efficiency and a rational for ignoring the local contexts in which IOs' decisions operate. The same critique is directed at those scholars who suggest to counterweight the dominance of the Western legal culture within supranational decision-making through reliance on the expertise of civil society actors. Critical accounts of technocratic expertise also raise the example of large consulting firms such as PricewaterhouseCoopers, KPMG or Andersen consulting that have established government consulting divisions for the purpose of advocating for more managerial approaches in government.

As part of the ICs, the technical component serves two aims. The first is internal and consists of the intellectual resources offered to the ICs' advocacy and lobbying. As advocacy campaigns are often critical of existing policies practices, alliances with well-reputed academics serve to lend some legitimacy to the campaigns. Clearly, commissioning policy reports and co-opting experts give the ICs a patina of scholarly rigour. The second aim served by the ICs' technical component is indirect. Through it, the ICs provide a source of technical expertise and knowledge to the decisional workflow of the IOs with whom the coalitions cooperate. A technical expertise demanded by IOs for various scopes (to provide advice, help arbitrate disputes, or review treaty implementation) but chiefly because it is better, or

[20] See also D. Stone, "Non-Governmental Policy Transfer: The Strategies of Independent Policy Institutes" (2000) 13:1 *Governance: An International Journal of Policy and Administration* 45.

[21] See generally www.simpol.org

[22] See generally www.globalfootprintnetwork.org

[23] See also K. Hewit (ed.), *Interpretations of Calamity, from the Viewpoint of Human Ecology* (Boston, Allen & Urwin, 1983).

cheaper, than the expertise that the internal structures that the IO itself would produce.

Despite the scientific presence in the ICs, they should not be confused with think tanks.[24] While the latter only include the technical component, the ICs also include a political component. This component includes the activists: individuals whose main task is to campaign around specific issues towards the IOs' bureaucrats, or, in the definition of Pamela Oliver and Gerald Marwell (1992), "people who care enough about some issue that they are prepared to incur significant costs and act to achieve their goals". Activists' methods, as we shall see in the following sections, differ from the work of epistemic communities. They are not "constrained by canons of reasoning", as John Peterson explains (1992), and may therefore include "mobilization of shame" (appealing to the public at large through the mass media) or set on more cautious approaches, in the form of dialogues with the IOs' bureaucracy. Because of their role, activists may be considered as key players in the ICs' objectives.

The differentiation between the ICs and think tanks, however, has three limitations. First, while this differentiation is valid to exemplify and highlight the weight of the political component in the ICs, it should not lead to assumptions that think tanks are excluded from membership into coalitions. Among the 27 EPLO members, for instance, individual NGOs, networks of NGOs, and charities, as well as think tanks are included. This is also the case with Alter-EU and ATM. Second, while it is true that many think tanks claim to function on a non-partisan or non-ideological basis, it is also true that others are overly partisan and ideologically informed. Ideological organizations widen the separation between think tanks and the ICs. Third, think tanks (and epistemic communities more generally) are transnational networks themselves. They compose domestic networks (together with political parties, universities and the media) as well as international networks (in partnership with other think tanks, NGOs and IOs). Early examples of think tanks' networking are covered by Diane Stone (2008). These include the networking from the institutes of international affairs in Europe and the US that formed the Versailles settlement, and then maintained lines of communication until World War II; and the sister institutes of Chatham House founded in a number of Commonwealth countries between 1930s and 1940s. Recent examples are those of the International Centre for Economic Growth and the Stockholm Network, whose members are worldwide and European market-oriented think tanks, respectively.

[24] See D.E. Abelson, *Do Think Tanks Matter? Assessing the Impact of Public Policy Institutes* (Montreal, McGill Queen's University Press, 2002); S. Boucher (ed.), *Europe and Its Think Tanks: A Promise To Be Fulfilled* (Paris, Notre Europe, 2004); S. Diane, *Capturing the Political Imagination: Think Tanks and the Policy Process* (London, Routledge, 1996).

3.7 The Dynamic Nature of Interlocutory Coalitions

The number of each component as well as the number of participants to a coalition (and therefore the size of coalitions) is subject to iterate variations, depending upon different circumstances. The ICs are in fact dynamic (in both processes and structures) rather than static entities. They often comprise a large number of participants, who frequently move in and out, and enjoy quite variable degrees of commitment or dependence upon each other. Again, the most interesting example is that of BetterAid. Section 3.5 has already described the transformation of BetterAid into a QUANGO. After having returned to its original composition, in 2009 BetterAid split again. Its members created a new platform: the Open Forum on civil society's organizations development aid effectiveness (hereinafter, the Open Forum). The Open Forum aimed at defining and promoting the roles and effectiveness of CSOs in development, moving from a shared framework of principles. In the following 3 years the Open Forum managed to adopt, first, the "Istanbul Principles" on CSOs' development effectiveness and, later, the "Siam Reap Framework" to implement those principles. In 2012 BetterAid and the Open Forum merged into a new coalition: the CSO Partnership for Development Effectiveness (CPDE).[25] Participants to CPDE represented all regions of the world including faith-based, feminist, labour, rural sectors, and international CSOs. The structure of the coalition changed a great deal across its variations. BetterAid was probably the loosest structure, with only a Coordination Group holding biannual meetings. The Open Forum added a layer of governance, creating a global facilitation group and a consortium. Ultimately, the structural posture of the CPDE is much more complex. It includes a Global Council, a Coordination Committee, a Global Secretariat and an Independent Accountability Committee.

Also because of the dynamic nature of the ICs, it may be the case that that more coalitions connect into a single, larger network. While this aspect will be discussed in more details in the last chapter of this volume, for the moment it suffices to note that networks of coalitions, or meta-coalitions, represent an interesting trend in the possible future evolutions of supranational civil society's organizational structures.

3.8 Volunteering and Interlocutory Coalitions

Second, and decisively, support to the ICs' activities is provided on a voluntary basis. Membership is contingent on consent, rather than being compulsory. Participants in an IC are autonomous NGOs and/or other non-state actors (including individuals) that share a common purpose or a common set of values. In certain cases, the autonomy of the members is expressly written in the IC's funding

[25] See generally www.csopartnership.org

documents/agreements. For instance, the first principle of the CAN's "Network Rules and Guiding Principles" specifies: "Members (of CAN) are autonomous and independent. Many of these members have their own forms of organization and their own national or regional rules".

To this extent, these coalitions resemble what Romans defined as *universitas* and indeed depart from modes of association based exclusively on reasons of legal nature: what Romans used to define as *societas*. Grossly simplifying, *societas* comprised individuals grouped into an association not in the pursuit of common substantive purpose, but rather because of loyalty. In consequence, *societas* did not denote a relationship in terms of common action. Rather, they acknowledged a mere legal arrangement. Of course also the ICs are devoted to legal arrangements (and it will be discussed some in the following sections) and use it to regulate their connections. Yet reasons motivating the presence of such legal constrictions do not draw from the necessity of the coalitions' members to be accredited a status of formal legality, or at least not exclusively. While minor NGOs might have an interest to this extent, larger NGOs already operate on a legal status due to the accreditation by the IOs. It might be then argued that moving into a coalition denotes a joint undertaking in pursuit of a common substantive objective (which is precisely what pursued *universitas*).[26]

This metaphor of *societas* and *universitas* is also helpful to separate qualitative from quantitative memberships. Obviously, a coalition is stronger if it relies on a major number of members. Yet, its leverage is considerably higher if the IC constructs a "dense" relationship, which involves equal conditions for all members to influence the position of the coalition. Not by chance, the density of a coalition is at the origins of a serious concern of legitimacy in the ICs, to which Chap. 4 will devote further analysis. The possibility that powerful members (e.g. multi-national NGOs) may dominate a coalition, while weaker members would suffer serious costs by not participating, may in fact denote the latter's consent as not genuinely voluntary.

For the same reasons, the ICs fit into John Peterson's distinction (1995) between communities and networks, the former being composed of actors provided with adequate technical knowledge but small coordination, the latter instead being constituted by the parts of a given community that choose to coordinate themselves in order to have a more effective access to the decision-making channels. According to the author, the formation of networks responds to the need for technical knowledge related with the formulation of broader policies from IOs. Other scholars, however, have argued that the same need for technical knowledge also occurs in communities.[27]

There are a further four implications of volunteering to work for the ICs. The first regards compensation, the second with access-fees, the third with the opt-out rules, and the fourth with the ICs' leadership. Regarding compensation, the general

[26] See S. Tierney, S. Toddington, "*Societas, universitas and the third order of the political*" (2005) 16 *King's College Law Journal* 215.

[27] See F. Longo, *Unione Europea e scienza politica* (Milano, Giuffrè, 2005).

rule is that the representatives of members do not get any compensation for their work. They usually have to pay for travel and subsistence costs by themselves, although there are exceptions to this. The members of the Standing Committee of CINGO, for instance, have their travel costs reimbursed by the COE for the four ordinary annual sessions of the Conference. Partial reimbursements of costs provided by IOs have consequences for the typology of agreements governing coalitions. As it will be later explained in more details, IOs are not against compensations to coalitions' costs. However, they are more likely to invest on the ICs with whom a long-term relationship is established. That is why coalitions regulated by vague and open-ended agreements are less common.

A second implication concerns access-fees. Volunteering does not necessarily means that membership to the ICs is granted for free. Access-fees may vary upon several factors, including the need to fund the coalition's activities, or the necessity to maintain a small and exclusive membership. In some cases, accession to a coalition is granted for free, as in the cases of CINGO, the Consultative Platform and Alter-EU. Predictable as it may seem, when no membership fee or any other obligation for accession is requested, new members may be invited to endorse the values and principles of the concerned IC. In other cases, fees are set in accordance with the size of the future member. ATM, for instance, recommends an annual fee of 100€ for small organizations; 500–2000€ for medium-sized organisations; and 10,000€ or more for big organisations. However, the same coalition admits different forms of support in exchange to the membership (e.g. regular spread of news about the alliance among the members of the joining organization; to get involved in national campaigns; or to actively participate in one or more of the working groups of the coalition). In the case of CONGO three different membership status are granted: (1) full membership is "open to all NGOs having Consultative Status with the UN through the Economic and Social Council ECOSOC", and comes at the cost of 250€; (2) associate membership is "open to all NGOs having formal relationships with the United Nations system – including NGOs affiliated with the Department of Public Information, NGOs accredited to UN Conferences, and NGOs accredited to treaty bodies", and comes at the cost of 100€; (3) friends-status and fellowship-status are provided to those (individuals and organizations) who are not necessarily interested in the administrative work of the coalition, but who wish to support it. Access fees for full and associate memberships are paid onetime. Instead, friend-status implies a minimum annual donation of 120$. Fellowship status is free.

Opt-out rules are a third implication of voluntariness. With a few exceptions, the majority of agreements governing the ICs do not provide procedures for opting-out. The exceptions will be further discussed in Chap. 4. Thus, in the absence of a clear regulatory framework, one could deduce that the decision to leave a coalition is left, to the discretion of the single participants, to the will of the IO whose network cooperates, or to the joint decision with the other participants. Except, of course, in the hypotheses in which the ICs' membership is temporary.

A last implication of the voluntary accession to the ICs is related to leadership. The fact that civil society actors are free to choose whether to join a coalition, as well to leave it, means that there are no single leaders to the ICs. None of the ICs considered in this volume has appointed a single leader. Even in cases as the CONGO, where a President exists, a General Assembly (the governing body of the coalition) and a Board (composed of the President and 20 members) are in control of all the important decisions. Moreover, the Presidential mandate is to a maximum of two consecutive periods of 3 years. Being the inclusiveness of the ICs' decision-making process a consequence of voluntariness, this in turn influences the internal mediation. Chapter 4 will discuss this aspect in further details.

3.9 Agreements Governing Interlocutory Coalitions: Type A

The ICs are not governed through public elections or governmental structures. Rather, they are controlled by their members through specific agreements aimed at providing regularity to their operations, whether or not they are formally constituted or legally registered. Having said that, agreements governing coalitions might have a variety of degrees in structure, from codes of conduct to more nuanced agreements, but usually come in three broad generic types. The ICs might be informal in nature, and thus founded on unofficial agreements among its participants rather than on conventional legal instruments. This is not, however, an unalterable rule. A higher degree of formalization may in fact occur at the moment in which networks are set in operation, or in a latter stage of their existence.

Agreements of type "A" contain detailed rules and procedures on coalitions' activities and generally adopt collegial methods of decision-making to coordinate its members. It is interesting to note that the adoption of A-type agreements depends on the fact that the coalition is created out of the will of its members (as it is generally the case), or it is generated by an IO's decision. In the former, the choice to coalesce under detailed rules may be driven by the members' need to maximize their leverage over the target of their actions. In the latter case it is almost a given condition that the coalition's rules of procedure will adopt the A-type agreements to guarantee functional and rapid interactions. The best-known examples coming under this heading is the Transport Forum. As explained in Chap. 1, this was established with an official act from the Commission (Decision 2001/456/EC). The Commission Decision sets the rules for the membership to the Forum, the procedures for submitting opinions and reports to the Commission and the terms of the Meetings. Another noteworthy example is provided by the Consultation Forum established by Regulation (EC) No 1980/2000 on a revised Community eco-label award scheme. Article 13 of the Regulation creates the European Union Eco-Labeling Board (EUEB), an intra-governmental body composed of Member States' representatives. Article 15 disposes that the EUEB cooperates with a Consultation Forum. Members of the Forum are all the relevant interested parties concerned, such as industry and service providers, trade unions, traders, retailers, importers, environmental protection groups and consumer organizations. According to article 15 of the Regulation, the Commission establishes the rules of procedure of the Forum.

Among the ICs that are created out of the will of its members and adopt A-type agreements are the Consultative Platform and the CINGO. Both these coalitions regulate its overall institutional relations, discipline internal affairs, and provide rules for the formation of its policies with a composite set of by-rules and terms of reference. The CONGO is another significant case in point. The rules governing the coalition not only regulate its aims, membership and governing structure, but also define in details the procedures governing the adoption of resolutions, the organization of meeting, the finance and the elections of the coalition.

3.10 Agreements of Type B

Agreements of type "B" are relatively vague and open-ended agreements primarily designed to create a framework for cooperation among civil society actors with mutual interests and goals. The defining aspect here is not whether the coalition is legally or formally recognized but whether it has some organizational permanence and regularity as reflected in regular meetings, a membership, and a set of procedures for making decisions that participants recognize as legitimate. In this sense, agreements of Type B remind the description provided by Keck and Sikkink of transnational advocacy networks as "political spaces". Places in which, they explain, "differently situated actors negotiate – formally or informally – the social, cultural, and political meanings of their joint enterprise".[28] Indeed, agreements of type B represent a resource in periods of emergency or crisis, since they can respond with greater speed and greater flexibility than IOs.

The Pan-European ECO Forum and the NGO Forum's Agreements fall within this second category. The same kind of agreement is also used by Alter-EU and CAN. The latter is particularly instructive to show how a B-type Agreement is conceived. At the commencement of the CAN Charter, it is written that its purpose is "to facilitate and enable decision-making, rather than prescribe rules". Added later in the document is: "The network of independent members of CAN act in terms of their own mandates and organizational aims and objects. This Charter does not create a new organization; rather, it establishes rules and guidelines which members will adhere to in formalizing their national, regional and global co-operation".

Thus, guidelines, not rules, are provided by Agreements of type B. It is, however, possible that agreements of type B develop more detailed rules to govern the relations among its members. Reasons for bolstering formalization on the part of the members of a coalition generally follows increased interaction and mutual confidence among them, and is aimed at increasing the political resonance of their activity. The Pan-European ECO Forum is exemplary to this extent. IOs' interest in introducing legally binding provisions towards networks' participants is due to the necessity to certify networks' legal authority. The NGO Forum, for instance, was

[28] See M.E. Keck, K. Sikkink, *Activists Beyond Borders*, see chapter 1 at section 1, chapter 1 n 60 and n 68, chapter 4 n 29 and chapter 6 n 24, at 3.

created upon the proposal of the ADB President, following the huge protests by NGOs and affected communities of ADB projects at the ADB 2000 annual meeting.

3.11 Agreements of Type C

A last variant consists of Agreements of type "C": codes of conduct designed to spur harmonization through political convergence towards a common focal point. Albeit similar to agreements of the B type, these agreements differ from the latter in that their chances to evolve into more complex forms of cooperation are remote. The relationship between the NGO Advisory Body and the Informal Council is an example. This is also the case of the Consultative Board on the Future of the WTO, created by the Director General of the WTO for advice and communication on WTO issues and the concerns of civil society.[29] Although all of these *consortia* were designed to provide a platform for dialogue, in none of these cases the original informal agreements turned into more formal partnerships. Agreements of type C, however, remain an exception. They are not functional to IOs' long-term purposes. While IOs are willing to pay the costs related to the official recognition of a coalition – which include expenditures of both material and immaterial resources – it may be assumed that they expect the benefits to outweigh these costs, over time. Thus, coalitions of this kind are useful only to a short or mid-term basis.

3.12 Membership of Interlocutory Coalitions

Third, the membership of ICs is not exclusive. The participating members are allowed to conduct their own programs and activities as well as to join other networks. It might be useful, however, to draw a line between the juridical status of single participating members and the coalition's juridical status. There are no regulations under international law governing the legal status of non-state actors. As a general rule, non-state actors are embedded in the system of law of their home as well of their host state, and therefore do not benefit from the special privileges, standing, facilities or immunities under international law that may be accorded to IOs. International law scholars, however, have long been aware of the problem. Wilhelm Kaufmann (1908) invoked a regulation of international non-state actors in order to preserve the international general interest; to effectuate the formation and functioning of these non-state actors; and to ensure that single state could not retard or hinder their activities with domestic norms. Two years later, both the *Institut de*

[29] See P. Van den Bossche, "NGO Involvement in the WTO: A Lawyer's Perspective on a Glass Half-full or Half-empty" (2006) *Maastricht Faculty of Law* Working Paper 10, available at www.unimaas.nl/bestand.asp?id=6981

droit international and the International Law Association began to promote consideration of a convention to grant legal personality to international NGOs. In 1923 the former adopted a draft Convention on the legal position of international associations. The proposed treaty, however, did not gain any adherents.

In a famous 1949 Advisory Opinion on the "*Reparation for Injuries*" case, the International Court of Justice recognized that "the subjects of law in any legal system are not necessarily identical in their nature or the extent of their rights, and their nature depends upon the needs of the international community".[30] In so doing, the Court paved the way for the adjustment of the doctrine of legal subjectivity to the new demands of the international community. NGOs and other civil society actors may not yet have reached the stage of being fully fledged subjects of international law, seemingly stated the Court, but they could contribute to creating a "*social milieu*" or "*ambiance*" (to use the telling words of Dietrich Schindler)[31] in international life out of which new legal structures and entities might grow. In fact, while only few writers argue that Reparation for Injuries only applies to State-created bodies such as the UN,[32] governments have broadly interpreted the Opinion from the Court, and increasingly they have made international commitments regarding NGOs. However, for the time being, the only international agreement on the legal personality of NGOs is the European Convention on the Recognition of the Legal Personality of International Non-Governmental Organizations, which came into force in 1991.[33] Occasionally, special treatment has been granted to NGOs as parties of specific international instruments. The broadest acknowledgement of the non-governmental sector is included in Article 71 of the UN-Charter, which enables the Economic and Social Council to consult with NGOs that are concerned with matters within its competence.[34] Under international law, a special status is also given to the International Committee of the Red Cross.

Broadly speaking, both non-state actors and ICs do not have an international legal personality. Yet, while the laws of the State in which they are incorporated govern the former, the latter are not subjected to national laws but rather gain

[30] See 1949 ICJ Reports, p. 178. See also J. Klabbers, (I Can't Get No) Recognition: Subjects Doctrine and the Emergence of Non-State Actors", in J. Peterman, J. Klabbers (eds.), *Nordic Cosmopolitanism: Essays in International Law for Martti Koskenniemi* (Leiden, Kluwer Law International, 2003).

[31] For further details on Dietrich Schindler's view See D. Thurer, "The Emergence of Non-Governmental Organizations and Transnational Enterprises in International Law and the Changing Role of the State", in A. Bianchi (ed.), *Non State Actors in International Law*, see chapter 1 n 72 and chapter 4 n 52.

[32] See A. Orakhelashvili, "The Position of the Individual in International Law" (2001) 31 *California Western International Law Journal* 241.

[33] See S. Charnovitz, *Two Centuries of Participation* see text n 38 and chapter 1 n 68;K. Martens, "Examining the (Non-)Status of NGOs in International Law" (2003) 10 *Indiana Journal of Global Legal Studies* 1.

[34] See Resolution 1996/31 concerning "Consultative relationship between the United Nations and non-governmental organizations", adopted by the Economic and Social Council at its 49th plenary meeting on 25 July 1996.

indirect international legal recognition from their cooperation with IOs. Moreover, from the distinction between the legal personality of single non-state actors and the ICs two corollaries stand out conceptually. First, to be discussed below, is the extent to which the participating actors operate on a partnership basis with the coalition – and thus become an integral part of it – they temporarily abdicate their autonomy. This explains why, in the first place, ICs are often federated. They dispose of a secretariat and a lead organization, which provide coordination to the network (unless administrative tasks are attributed to one of the ICs' members, as it is in the case of the UNCAC Coalition, where Transparency International also functions as the Coalitions' secretariat). Also, it explains why initiatives and strategies taken by the coalitions are attributed solely to the coalitions' – and not to their members' – responsibility.[35] Nonetheless, an empirical perspective may suggest that through the membership to a coalition, single NGOs and civil society organizations receive indirect international legal recognition as participants in international law making.

3.13 Global Networks and Transnational Issue Networks

The discourse on membership is also useful to distinguish interlocutory coalitions from "global networks", "transnational issue networks", and "parallel summits". Global networks are generally defined as an informal web of different civil society actors (such as, for instance, grass-roots groups or SMs). But also, and primarily, they identify a geographical, rather than a conceptual, identity. While Section 3.15 of the present chapter will explain how and why the ICs do not rely on geographically homogeneous members, but rather accept members from different countries, it is important to remember that the ICs are defined – if not exclusively at least primarily – by a set of common values and principles. Even if the ICs are too large for its members to know each other, they are still coalitions of solidarity, based on their members' belief that they are united by some set of characteristics that differentiate them from outsiders. Thus, the ICs are networks that operate globally, but they are separate from the definition of Global Networks.

Differently from Global Networks, Transnational Issue Networks are gatherings of actors bound together by a core of shared values and working together on issues of international relevance exchanging information and services. However, these networks lack a defined structure to coordinate accession and membership, and exist only as long as the issue they oppose. The NGOs and trade unions coalition created in 1998, following the decision from the College of Commissioners to block some 800 million Euro of expenditure destined to support NGO activities, is an example. After having mounted a series of high profile actions ranging from public demonstrations to coordination of lobbying actions in Brussels with those at the local level, the network dismantled. The issue was resolved with an agreement

[35] These conditions are familiar to the idea of corporatism. See M. Ottaway, *Corporatism Goes Global,* see chapter 1 at section 7.1.

between the EU institutions that curtailed the budgetary powers of the European Parliament. Another recent case is the "Global Multi-stakeholder Meeting on the Future of Internet Governance", also known as NETmundial. This is described as a "bottom-up, open, and participatory process involving thousands of people from governments, private sector, civil society, technical community, and academia from around the world". NETmundial convened for the first time on April 2014 to discuss two important issues relevant for the future evolution of the Internet: first, the governance and the principles of Internet; and, second, the roadmap for the future evolution of the Internet governance ecosystem. Of the 180 contributions posted by stakeholders around the globe, a conclusive document was elaborated and approved by the participants of the meeting.[36]

3.14 Parallel Summits

Finally, parallel summits (or "unofficial conferences" in the words used by some scholars)[37] are events held contextually to inter-governmental summits, the scope of the former being to challenge the legitimacy of the latter. Examples of parallel summits date back to the nineteenth century. It is agreed that the idea of parallel conferences was inaugurated in 1899, with the Hague Peace Conference that attracted a mélange of voluntary associations. Women peace activists circulated a petition that acquired more than one million signatures from Europe, Japan and the US, and two of those associations (the International Council of Women and the Salvation Army) were also offered deputations. However, it was only in the 1990s that parallel summits gathered pace as a normal way of doing politics. Since then, parallel NGO meetings have taken place at almost all major international events. Mario Pianta (2001) shows that parallel summits increased from around 2 a year in the period 1988–1991 to over 30 a year in the period 2000–2001. Participation in these events also increased. Around a third involved more than 10,000 people and several involved tens of thousands, especially in 2000 and 2001.

Parallel summits have a narrower conceptual identity with respect to the ICs. Their activity is hinged on the topic(s) of the official summits, and therefore they dissolve as decisions are reached. There are five examples to test the correctness of this difference. At the Hague Peace Conference in 1899, non-governmental groups organised a parallel salon for diplomats to meet with concerned citizens.[38] This parallel event produced various petitions with numerous signatures that were submitted to the official conference, and a daily conference newspaper. During the 1972 UN Conference on Human Development (colloquially called the "Stockholm conference" in recognition of its host city), an official parallel conference was set up

[36] See the NETmundial Multi-stakeholder Statement here: www.irpa.eu/wp-content/uploads/2014/05/2014_04_24_NETmundial_Multistakeholder_Statement_-_NETmundial.pdf

[37] See P. Willets, *Pressure Groups in the Global System* (London, F. Pinte, 1982), at 15.

[38] See S. Charnovitz, *Two Centuries of Participation*, see chapter 1 n 68 and text n 33.

as a venue for NGOs aimed at discussing issues of common concern. This was called the Environmental Forum. The second case is the Earth Summit held in Rio de Janeiro in 1992. Notwithstanding NGOs' active participation within the conference, thousands of environmentalists and other NGOs gathered in a parallel forum to the Summit, the Global Forum. In 1998, when the representatives of the WB and the IMF convened, a public rally of 80,000 people organised public protests in the city. Two years later more the 500,000 protestors met in Barcelona to protest against a EU summit.

3.15 The Supranational Nature of Interlocutory Coalitions

A final characteristic of the ICs is that their activities are held primarily, and almost exclusively, at the supranational level. It is well known that interest groups positioned on a national level cooperate with similarly situated foreign interest groups in order to impose externalities on rival domestic groups.[39] In terms of practical actualisation of such cooperation, one may consider the example of producers' liaisons with their counterparts in different states in order to exploit consumers' groups. However, despite the transnational dimension of such cooperation between fellow groups, the scopes and benefits remain national. The ICs, on the contrary, are rooted in the perception that civil society constitutes a class with a common cause that transcends domestic boundaries. In this sense, the ICs are simultaneously designated as both a network of people and the infrastructure that sustain them. Thus, even when operating locally, the ICs maintain a close and constant relationship with the supranational regulatory level. As explained by Jan Scholte (2000), the concept of a GCS encompasses civic activity that, *inter alia*, addresses trans world issues, and works on a premise of supra-territorial solidarity. The "Transatlantic Consumer Dialogue" is an example of this. This is a *forum* of American and European consumer organizations that develop joint consumer policy recommendations to the US government and to the European Commission to promote consumer interest in EU and US policymaking. The European Commission, however, provides financial support and coordination to the *forum*.

The supranational character of the ICs implies that members from different geographical areas are admitted as members, even when the coalition has a very specific target. Some ICs are truly global in their membership, others have global support but are only organised in the West because it is here that major IOs are based. Yet other ICs are strong in the West and seek to exercise influence throughout the world. Interestingly, also the European ICs do not necessarily include only non-state actors from Europe. Supporters to Alter-EU, for instance, include members from Europe and a list of signatories from countries outside Europe, including US, Mexican and Brazilian NGOs, as well as a network of NGOs from Bangladesh.

[39] See E. Benvenisti, "Exit and Voice in the Age of Globalization" (1999) 98 *Michigan Law Review* 167.

Non-European Supporters to the ATM came from South America, Canada, Africa and Asia. In other cases, however, geographical limitations may be present (e.g. only Europe-wide NGOs are admitted as members to the Consultative Platform). This is due to the necessity to guarantee a greater degree of accountability, as Chap. 4 will explain in further detail.

References

Bruno, I., and E. Didier. 2013. *Benchmarking. L'état sous pression statistique*. Paris: Zones.

De Waal, A. 1997. *Famine crimes: Politics and the disaster relief industry in Africa*. Oxford: Oxford University Press.

Haas, P.M. 1992. Introduction: Epistemic communities and international policy coordination. *International Organizations* 46: 1.

Haunss, S., and D.K. Leach. 2007. Social movement scenes: Infrastructures of opposition in civil society. In *Civil societies and social movements*, ed. D. Purdue. New York: Routledge.

Kaufmann, W. 1908. Die modernen nicht-staatlichen internationalen Verbände und Kongresse und das internationale Recht. *Zeitschrift für Völkerrecht und Bundesstaatsrecht* 2: 434.

Oliver, P.E., and G. Marwell. 1992. Mobilizing technologies for collective actions. In *Frontiers in social movement theory*, ed. A.D. Morris and C. Mcclug Mueller. New Haven: Yale University Press.

Peterson, J. 1992. Whalers, cetologists, environmentalists, and the international management of whaling. *International Organization* 46: 149.

Peterson, J. 1995. Decision-making in the European Union: Towards a framework for analysis. *Journal of European Public Policy* 1: 69.

Pianta, M. 2001. Parallel summits of global civil society. In *Global civil society*, ed. H. Anheier, M. Glasius, and M. Kaldor. Oxford: Oxford University Press.

Sabel, C., and Zeitlin J. 2006. Learning from difference: The new architecture of experimentalist governance in the European Union. *European Governance*. Paper No. C-07-02.

Schachter, O. 1971. The twilight existence of nonbinding international agreements. *The American Journal of International Law* 71: 296.

Scholte, J.A. 2000. Global civil society. In *The political economy of globalization*, ed. N. Woods. London: Palgrave Publisher.

Stiglitz, J. 2000. Scan globally, reinvent locally: Knowledge infrastructure and the localization of knowledge. In *Banking on knowledge: The genesis of the global development network*, ed. D. Stone. London: Routledge.

Stone, D. 2004. Transfer agents and global networks in the "Transnationalization" of policy. *Journal of European Public Policy* 11(3): 545.

Stone, D. 2008. *The new networks of knowledge: Think tanks and the transnationalization of governance*. New York: The Social Science Research Council.

Chapter 4
The Activities of Interlocutory Coalitions: Mediation, Rule-Making and Implementation

4.1 The Focus of the Chapter

Previous chapters examined the way in which GCS coalesce in networks revolving around common values and needs, and pursue concrete benefits in interacting with IOs. Having named such networks "interlocutory coalitions", Chap. 3 has described their composition, membership, rules of governance and legal status. In this context, the ICs have been differentiated from other forms of networks, including Social Networks, Trans governmental Committees, think-tanks, SMs, Parallel Summits and QUANGOs. However, one central question remains unanswered. How exactly do the ICs elaborate their decisions and advocate them towards IOs? The current chapter addresses this question, with the focus of attention shifting away from an analysis of the composition and structure of the ICs to the processes governing the ICs' decision-making and advocacy.

The task of identifying and distinguishing the ICs' internal processes is not an easy one. The ICs seldom offer a detailed account of their advocacy strategies, and the reason for this is quite simple: listing the activities and functions of a coalition is also a sort of limitation. The ICs prefer to settle on general tasks, or to indicate only broad goals, in order to be able to pursue different strategies and perform various tasks, depending on the case. Exceptions are possible, but very rare. One is CAN. The Charter of CAN includes a detailed account of its strategies (including the active participation in the international climate change negotiations and all other relevant international and domestic *fora*; the raising of awareness to influence climate change decision-making processes; and the development and dissemination of knowledge) and its primary activities, namely: information sharing, capacity building, lobbying on common positions, coordination of media messages, coordination of research efforts, coordination with other NGOs groupings, and mobilization of public support and awareness.

G. Sgueo, *Beyond Networks - Interlocutory Coalitions, the European and Global Legal Orders*, Studies in European Economic Law and Regulation 8,
DOI 10.1007/978-3-319-28875-8_4

In broad terms, this book assumes that the ICs undertake three main tasks, which indeed are not mutually exclusive. To the contrary, the ICs perform a number of these activities simultaneously. At their heart, the ICs mediate. As we shall see presently, this all-encompassing definition includes a complex variety of processes, techniques and rules that depend on the context and the object of the mediation at hand. In the case of ICs, one can distinguish the discussion of the diverging positions carried out by the coalitions' participants and the promotion of policy alternatives to supranational decision-makers. From an early stage, the ICs mediate "internally" between the diverging members' interests; later, they mediate between these interests and the IOs' representatives. The ICs may also have enforcement powers. They may monitor the compliance of specific norms and rules, they may evaluate the degree to which these rules are successful, and they may report the possible breaches of these rules to the competent bodies. But, most decisively for the discourse of the role of the ICs in developing principles of administrative governance across supranational legal systems, the ICs may have "rule-making" powers. Of course, if by rule-making we mean the precise process that brings to the promulgation of norms and regulations, we would conclude that the ICs do not qualify. Their non-governmental nature would not permit these *consortia* to perform genuine rule-making activities. Be that as it may, the definition of rule-making appears nevertheless as the most appropriate way to describe the ICs' advocacy towards IOs. Two reasons support this assumption. To start with, rule-making seems to be an appropriate definition from a practical point of view. The lobbying pursued by the ICs into IOs' official negotiations, and/or into the other phases of the policy cycle, often results in influencing IOs policies and shaping IOs strategic directions.[1]

As the following paragraphs will explain in detail, the ICs may work as catalysts in calling for the revocation of rules that no longer work in the common interest. Furthermore, the ICs may influence the agenda-setting of the IOs. In the environmental field, for instance, the adoption of international environmental standard setting, despite being formally dominated by the IOs' governing bodies, is significantly influenced by the contribution of the ICs.[2] The role of loose transnational coalitions of environmental organizations in mobilizing interests and action on the ozone depletion and climate change issues are well acknowledged cases in point.[3] To continue, the ascription of the ICs' activities to the conceptual domain of rule-making becomes even more pertinent when we consider that in the supranational arena the

---

[1] See generally P.J. Simmons, C. De Jonge Oudraat (eds.), *Managing Global Issues: Lessons Learned* (Washington, Carnegie Endowment for International Peace (2001); P.J. Spiro, "New Global Potentates: Non-governmental Organizations and the "Unregulated" Marketplace" (1996) 18 *Cardozo Law Review* 958; A.M. Clark, "Non-Governmental Organizations and their Influence on International Society" (1995) 48 *Journal of International Affairs* 507.

[2] See A. Alkoby, "Global Networks and International Environmental Lawmaking: A Discourse Approach" (2007–2008) 8 *Chicago Journal of International Law*; S.C. Schreck, "The Role of Non-governmental Organizations in International Environmental Law" (2006–2007) 10 *Gonzaga Journal of International Law* 252.

[3] See W.E.F. Torrance, A.W. Torrance, "Spinning the Green Web: Transnational Environmentalism" in S. Batliwala, D. Brown (eds.) *Transnational Civil Society* see chapter 1 at section 6.1, at 101.

distinction between the private and the public sphere is less clear-cut with respect to the domestic level. The distinction between the private and the public spheres has informed Western political practice since antiquity. Greeks named with *Oikos* the possession of goods. Therefore *Oikos* implied a relationship between an individual and an object. *Polis* concerned the idea of ruler ship, and thus referred to a much broader community of interests and people. Conversely, the Romans defined the former in terms of *res publica,* while the second was referred to as *dominium.* However in the supranational arena the formal distinctions between the two spheres have blurred. By the 1930s, Carl Schmitt (1932) had already observed that the distinction between public law and private law was one of the greatest dualisms of his time (the other being the distinction between international and domestic law). The twenty-first century, observed Don Eberly, "will be about social entrepreneurs, private philanthropy, public-private partnerships, and global grass-roots linkages involving the faith and civic communities".[4] As a consequence of these transformations, sectors traditionally regarded as public experienced varying degrees of privatization, to the point that it has become virtually impossible to draw a clear division of roles between the public sphere and the private interest in the supranational arena. Lorenzo Casini (2013) estimates at 2000 the number of hybrid regulatory regimes operating beyond the State. Examples include the health sector, the environment, the governance of the Internet, cultural property, and the field of security and peacekeeping.[5]

This blurred governance, portrayed as a "balancing process" between formerly separate interests, takes different shapes. Grossly simplifying, however, there are two main profiles. On the one hand, global governance has enhanced the significance of the private sphere in the creation and enforcement of policies and norms; on the other hand, global governance has pushed public powers (both governments and IOs) to make increasing use of private law instruments when exercising regulatory powers. Indeed both shapes are of importance for the purpose of elucidating the ICs' rulemaking powers. This brings us to a number of considerations. First, it is suggested in this volume that GCS in general, and the ICs in particular, have benefited from this process, becoming legitimate partners of IOs in decision-making processes. After all, the rise of PPPs has been triggered from the necessity to satisfy the basic needs of governing: to provide for accountability, to heighten controls of legality, to broaden the participation of stakeholders, to enhance transparency, and to rely on more flexible and less bureaucratic implementation, to name but a few.[6] As a further consequence, it is submitted that the partnership between IOs and the ICs has contributed to the development of a set of administrative law and principles

---

[4] See D. Eberly, *The Rise of Global Civil Society* see chapter 1 n 68, at 1.

[5] See S. Chesterman, A. Fisher (eds.), *Private Security, Public Order: The Outsourcing of Public Services and Its Limits* (Oxford, Oxford University Press, 2009).

[6] In disagreement with this opinion is E. Benvenisti, *The Law of Global Governance* see chapter 1 at section 1, chapter 1 n 10, n 22 and n 96 and text n 33, at 53. Benvenisti describes public-private institutions as institutions that operate almost exclusively in the sphere of health regulation, oftentimes as a result of the efforts put by big pharmaceutical companies to enhance their market shares.

shared across diverse supranational legal regimes (see Chap. 6 for a detailed analysis on this point). Finally, it is suggested that, despite (or perhaps as a consequence of) this public-private hybridism the ICs may experience shortcomings. One is the "taxicab delegation" pathology, described by Jonathan Pincus and Jeffrey Winters (2002). This pathology occurs when delegating processes are not as clear in practice as they are in principle. Delegates are told they are in the driver's seat, but in fact they are told where to go by the delegators. Interestingly enough, while Pincus and Winters used the taxicab metaphor with reference to the case of the WB, the same problem may arise with delegation of powers from IOs to other ICs. A second possible limitation deriving from public-private hybridism in supranational governance will be discussed in Chap. 6: it concerns the suggestion that such hybridism may oppose the process of administrative convergence.

The following sections will illustrate the ICs' activities in more specific detail. Section 4.2 will discuss the distinction between the ICs' internal and external mediation. Following this, Sect. 4.2.1 will describe the processes governing internal mediation through a number of examples. Analysis of the external mediation activities will follow from Sects. 4.3–4.5. Various issues will be detailed, including those of the legal value of the outcomes of the ICs' advocacy, as well as the discourse about the importance of soft law.

4.2 Internal and External Mediation

As Sect. 4.1 explained, the first and main function of any IC consists of mediation. In technical legal parlance, mediation is described as the attempt to settle a legal dispute through the active participation of a neutral third party who works to encourage cooperation between the parties in conflict.[7] A number of authors use the word "campaign" to address mediation and a broad set of complementary actions, including mobilisation, lobbying, and the production of information and research.[8] While this volume prefers to settle on the former term, it also gives it a broader definition with respect to common legal parlance. More specifically, mediation in the ICs is viewed in this volume as a multi-level and multi-directional activity, which not only involves the bargaining between the positions of participants (internal mediation), but also encompasses negotiations with governmental representatives/IOs and, in a latter stage, implementation (external mediation).

[7] See generally C. Menkel-Meadow, "From Legal Disputes to Conflict Resolution and Human Problem Solving: Legal Dispute Resolution in a Multidisciplinary Context" (2004) 54 *Journal of Legal Education* 7; "When Litigation is Not the Only Way: Consensus Building and Mediation As Public Interest Lawyering" (2002) 10 *Washington University Journal of Law and Policy* 37.

[8] See, for instance, L. Hinojosa, D. Pearce, S. Dumpleton, "Contesting Unfair International Capitalism: Assessment of the Effectiveness and Impact of Campaigning and Advocacy From the NGO Sector" (2007) *Brooks World Poverty Institute* Working Paper n. 2, available at www.manchester.ac.uk/bwpi, at 3.

Thus understood, both internal and external forms of mediation are crucial to the ICs' existence. Internal mediation is key to the ICs because the adoption of uniform approaches to specific matters defines the first key-step in the process of advocacy. While in fact it is true that non-state actors primarily partake in ICs with similar interest and ideological character, it is also quite common to find a wide range of approaches among the ICs' members, ranging from impatient radicals wanting to see immediate progress through cautious conservatives. As Annalise Riles (2001) explains, actors in civil society networks do not necessarily share much in terms of culture or lifestyle. Network theorists suggest that networks with weak ties and connections may result in a higher probability of introducing new ideas and opportunities.[9] In the case of the ICs, however, weak connections are counterweighted by the attempt to maintain some degree of autonomy, so not to risk dissolution of the coalition. Civil society actors may well decide to become members of an IC precisely because they disagree over the issues in which they are jointly implicated, or because they have divergent opinions on the ways in which these are to be addressed. However, if members of an IC perceive it as not being sufficiently successful in addressing the issues of their interest, there can be a split about the methods of political actions. In extreme cases, there may be a widening in the number of the members of the coalition (who would join another IC, or form their own coalitions). Consequently, the IC would suffer from a weakening in its political leverage. The conclusions of this book will deal with the issues of competition and uniqueness among the ICs thoroughly. The present chapter will instead concentrate on decision-making in ICs, and specifically it will see how the ICs' members manage and resolve disagreements.

Thus the ICs have to balance cooperation with differentiation. That is, they have to be different enough as to attract new members (and its resources); and, at the same time, they have to be able to reach consensus in a possibly fast and efficacious manner. Considered from this angle, we can compare the ICs' internal mediation to a consultative process. Topics are initially isolated and distinguished by single members; then they are promoted to other members. Decisions are thus taken after debate among participants. In deciding, those participants must examine their own interests in the light of other participants' requests and needs. Interests unsupported by general considerations are destined to carry no weight.[10] In many respects, this process of internal mediation is reminiscent of what Beth Noveck (2009) named "collaborative democracy" to describe practices of crowdsourcing from governments. Noveck suggests that the model of collaborative democracy could be applied to engage niche groups in society. It is arguable, says Noveck, that if institutions adopted this approach, and regularly engaged non-representative samples of individuals on niche issues that they are affected by, then rates of participation should increase, achieved through diverse, specialized engagement efforts that focus in on particular groups and issues. Similarly, in the ICs interest in particular issues or

---

[9] See, for instance, M. Granovetter, "The Strength of Weak Ties" (1973) 78 *The American Journal of Sociology* 1360.

[10] See J. Cohen, C. Sabel, "Directly-Deliberative Polyarchy" (1997) 3 *European Law Journal* 313.

topics is usually raised through efforts to seek collaboration amongst other members. Collaborative efforts from the ICs' members can be better grasped also having in mind Charli Carpenter's description (2009) of the "issue emergence" process, as he names it.[11] This process is divided in two phases. Phase one revolves around the definition of new issues for advocacy. Non-state actors are involved in demonstrating that, *first*, a given state of affairs is a problem; that, *second*, this problem has a possible solution; and that, *third*, a number of policy actors, including IOs, are necessarily involved in the search for its solution. Phase two of the issue emergence process begins when a major player recognizes the problem as such, and in so doing gives it political salience at the international level. Carpenter reminds us how crucial is the leverage of a major player that recognizes an issue as a problem worth to be advocated. He brings up the case study of David Lake and Wendy Wong (2006), who demonstrated the "contagion effect" within the human rights community produced by leading NGOs such as Amnesty International when referencing new issues. Following Carpenter's line of thinking, the ICs may be considered as major players within GCS' plethora of actors. As also clarified in Chap. 2, this helps to explain why NGOs and other non-state actors join the ICs – because of the benefits they will receive in terms of leverage at the international level. It is however important to observe that, in spite of the importance of internal mediation to the effectiveness of a coalition, the ICs' efforts to attain genuine reach become visible to the international community only through the activities clumped under the umbrella of "external mediation". It is in this moment that the impact of the ICs on international policy-making becomes measurable because strategies for advocacy towards IOs, governments and the domestic and international judiciary translates into concrete means.

4.2.1 Internal Mediation in the Pan-European ECO Forum, the CAN and CPDE

Based on the current empirical observations, the cases of the Pan-European ECO Forum and the Consultative Platform have been used to illustrate internal mediation in the ICs. The CAN, the European Transport Forum, the CINGO, the CPDE, the ATM and the Global Climate Coalition will be considered as examples. Both the Pan-European ECO Forum and the Consultative Platform are particularly significant for the purpose of mapping the attributes of internal mediation due to the differences in the rules governing their activities. In the ECO Forum, accession and membership are subjected to simplified and informal procedures. In contrast to the latter,

[11] See C. Carpenter, Governing the Global Agenda: "Gatekeepers" and "Issue Adoption" in Transnational Advocacy Networks, in A. Peters, L. Koechlin, T. Forster, G Fenner Zinkernagel (eds.), *Non-state Actors as Standard Setters* see chapter 3 n 18, see text n 32 and see chapter 5 n 31.

the Consultative Platform adopts a more formalized system of rules, which affects – *inter alia* – the mediation among its members.

The first case to be analysed is the Pan European ECO Forum. Every NGO that operates within the United Nations Economic Commission for Europe (UNECE) region, and shares the goal of promoting sustainable development, is a potential eligible member in the ECO forum. Acceptance of the coalition's agreement is also requested. Membership can be applied for by a simple letter to the Secretariat of the coalition or by registration for the Plenary. Accordingly, membership can be cancelled with a letter without need to indicate reasons. Obviously, while facilitating conditions to access the coalition encourage a large participation, they also necessitate a fast and efficacious way to mediate any diverging positions amongst their members, and thus to avoid the coalition becoming inactive. As noted by some authors with regard to administrative colleges made up of hundreds of delegates, their excessive size may transform joint decision-making processes into "joint decision traps".[12]

To prevent this risk, the ECO Forum employs two correctives. The first corrective relies on the organization of the Forum. The coalition is structured hierarchically, with the Plenary on the top of the structure, the Coordination Board and the Secretariat at the centre, and a number of Issue Groups and Focal Points situated at the periphery. The Plenary makes common policy statements and defines the strategies of the Forum. Yet, the content of such statements and strategies results in a multi-level process of bargaining between the members held during the working sessions of the Issue Groups. These are subject-related coalitions (also termed "content coalitions") appointed by the Plenary and subjected to the duty to report to it. The process of bargaining is completed by the presence of the Focal Points, whose main task is to guarantee the coordination between the members of specific UNECE regions, its key-issues, and the Forum itself. Informal coordination between the Focal Points and the Issue Groups is organized on a daily basis. A more formal coordination is guaranteed by the Coordination Board, which is composed of the representatives of the two organs. The second corrective to avoid inactivity of the coalition, given the considerable diversity among the members NGOs, entails the rules governing the voting within each organ. Each member gets one vote. The Plenary takes decisions by consensus. When consensus cannot be reached, the rule of majority applies and decisions are taken by the two thirds of the participating members. All the other bodies decide by consensus.

Very close to the approach adopted by the ECO Forum is that of the CAN. As in the former IC, eligibility criteria to obtain CAN's membership is not particularly demanding. All NGOs that do not represent industry, have an interest in the promotion of sustainable development, and are active in climate change issues are eligible

[12] See F.W. Scharpf, "The Joint-Decision Trap: lessons from German Federalism and European Integration" (2007) 66 *Public Administration* 239; M. Savino, *The role of Transnational Committees* see chapter 3 n 8, at 13.

to become members of CAN. NGOs and individuals who do not qualify (or prefer not to apply) for full membership may be still granted the status of observers. They do not, however, have rights to influence the determination of consensus at the point where a decision is being finalized. The easy accessibility to the CAN is in fact balanced by strict rules governing the consensus-building of the coalition. To begin with, the CAN General Assembly is the sole body of the coalition entitled to assume official positions. The rules of the coalition states that, having CAN membership not equally representative of all national, regional and other constituencies, "consensus will be strived for" in General Assemblies in order to guarantee decisions as much fair as possible. However, it is added in CANs rules that in special circumstances full consensus is equated to "sufficient consensus". These are the circumstances in which most of the members in a given constituent group support a decision, with only a small minority dissenting. It is in the faculty of "facilitators", who assist the workings of General Assemblies, to decide when it is the case to opt for sufficient instead of full consensus. In the extreme case, the representatives whose views are overruled by the majority are entitled to declare a formal dispute against the decision. The dispute is then referred to the CAN Board. The Board makes a first attempt to resolve the dispute by mediation. Should this fail, it can confirm or overrule the decision, and may refer the issue back to the General Assembly for further debate.

As the ECO Forum and the CAN examples suggest, the combination between a multi-level bargaining system and consensus rules may be used to overcome competing visions – a by-product of interest heterogeneity – and to foster compromises. Thus, internal mediation is pursued through a subtraction of the most controversial issues, which are "filtered" in the passage from working groups to the plenary body. A solution further illustrated by the case of the CPDE. It has been already mentioned that the CPDE is the result of a 5 years transformation process that progressively brought complexity to the original structure. Currently the CPDE's main body is the Global Council, where members geographically and thematically close gather. There are five co-chairs that support the Global Council. These co-chairs are obligated to include at least two members from the "Global South" and two women. A Coordination Committee oversees the work of the coalition, supported in its task by a Global Secretariat. Fascinatingly, the Global Secretariat is hosted by a single NGO, IBON International, which focuses on capacity building and it is based in the Philippines. An Independent Accountability Committee completes the structure. The Committee's goal is to ensure that evaluation and audit mechanisms and other accountability measures are in place and functioning. But most importantly, the CPDE aims at dealing with internal mediation with a vast number of focus-oriented committees. As an alternative to working groups, the above cases show how diverging positions can be mediated through scaling down the impact of the coalitions' decisions over its members. Strategies are defined only in their outsets and then single NGOs are left the option to promote their positions individually.

4.2.2 *The Cases of Alter-EU and ATM*

Surprising as it may seem, there are cases in which the ICs decide to avoid any formal coordination, and therefore adopt only light correctives, Alter-EU and the ATM being paradigmatic examples. The only effort towards the coordination of Alter-EU consists of the creation of two bodies, one for the political organization of the network, and one devoted to the administrative management. The Steering Committee is the politically responsible body of Alter-EU. There are almost 200 members of Alter-EU. Yet, only a few and selected of those are in charge for its political coordination. Currently, only seven members sit in the Steering Committee, each of those representing civil society actors that are also members of the coalition. Although no specific information is provided on this point by Alter-EU documents, it seems that being part of the Steering Committee implies a duty to contribute to the funding of the coalition (which may also be described as a corrective). Moving to administrative coordination, the solution adopted by Alter-EU is that of creating another organization to the only scope of serving administrative duties. This is "Alter-EU asbl", an organization with legal not for profit status registered under Belgian law which looks for (and administrates) funding opportunities, and – as indicated on the website of Alter-EU – "provides administrative support to allow the coalition to organize its activities".

Similarly to Alter-EU, the ATM establishes that the representatives of the member organizations and networks meet at least once a year and take the main strategic decisions in an alliance meeting. However, in the time between one meeting and the next one, a "Coordination Group" composed of six members, is in charge. Correctives are very poor. Firstly, there is a "Writing Group" that operates during the annual meeting to draft and coordinate the written outcomes of ATM. Secondly, for each consultation organized by the ATM, a group of organizers is established. Each group has a coordinator, who ensures the exchange of information between the consultation groups on the one hand, and the coordination group and writing group on the other hand. Thirdly, and finally, one overall coordinator of the whole project is contracted to support and coordinate the work of the coordination group. In basic terms, it could be affirmed that the ATM approaches internal mediation not as a general rule, but to the specific aim of approving single documents. Explanatory is the process that brought to the publication of the report "Trade: time for a new vision".[13] The proposals included in the document were developed in a 4 years process, with public workshops held all over Europe to which engaged a wide range of civil society groups from both within and outside the EU. However, in the forewords to the document it is clearly stated: "the members and supporters of the ATM do not necessarily agree with each and every detail in this paper, but support the general line of thinking". Moreover, the process of mediation did not finish with the

[13] The document is available at the following web address www.alternativetrademandate.org/wp-content/uploads/2013/09/ATM-Document-Final-EN.pdf.

official presentation of the document. A series of papers with more detailed proposals on several pressing issues was circulated in order to open topic-oriented discussion with the ATM members.

4.2.3 Internal Mediation in the Consultative Platform

Yet, leaving the application and enforcement of a strategy entirely to the willingness of members may be risky. This is especially true when highly political problems come into discussion. It is for this reason that other ICs adopt more formalized agreements. Consider the case of the Consultative Platform. According to the terms of reference of this coalition, NGOs, stakeholders' organizations representing consumers, and food operators active in the food chain are all permitted to join the coalition.[14] Accession, however, is precluded to organizations that do not comply with geographical, functional, and practical conditions. More specifically, the accessing organizations are requested to set their activity on the European level; they are requested to be competent in the areas of work of the EFSA; they also have to be in frequent contact with the EFSA. To complement the conditions to access the coalition, the terms of reference introduce two additional criteria. First, members of the MB, the Advisory Forum, the Scientific Committee, and the various Panels of experts of the EFSA participate in the meetings of the Consultative Platform. They do not, however, take active part in internal mediation. Their role is aimed solely at ensuring a proper exchange of information among participants, and at providing administrative support to the coalition. In order to coordinate the discussion, the Consultative Platform also designates a Chair and two Vice-chairs from among its members. Second, detailed rules discipline the maximum number of participants to the coalition (never more than 30), the frequency of its meetings (twice a year), and locations (preferably in Parma).

Differently from the case of the Pan-European ECO Forum, the example of the Consultative Platform suggests that a higher degree of formalization may be used to the scope of facilitating the coalitions' effectiveness and to avoid its inactivity. This option, however, has its shortcomings from a democracy-theory perspective. Arguably, the stricter are the conditions to access the coalition, the lesser is the number of civil society actors that fulfil these criteria. Needless to say, a narrow number of participants may influence the coalitions' specific weight on the international level and thus undermine its chances to obtain successful outcomes. As Chap. 3 already had the opportunity to explain, many ICs admit associated (or not permanent) members to overcome this problem. Not accidentally, the Consultative Platform permits different classes of membership.

A higher formalization of rules may also give origin to a closer control from the part of the IO management on the internal activities of the coalition. This point is

---

[14] See MB 12/09/2006, No. 6. See also H.C.H. Hofmann, A. Turk, "The Development of Integrated Administration in the EU and its Consequences" (2007) 13 *European Law Journal* 253, at 260.

illustrated by the WTO Informal Council and the Consultation Forum on a revised Community eco-label award scheme. As Chap. 3 explicated, the WTO Director General created the Informal Council in 2001 in the attempt to increase the cooperation between NGOs and the WTO. However, when two similar initiatives were issued in 2003, a number of influential NGOs, such as Oxfam International and Friends of the Earth, refused to take part in these bodies claiming that they did not represent civil society and that controls from the part of the IO management was too severe.[15] According to Peter Van den Bossche, the rejection of this invitation was due to the fear of both criticism from other NGOs and potential bad publicity. To confirm this interpretation, there is the fact that the NGOs that accepted to join the new initiatives requested that its activities not be made public (and it is possibly for this reason that no information has been made available on the WTO website).[16] The same discourse applies for the Consultation Forum, also introduced in Chap. 2. Article 15 of the Regulation (EC) No 1980/2000, which established this umbrella organization, states that is up to the Commission to establish the rules of procedure of the Forum.

4.2.4 Internal Mediation in the European Transport Forum and the CINGO

As the examples of the Alter EU and ATM show, a number of ICs sit between the two extremes cases represented by the ECO Forum and the Consultative Platform. In other words, the ICs often adopt mixed rules to delimitate the boundaries of full membership and to oversee the decisional workflow. The European Transport Forum and the CINGO may be used to examine how consensus is built through mixed process of internal negotiation. The European Transport Forum combines the rules regarding the membership with a number of restrictions regarding the organization of its workings. The members of the Forum were selected following a call for applications published in the Official Journal of the European Communities (with the only exception of the members representing trade unions).[17] With regard to the workings of the Forum, three correctives have been introduced to guarantee successful mediation among the members. To begin with, Commission Decision 2001/546/EC (article 4) establishes that the Forum may set up ad hoc working parties, but these can exceed a maximum of 11 members and are subjected to the prior Commission's approval. Experts may be invited to participate in the Forum workings, provided that (article 5) they only take part in the discussions regarding the topic for which they are invited. Most relevantly, according to article 9, all meetings

[15] See M. Ratton Sanchez, "Brief Observations on the Mechanisms for NGO Participation in the WTO" (2006) 4 *International Journal of Human Rights* 103.

[16] See P. Van den Bossche, *NGO Involvement in the WTO* see chapter 3 n 29.

[17] The EU Commission called upon the European Trade Union Confederation to appoint six members to represent the fields of energy and transport.

of the Forum must be authorized by the Commission (who will also have a voice in the choice about the place of meetings).

The rules of procedure of CINGO provide detailed instructions about accession and consensus building. The main body of CINGO is the Conference of INGOs. This is the place where all INGOs enjoying participatory status with the COE have a seat. The Conference meets at least twice a year, during ordinary sessions of the COE's Parliamentary Assembly. Each member only has one vote. To this end, the Conference Secretariat gives the delegates one voting card for each of the members present and represented. Internal mediation is encouraged through a number of incentives. First and foremost is the fact that invitations to the Conferences (accompanied by the agenda) must be sent out at least 1 month before the day of the meeting. As a further effort to have an informed discussion among the participating members, all documents for the meeting are made available at least 2 weeks before the meeting. All the decisions of the Conference require a relative majority of the INGOs present and represented. Decisions are normally made by a show of hands, unless the President of the Conference, or one third of the INGOs present and represented, requests a secret ballot. Finally, the CINGO establishes a number of committees to the extent of facilitating coordination about the members in specific interest areas. To avoid dispersion of opinions, the rules of procedures of CINGO dispose that committees shall plan their work to reflect the general lines and the programme of activities pursued by the Conference of INGOs, and that they have to ensure coordination of its work with that of the other committees.

4.3 External Mediation as a Collaborative Effort

Once a strategy is settled, an official position is agreed upon, or the contours of an action are defined, the activity of the ICs develops into external mediation. Having in mind what has been told about external mediation in Sect. 4.1 of this chapter, this can be better grasped by making reference to the concept of PPPs. PPPs in the supranational legal arena are the expression of a collaborative effort in governance that involves public and private actors. Case in point, the UN General Assembly defines the PPPs as "voluntary and collaborative relationships between various parties, both State and non-state, in which all participants agree together to achieve a common purpose or undertake a specific task and to share risk and responsibilities, resources and benefits".[18] Of the many examples that may be used to illustrate PPPs, two are worth a brief mention. The first is the Global Alliance for Clean Cook stoves, which brings together over 175 government agencies, corporations and NGOs to secure the adoption of 100 million clean cook stoves by 2020.[19] The aim

[18] See UN General Assembly, Enhanced Cooperation Between the United Nations and All Relevant Partners, in Particular the Private Sector. Report of the Secretary General, A/60/214, 2005, available here www.un.org/partnerships/Docs/partnershipreport_a-56-323.pdf

[19] See generally www.cleancookstoves.org

of this PPP is to reduce carbon emission, to improve the health of tens of millions of families and to increase the security of millions of women. A second example of PPP is the Partnership for a New Beginning, involving the US State Department, the Aspen Institute and several corporation and universities in the US, Algeria Egypt, Indonesia, Morocco, Pakistan, the Palestinian Territories, Tunisia and Turkey.[20] Thus far this PPP has supported over 70 projects connected with science and technology, economic opportunity, and education.

All activities labelled in this chapter as "external mediation" are concerned with collaboration between the ICs and IOs. At one end of the continuum stands the elaboration of communication strategies; elsewhere, further along the continuum, there are standard setting and IO's agenda-setting activities; then, at the opposite end of the continuum, we find the implementation of rules. Collaboration may sometimes look evident, as in the case of agenda setting; or it may instead appear less tangible, as for the elaboration of communication strategies. However, if we conceive it as a "process", instead of a sequence of isolated actions, then the collaborative nature of external mediation is clearly present. This, in turn, produces a number of effects. Chief among them is the fact that most of the actions carried by the ICs escape precise legal categorisation, and therefore fall into the definition of soft law[21] (a typical outcome of PPPs that will be analysed in Sect. 4.4 of this chapter). A second outcome of the collaborative nature of the IC external mediation process is concerned with the convergence of principles of administrative governance, and it will be discussed in Chap. 6 of this volume.

4.3.1 Communication Strategies by Interlocutory Coalitions

Chief among the previous academic accounts of tactics used to mediate and advocate by networks of civil society actors with IOs is that of Keck and Sikkink, who identify four typologies of tactics to apply pressure. First is what they name "information politics", described as the ability of a network to quickly generate politically usable information and move it to where it will have the most impact. The second tactic described by Keck and Sikkink is "symbolic politics", intended as the ability to call upon symbols, actions or stories that make sense of a situation for an audience that is far away from the place of action. Information and symbolic politics – unified by Sabine Lang under the "public advocacy" label – attempts to achieve policy success by engaging broader publics and stimulating their engagement. Thus, information and symbolic politics, as well as Lang's public advocacy, are all concerned with the first of the ICs' actions to mediate externally: communication.

When talking about how communicative strategies work and why they are at the base of advocacy efforts by the ICs, one can draw a distinction between two main

[20] See generally www.state.gov/s/partnerships/newbeginning/

[21] For a definition of "soft law" and an analysis of its virtues See A. Schafer, "Resolving Deadlock: Why International Organisations Introduce Soft Law" (2006) 2 *European Law Journal* 194.

functions: information and knowledge. It is posited in this volume that information and knowledge are two mutually reinforcing dimensions of communication that cannot be understood in isolation from one another. Information involves both internal and external mediation. In fact, it consists of sharing facts and data among the participants of a coalition, and eventually outside of it. It is quite telling that many ICs dispose of their own media facilities. Within few hours they can provide photographs and information to newspapers and magazines, or upload videos on YouTube and other websites. After all, there is a well-known practice of NGOs collaborating with journalists to produce daily newspapers during important international meetings and conferences in order to provide a communication channel between the official and unofficial events. Knowledge, in turn, is more strictly related to external mediation. It is actually created out of information, and overlaps with the usage of reasons to induce or move someone to believe something or perform some action. Thus, knowledge comprises and shares not merely facts, but also experiences, technical expertise and values.[22]

Can information and knowledge may be regarded as forms of rule-making? As observed by the German Constitutional Court in the 1994 International Military Operations Case, concerning the right of participation of the Federal *Bundestag* in decisions on the deployment of German armed forces within the framework of operations undertaken by the NATO and the Western European Union for the implementation of the UN Security Council resolutions,[23] changes in the contents of an international treaty might be well brought about by interpretation (rather then by a formal amendment) of an existing international treaty. This is exactly what happens when information and knowledge are spread through the activity of the ICs. They do not necessarily support radical changes. Rather, information and knowledge develop moderate modifications through interpretation of IOs' policies, decisions, rules, and more generally of administrative principles of governance at the supranational level. This process has been qualified by Dorothy Thomas (1993) as the "methodology" of human rights activism. A methodology, Thomas explains, made of "promoting change by reporting facts". How is promotion of change made through information and knowledge? There are three different possible ways. First is mobilization of public scrutiny. The ICs gather public attention towards a

[22] See V. Allee, *The Future of Knowledge: Increasing Prosperity through Value Networks* (Boston, Routledge, 2003). See also J.L. Martinez, "Communication Conflicts in NGO: A Theoretical Approach" (2002) *Instituto de Empresa* Working Paper n. WP 2/02, available at www.ie.edu. A second difference between information and knowledge concerns its concrete effects. Information, differently from knowledge, may lead to an "informational paradox", as argued by Keck and Sikkink. In short, when ICs start to gather public attention towards an issue, before beginning to advocate towards IOs, they contribute to make the issue of their interest more visible. Observers may have the impression that, regardless the activists' efforts, the problem is getting worst, because information portray the issue as worse than it actually is. This may also have implications in evaluating the networks' effectiveness.

[23] On alternatives to traditional treaty-based law-making See S. Kirchner, "Effective Law-Making in Times of Global Crisis – A Role for International Organizations" (2010) II *Göttingen Journal of International Law* 267.

topic of interest, in order to substantiate their advocacy strategy towards IOs. There is a great deal of empirical evidence of single non-state actors (NGOs in particular) using this strategy. A very well acknowledged case is that of Amnesty International. Amnesty may not have been the inventor of communication for advocacy, but it probably perfected it. Peter Benenson, a London attorney, created Amnesty in 1960, after having read a news report of two Portuguese students sentenced to prison by the Salazar dictatorship. In response to it, Benenson bought a full-page in the Sunday newspaper, the Observer, where he called for a 1-year campaign for the release of the "Forgotten Prisoners". In so doing, Benenson fashioned a strategy consisting of a mobilization of public attention through an international letter-writing campaign to pressure governments to release those "prisoners of conscience". In the decades since, tens of thousands of Amnesty International letter-writers have been moved to imitate this strategy.

A second way ICs use communication for advocacy purposes is when they present official written statements during sessions or meetings in order to influence officials and governmental representatives, and to reduce the abstractness of IOs' officials questioning towards governmental representatives. The flow of information provided by the ICs may reduce the likelihood of mistaken analysis and may enrich the quality of the final reports by IO's officials. A quality that is further increased by the extended creativity that, scholars believe, civil society actors better exercise compared to government officials. In the telling words of Paul Reinsch (1909), private initiative "can be far bolder and more optimistic than that of the state. It is not beset by ever-present care to preserve national sovereignty intact". Specific empirical evidence on this point may be derived from the activity of the Consultative Platform and the Pan-European ECO Forum. Over the years, the Consultative Platform has contributed to shaping EFSA's policies through providing scientific advice on health claims' management, genetically modified organisms, and emerging food-chain related risks. To this goal, members of the EFSA's Scientific Committee and the panels of experts – both highly specialized units which carry out risk assessment work in their respective fields – participate on a regular basis to the Platform's meetings. In a similar vein, the Issue Groups of the Pan-European ECO Forum make scientific information available to other coalition's members and governmental representatives involved in the MOP of the Aarhus Convention.

Finally, there are all the cases in which ICs make a proactive use of communication. In this third hypothesis, differently from the previous two, the scope of communication is not necessarily linked to the scope of advocating an issue towards IOs. Information and knowledge in this case are spread proactively in order to expand the general knowledge of the existence of the coalition, to support campaigns from other GCS' actors, to the simple end of contributing to the public debate, or even for the scope of creating new ICs. Examples include the vast number of public events organized by ICs on topics of different nature (e.g. the CINGO public meetings held in the most important European cities to debate topics such as democratic participation, inclusiveness or poverty)[24]; the publication of books and reports (e.g. the periodical assessments from the European ECO Forum on climate change, pollutants or more generally the protection of environment); the organization of public actions to be held in different part of the words and related to the same topics (e.g. the initiative from the GCAP, called "I Move Against Injustice, Inequality and Insecurity" and aimed at demanding that local and global leaders to deliver on promises to uphold the rights of all women, men and children)[25]; or even the organization of contests in which citizens and other civil society actors are invited to participate (e.g. the International Social Innovation Competition launched by the Euclid Network in partnership with UniCredit Foundation and Project Ahead to acknowledge a prize to social innovators from around the world).[26] To exemplify how communication may lead to the creation of new ICs, the cases of Alter-EU and AskTheEU will be considered. Alter-EU formalised as a coalition in July 2005 in response to the "European Transparency Initiative" launched by Siim Kallas, at that time European Commission Vice President; while AskTheEU is a project formally promoted by a single not-for-profit human rights organization, Access Info Europe, based in Madrid and active in the field of institutional transparency. Although a sole actor runs AskTheEU, the project gets financial and operational support from a coalition of European and international organisations, including MySociety (an organisation aimed at making governments more accountable), the German chapter of Open Knowledge Foundation, and the Chilean *Acceso Inteligente* project. Basically, AskTheEU collects information, brings to light facts and materials concerning disputed and/or controversial situations which would otherwise be neglected or forgotten by public opinion, to the scope of promoting transparency.

4.3.2 Agenda-Setting

The third tactic adopted by supranational advocacy networks in the description provided by Keck and Sikkink involves "leverage politics", and it is described as the ability of networks to influence other actors (external to those networks). The very same concept, i.e. the attempt to influence IOs' decision-making by gaining some degree of insider status in it, is identified by Sabine Lang under the label of "institutional advocacy".[27] As for the case of communication strategies, there are a vast number of actions that can be described according to the conceptual domain of institutional advocacy and/or leverage politics. A long line of cases illustrates non-state actors influence's on the agendas of IOs and on international conferences. "Individuals" – report Thomas Davies – "had petitioned intergovernmental meetings

[24] See generally www.coe.int/t/ngo/events_en.asp

[25] See generally www.whiteband.org/en/news

[26] See generally www.euclidnetwork.eu/projects/current-projects/european-social-innovation-naples-20.html

[27] See S. Lang, *NGOs, Civil Society and the Public Sphere* see chapter 1 at section 6.2, at 22.

since at least the Congress of Breda in 1667".[28] John Humphrey (1984) reports the famous case of the 1945 conference held in San Francisco to establish the UN. Humphrey explains how the role played by NGOs, trade unions and peace movements was pivotal in securing the inclusion of human rights language in the final UN charter. These actors lobbied in favour of human rights in a way "there is no parallel in the history of international relations". A major milestone in citizens' petitions at the supranational level dates back to 1928, during the sixth Pan-American Conference. After women's groups journeyed to the Conference venue, the governments agreed to hold a plenary session to hear them, and accepted their proposition to create the Inter-American Commission of Women. NGOs are officially recognized as having assisted in the drafting of the 1989 UN Convention on the Rights of the Child and the 1979 Convention on the Conservation of Migratory Species of Wild Animals. Recent examples of leverage politics/institutional advocacy from GCS actors include the 1992 Rio Conference on Global Environment, the 1993 World Conference on Human Rights in Vienna, the 1994 Habitat Conference in Cairo, the 1995 Social Summit in Copenhagen, and also the 1995 World Women's Conference in Beijing. These are all cases in point when non-state actors have moved "from the corridors to sessions", as Karen Knop (2002) once tellingly explained. More generally, the three areas where the active role of non-state actors is most acknowledged are those of international humanitarian law (especially due to the support of the International Committee of the Red Cross), the sector of competence of the International Labour Organization (thanks to the help provided by trade unions and employer organizations), and the environmental sector.

Given the variety of actions used by GCS' actors to advocate institutionally towards IOs, the present and the following sections will concentrate on two actions from ICs. The first is agenda setting, and it will be dealt presently; the second is standard setting, and it will be explicated in Sect. 4.4. Before embarking on the detailed description of agenda and standard setting activities, it might be useful to recall that this is not a general condition. ICs' activity, practically speaking, may also not result in any specific outcomes or forms of legal regulation, as in the case of the NGO Advisory Body. This IC meets regularly (generally once a year) to discuss the state of play in the on-going trade negotiations. Thus far, however, these meetings have not produced official meeting reports or official statements. Yet, when the formulation of rules is encountered in ICs, it may be well considered as the second and more genuine rule-making function.

The agenda setting activity is the first example of this kind. It consists of raising points to be discussed and analysed during the meetings between civil society activists and IOs' bureaucrats. Significantly, in Keck's and Sikkink's taxonomy, agenda-setting is described as the first stage of network's attempt to advocate.[29] As such, agenda-setting is followed by the attempt to influence on discursive positions of

[28] See T. Davies, *NGOs, A New History of Transnational Civil Society* see chapter 1 at section 6.2, chapter 1 n 77 and n 79, at 28.

[29] See Keck, Sikkink, *Activists Beyond Borders* see chapter 1 at section 1, chapter 1 n 60 and n 68, chapter 3 n 28 and chapter 6 n 24, at 25.

states and IOs; then by the influence on institutional procedures; later on, by the influence on policy change in target actors; and, finally, by the influence on state behaviour. As for the case of single non-state actors, ICs are also interested in influencing the IOs' *travaux préparatoires* through pursuing the agenda-setting function. Firstly, this is because it is during this phase that the founding principles for the final documents are usually agreed upon; and, second, it is through agenda-setting that the ICs can contribute to the development of new guiding principles from the IO with whom they cooperate. Some examples should help to make this point clearer. During its 11th meeting held in Parma in December 2009, the Consultative Platform suggested that the EFSA create a Working Group on Emerging Risks to deal rapidly with food/feed chain risks. The proposal stressed the opportunity to involve stakeholders in the Working Group. The NGO Forum is actively involved in the annual meeting of the ADB's Board of Governors, during which decisions are made to set the ADB's policies and programs. In 2008, for instance, the NGO Forum insisted upon the substantial revision of the ADB's policies on the environment, involuntary resettlement and indigenous peoples. Further examples include the CONGO and the GCAP. CONGO's efforts to influence the ECOSOC agenda-setting include the organization of theme oriented activities, such as the annual Civil Society Development Forum. This is a parallel summit whose main scope is to set the focus on the topics of interest to the members of CONGO, and advocate for their inclusion in the ECOSOC agenda. The GCAP is directly involved in G8 and G20 meetings, where it lobbies government delegates to include in the agendas for future actions the Millennium Declaration goals.

One last matter should be mentioned before proceeding to the discussion of external mediation in the ICs. In all the activities concerned with agenda-setting, interactions between the ICs and IOs can be held on a formal or informal level, depending upon the framework of the IOs' rules and procedures on the relevant matter, and upon the ICs' perception of what is the most appropriate solution on a case-by-case analysis. Broadly speaking, the two conditions are joined in a cause-consequence relation: the stricter the IOs' rules are, the greater the use is of formal ways of interaction.[30] During the negotiations for the UN Convention for the Climate Change, for instance, the observers from CAN were allowed to present oral interventions and written submissions. However, during the negotiations for the Kyoto Protocol, the same representatives could only attend the official session and deliver formal statements. Consequently, they turned to informal means of influencing the state delegations through advice-giving. Exceptions are, however, possible. The CINGO and the Consultative Platform, to take an example, are hinged to the respect of strict rules concerning their relations to IOs. Yet, both these ICs rely upon informal channels of influence, such as informal meetings with IO's staff, as meaningful ways of action. In contrast, in cases like the NGO Forum or the Pan European ECO Forum, the opposite trend exists: these ICs attempt to improve the formality in contacts with the ADB and the MOP.

[30] See A. Alkoby, "Global Networks and International Environmental Lawmaking: A Discourse Approach" (2007–2008) 8 *Chicago Journal of International Law*, at 390.

4.4 Rule-Making Through Standards

Alternatively, the ICs may influence the behaviours of IOs by formulating and spreading rules autonomously. Or they may do it by "forum shopping": i.e. borrowing rules from a court or other legal venue that are favourable for their needs and then employing those rules in another legal venue (and, in so doing, "becoming granular", in the sense used by Susan Sell (2013): they can target individuals in their advocacy pursuits). These are known as the standard-setting activities. The term "standard" is often used in scholarly writing with quite different meanings. Academic researchers refer to standards in terms of technical harmonisation (e.g. in the EU harmonisation of technical standards is used to indicate the removal of barriers to trade) or, in the common law tradition, as specific sources of law opposed to rules. International law scholars make use of the concept of standards mostly in economic, environmental and human right laws. These, it is generally supposed, consist of a wide array of non-binding sources of law, including principles (i.e. general statements that allow a great flexibility in their interpretation and implementation), recommendations, official reports, codes of conduct, declarations of intents, methodologies and guidelines providing detailed guidance on requirements to be met for its implementation. The importance of such standards at the supranational level, it is generally assumed by international scholarly research, is great. As Anne-Marie Slaughter recognizes, addressing the questions issued by standards at the supranational level has been the source of euphoria and anxiety.[31] While in fact in domestic legal systems these forms of legal regulation – that could be amorphously analysed under the "soft law" rubric – receive minor acknowledgement with respect to formal norms, the opposite is likely to occur in the supranational legal space. Here rigid and difficult-to-amend treaty law tends to be supplemented with new legal strategies, such as interim applications, flexible amendment procedures, or standards.

Indeed, the concrete effects of non-state actors' intervention through the dissemination of autonomous standards are much debated. Opinions diverge. Some scholars posit that the effect of standards cannot really be measured. First, because the main channels of influence through which standards are developed are informal; and, secondly, because the effectiveness of standards seems to depend not only on their quality/quantity, but also on the legitimacy of their authors. Thus, following in the footsteps of the on-going debate on non-state actors' representativeness and reliability, these authors assert that standards are not measurable, at least not in terms of effectiveness. The "shadow of hierarchy" hypothesis, formulated by Fritz Scharpf (1997), is pretty much illustrative of this critique. Scharpf postulates that non-state actors agree on a standard only in the case in which a credible threat of governmental, "hierarchical" law making exists. In the contrary hypothesis, he states, there will be only endless bargaining. Differently from this opinion, there is a growing body of scholarly work that supports the importance of soft law in the international legal arena.

[31] See A.M. Slaughter, *A New World Order* see chapter 1 at section 1, at 8.

It is particularly the case of analysis by Anne Peters, Till Forster, Lucy Koechlin, and Gretta Fenner Zinkernagel.[32] According to their view, soft law may work as "peacemaker" for subsequent hard law; it can substitute legislation, and thereby fulfil a "para-law" function; and, in the third place, soft-law can even complement hard law, by making it more concrete, or by guiding its interpretation. After all, it is further noted,[33] standards escape the need of formally binding norms, because legal formality is not considered the only way to make them widely effective. Chapter 6 of this volume will expound more profoundly this topic. For the moment it will suffice to know that scholars who studied policy transfer dynamics at the supranational level stressed the prominence of non-state actors in supporting "soft" forms of transfer (concerning ideas and knowledge rather than norms) as a necessary complement to the "hard" transfer of policy tools.[34] In facilitating the exchanges of such ideas and knowledge across countries at any one time, non-state actors are regarded as "policy transfer entrepreneurs".[35]

That said, GCS in general, and the ICs in particular, remain among the most prolific producers/borrowers of standards, or soft-law, in the supranational legal space. And there are two specific motivations for this. The first, and obvious, reason is related to the practical outcomes of standard-setting. By developing and publicizing such standards, the ICs seek to make them more widespread and influential, in order to let them acquire a sort of increased value which could eventually bind upon IOs[36]; and, indeed, they aim at increasing their leverage at the international level. Here a fundamental point to emphasize is that even in circumstances when the ICs' standards are not intended to directly constrain the behaviour of the underlying IOs, they may be nonetheless directed to the borrowers of these institutions, who are obliged to take them into account during the implementation of the projects. Such prescriptions are often designed to increase fairness, responsiveness, and efficiency in national governments. This is the case, for instance, of the NGO Forum, who works in close contact with the governments of the Asian and Pacific areas. By developing uniform standards towards' ADB's borrowers, the NGO Forum aims at strengthening the existing standards and increasing its influence. A second example

[32] See A. Peters, L. Koechlin, T. Forster, G Fenner Zinkernagel (eds.), *Non-state Actors as Standard Setters* see chapter 3 n 18, see text n 11 and chapter 5 n 31, at 500.

[33] See E. Benvenisti, *The Law of Global Governance* see chapter 1 at section 1, chapter 1 n 10, n 22 and n 96 and text n 6, at 57.

[34] See M. Evans, J. Davies, "Understanding Policy Transfer: A Multi-Level, Multi-Disciplinary Perspective" (1999) 77 (2) *Public Administration* 361; D. Stone, *Transfer Agents* see chapter 3 at section 1.6.

[35] See D. Dolowitz, D. Marsh, "Learning From Abroad: The Role of Policy Transfer in Contemporary Policy Making" (2000) 13 *Governance: An International Journal of Policy and Administration* Vol. 13, 5.

[36] See generally D. Shelton (ed.), *Commitment and Compliance: The Role of Non-Binding Norms in the International Legal System* (Oxford, Oxford University Press, 2000). On the relation between networks of NGOs and the formation of international standards See D.B. Hunter, "Civil Society Networks and the Development of Environmental Standards at International Institutions" (2007–2008) 8 *Chicago Journal of International Law* 437.

worth a brief mention concerns the global garment industry. In recent years, political coalitions of NGOs and trade unions have promoted an agenda of "core labour standards" as a mean of imposing democratic restraints upon the exercise of corporate power. Violations of these labour standards (and their inner values of equality) have been advocated towards the factory level to the diverse sites of decision-making within global production and supply chains.[37]

The second reason that motivates the massive usage or adaptation of standard-setting by the ICs is to be found within the blurring distinction between the public and the private spheres in supranational governance. The ICs may be considered as legitimate partners of IOs in decision-making processes. This increases their chances of being actively involved in the production of standards. Jessica Green (2010) explicates this phenomenon by addressing the concept of "entrepreneurial authority". Green separates from the traditional definition of authority as the mere capacity to enforce obedience. She actually describes entrepreneurial authority as opposed to the delegation of authority to private actors in the context of multilateral environmental agreements (what she calls "delegated authority"). As a dynamic and fast-growing form of private authority, entrepreneurial authority, in the opinion of Green, moves beyond traditional conceptions of non-state actors as lobbyists, seeking to influence the rules made by governments. Rather, actors exercising entrepreneurial authority strike out on their own, serving as de facto rule makers. Not incidentally, notes Green, such form of authority is becoming increasingly common in certain areas ranging from organic food to green building practices to sustainable tourism. Green reports two interesting examples. The first relates to forest certification. In 2007, nearly 8 % of world's forest cover was already certified as sustainable according to private environmental codes. The second is concerned with sales of fair-trade products. The Marine Stewardship Council certifies the sustainability of dish sold in retail giants worldwide, such as McDonalds, Walmart, and Carrefour. Other well-known cases of "civil regulations", as Green names it, are those of the Clean Clothes Campaign and Transparency International. The Clean Clothes Campaign is a network of European NGOs and trade unions that fight for fairer working conditions in the clothing industry.[38] The Campaign promotes codes of conduct that are grounded in the existing ILO Conventions. Those companies who voluntarily adopt these standards receive a "reward" in terms of more ethical public image. Transparency International publishes an annual corruption ratings list, together with a transparent contracts scheme for developing countries. Such forms of advocacy through codes and standards may even turn into helpful outcomes for the convergence of administrative principles of governance between the GAL and the EAS. They are in fact increasingly drawing on existing ones and incorporating them into their own new rules. Chapter 5 will investigate into this more profoundly.

---

[37] See T. Macdonald, K. Macdonald, "Non-Electoral Accountability in Global Politics: Strengthening Democratic Control within the Global Garment Industry" (2006) 17 *European Journal of International Law* 89.

[38] See generally www.cleanclothes.org

To effectively demonstrate the dynamics of autonomous formulation (or adaptation) of standards and rules by the ICs, five cases will be considered: the Coalition for Environmentally Responsible Economies (CERES), the CINGO, the Consultative Board on the Future of the WTO, the ATM, and the WTN. Let us begin with the example of CERES. CERES does not exactly fit into the definition of the ICs, since it includes members from the public sector (e.g. the California state pension fund). However, it exemplifies the importance of codes of conduct within the supranational legal sphere. CERES was created in September 1989 with the aim to introduce criteria for auditing the environmental performance of large domestic and multinational industries. As a result of their efforts, the "CERES Principles" were adopted in 1989.[39] These are considered as a sort of code of environmental conduct. The CERES principles are in fact a ten-point code of corporate environmental conduct to be publicly endorsed by companies as an environmental mission statement or ethic. For more than 20 years the CERES Principles have served the scope for which they had been created. Investors use it as a guide to determine which companies practice socially responsible investment; whereas environmentalists use the code to measure and, if the case, criticize corporate behaviour. In 2010 the CERES published a "Roadmap for Sustainability", aimed at providing a more robust and comprehensive set of guidelines than the Ceres Principles.[40] The Roadmap is designed to provide a comprehensive platform for sustainable business strategy and for accelerating best practices and performance.

Second in line is the example of CINGO. One of the main actions adopted by this IC consists of official recommendations. These are documents following an official decision from one of the COE's institutions in which the CINGO expresses its position and recommends further actions to be taken by the Committee of Ministers. The most recent proposals include suggestions to introduce formal time limits for decision-making by competent authorities, to foster greater transparency, and to support further reasoning in decision-making. CINGO's recommendations also address general issues such as human rights' protection. To the same scopes of influencing IOs' decision-making serve official reports. The Consultative Board on the Future of the WTO, for instance, in 2005 issued an official report (the so-called "Sutherland Report") aimed at recommending how the WTO could meet its challenges.[41] The report dedicated an entire section to the improvement of transparency and civil society involvement in the WTO.[42]

Third to be addressed is the case of ATM. In November 2013, a week before the departure of the EU ministers and European Commission for the WTO negotiations in Bali, the ATM launched a 20-pages proposal on enhanced human, labour and

[39] See generally www.ceres.org/about-us/our-history/ceres-principles

[40] See generally www.ceres.org/company-network/ceres-roadmap

[41] See Peter Sutherland et al. (eds.), *The future of the WTO: Addressing Institutional Challenges in the New Millenium* (Geneva, WTO, 2004). See also the "Mini-Symposium on the Consultative Board's Report on the Future of the WTO" (2005) 8 *Journal of International Economic Law* 287.

[42] The document is available at the following address: www.wto.org/english/thewto_e/10anniv_e/future_wto_chap5_e.pdf

environmental rights to drive the EU trade policy. On several areas, such as food, work, money and raw material, the document contained detailed proposals for change. As an example, the document suggested that the EU become more self-sufficient in protein and oil crops as alternatives to imports of (genetically-modified) soybeans, palm oil and agro fuels. Most importantly, the document called on EU to hold European corporations accountable for human rights violations, environmental destruction, tax avoidance and tax evasion. A set of standards for initiating, negotiating and finalising trade and investment agreements with attention on civil society participation were explained in the document. Thus not only the EU, but also the WTO, was concerned by the document.

The WTN concludes this brief account of standard-setting activity by ICs, and serves as prominent example of forum shopping. In 2004 the WTN, together with other non-state actors such as the Access to Knowledge movement and the Electronic Frontier Foundation, deliberately regime shifted from the WTO regime on intellectual property rights to the regime of the World Intellectual Property Organisation (WIPO).[43] The shift was motivated by the fact that the development agenda implemented by the WIPO was more favourable in terms of technical capacity building and technology transfer to developing nations than the agenda of the WTO (where the interests of states like the United States were predominant). In substance, the WTN's exited from the regime of the WTO and borrowed from the WIPO's regime the rules and standards that it could reinterpret in way more favourable to its needs.

4.4.1 Implementation by Enforcement

The third dimension of external mediation by ICs includes the implementation and the enforcement of international norms and rules. Since many international agreements lack forceful mechanisms for implementation, and IOs struggle to manage a growing number of programs, GCS' actors have been often delegated a certain degree of authority and independence by IOs to implement rules at the domestic level, serving as an additional tool for enforcement. This is, at the core, what Keck and Sikkink describe as the fourth typology of tactic. They name it "accountability politics", to address the effort from civil society networks to hold powerful actors to their previously stated policies and principles. Actually, enforcing compliance by non-state actors at the domestic level is so widespread, that until recent years some states acted directly against NGOs, even if in breach of international law. The most telling example is that of Greenpeace and the French state. The persistent activities of the former against French nuclear testing in the South Pacific led to the French

[43] As explained by Jonathan Kuyper, the regulation of intellectual property rights at the international level is shared between the WTO and the WIPO. Although the WIPO and the WTO have agreed on some harmonised policies, on many others (e.g. open-source innovation or access to medicines) there is disagreement. For further details See J.W. Kuyper, "The Democratic Potential of Systemic Pluralism" (2014) 3 *Global Constitutionalism* 170.

government ordering some of its agents to sink the Greenpeace "Rainbow Warrior" in a New Zealand harbour. As a consequence of this breach of international law, the Special Arbitration Tribunal stated that France had to pay compensation to New Zealand for interference in sovereignty (but not to Greenpeace).[44]

Robert Putnam (1988) once suggested that international negotiations are structured as a "two-level game", simultaneously played by governments at the international level (with the representatives of foreign governments) and at the domestic level, with representatives of domestic interest groups. Drawing from this interpretation, scholars have concentrated mostly on civil society actors' capacity to "play the game" at the domestic level. Examples include NGOs capacity to respond to free-riding attempts by other sub-state actors with public opinion campaigns, or to petition domestic courts for judicial review. Yet, to the extent of which the ICs are involved in enforcement and implementation activities, no account of its peculiarities can be found in scholarly research. To supplement this, and to discuss what exactly implementation by ICs means, the current section will primarily focus on describing this practice, as well as critically address the related problems.

In looking at implementation by the ICs, two key characteristics should be focused upon. The first is implementation by means of enforcement. The second is implementation by conflict-resolution. Both forms of implementation, as it will be discussed below, may come in formal or informal ways. To begin with, implementation by means of enforcement is linked with ICs' participation in the enforcement of international treaties. This is a practice particularly established in the environmental and human rights fields.[45] The Pan-European ECO Forum, for instance, over the years has launched many initiatives aimed at examining whether citizens of the Member States who signed the Aarhus Convention are given adequate and effective access to environmental justice. The findings of these initiatives have been widely published. Recommendations to the concerned governments have followed.[46] TRAFFIC is also a case in point.[47] This is a network of NGOs that collaborates with

[44] See Rainbow Warrior Arbitration (*New Zealand v France*), Special Arbitration Tribunal (1990), 82 ILR 499.

[45] Formal implementation has already received significant attention in international legal scholarship. See P. Alston, J. Crawford (eds.), *The Future of UN Human Rights Treaty Monitoring* (Cambridge, Cambridge University Press, 2000); S. Jasanoff, "NGOs and the Environment: From Knowledge to Action" (1997) 18 *Third World Quarterly* 579; R. Charlton, R. May, "NGOs, Politics, Projects and Probity: A Policy Implementation Perspective" (1995) 16 *Third World Quarterly* 2; J. Smith, R. Pagnucco, G.A. Lopez, "Globalizing Human Rights: The Work of Transnational Human Rights NGOs in the 1990s" (1998) 20 *Human Rights Quarterly* 379.

[46] More widely on the relationship between the Aarhus Convention and international environmental law See T.S Mullikin, N.S Smith, M.T Champion, "Inextricably Intertwined – Environmental Management and the Public" (2004–2005) 17 *Georgetown International Environmental Law Review* 421; S. Atapattu, "The Public Health Impact of Global Environmental Problems and the Role of International Law" (2004) 30 *American Journal of Law and Medicine* 291; C. Noteboom, "Addressing the External Effects of Internal Environmental Decisions: Public Access to Environmental Information in the International Law Commission's Draft Articles on Prevention of Transboundary Harm" (2003) 22 *NYU Environmental Law Journal* 246.

[47] See generally www.traffic.org

the secretariat of the Convention on International Trade in Endangered Species of Wild Fauna and Flora (CITES)[48] to assess how effectively member states implement the Convention. TRAFFIC was originally established as an independent initiative to track trade in endangered species. Following the progressive expansion of its network and the convergence of objectives with CITES, in 1999 TRAFFIC signed a memorandum of understanding to strengthen the cooperation with CITES. The cooperation included the capacity building of national CITES structures, on the field assistance, assessment of country-specific violations and critical evaluation of States compliance reports.

As a second option, informal implementation by enforcement may arrive through simple dissemination of information. Given the well-known reluctance of states to complain publicly about their fellow states in cases of violation of international agreements, dissemination of information may be a way to draw attention to such violations. Several ICs, for instance, have developed their websites into tools for advertising project-related activities. The NGO Forum highlights through its website the public debate on the ADB's development strategies in order to involve its members in monitoring the enforcement and review of ADB's policies. The NGO Forum also publishes a quarterly newsletter called "Bankwatch". In a similar way to the NGO Forum, the Pan-European ECO Forum distributes a monthly newsletter among its members and the general public. The use of such newsletters is aimed at revealing the current state of the negotiating processes with IOs and at helping to clarify certain diplomatic issues to the public. The Consultative Platform publishes the minutes of all the official meetings with the EFSA's representative. Finally, all the official recommendations and the related follow-ups from the CINGO to the COE's institutions are given publication on the coalition's website. Other ways to compel enforcement through information are provided by publications related to specific projects' issues. Both the NGO Forum and the Pan-European ECO Forum diffuse these kinds of publications on a regular basis.

4.4.2 *Formal Implementation by Conflict-Resolution.* Amicus Curiae

Conceptualized in terms of conflict-resolution, implementation by the ICs relates to formal interventions through which civil society actors participate in complaint proceedings taking place before international jurisdictions, as well as the informal mechanisms of intervention of civil society actors within international judicial *fora*. Chapter 1 mentioned the increased involvement of a panoply of actors, both public and private, in judicial activities from supranational courts. In a related manner, the very concept of legality review has undergone considerable changes. Moving from an orthodox concept of scrutiny of the adherence to a given set of rules, the

[48] See generally www.cites.org

present-day mechanisms of review at the global level have broadened, and adopted mixed methods. Respect for the norm in question is no longer the only consideration; focus is also now placed on fulfilment of policy goals, conformity with standards and, to a far greater extent, the recognition and acceptance of the possession and use of power. In the end, compliance is blended with implementation.[49] Formal ways of intervention essentially consists of three possibilities: the first is to present *amicus curiae* (friend-of-the-court) briefs; the second consists of the autonomous initiation of cases, through the dispute-resolution mechanisms created by IOs; the third is the creation of alternative review mechanisms. In the following pages, the three possibilities will be discussed, beginning with the *amicus curiae* case, then moving to the hypothesis of the autonomous initiation of cases in front of IO's dispute-resolution mechanisms, and finally concluding with the case in which independent review mechanisms are created.

Even if, as a matter of principle, the *amicus curiae* role is not the same as a formal legal right to bring cases to a court, it is nonetheless a way to engage civil society interests' within the judicial proceedings and raise public awareness. It is for this reason that several NGOs have continually pressed the WTO about this issue in recent years.[50] *Amici* are not the same as an expert or a witness, but they may occasionally overlap with these other categories. *Amici* can also provide legal expertise and factual information; they can provide assistance to persons and entities that may be affected by a decision in accessing the court; or act on the basis of public interest considerations, for the protection of common interests. In her 1994 study, Dinah Shelton (1994) found that all major international tribunals, except the ICJ, had developed procedures to enable NGOs to submit information or statements on pending cases.[51] Since then the trends she documented have continued apace. International tribunals' jurisprudence has underlined the distinction between participation in judicial proceedings and its transparency. The declarations of Canada, Turkey and Argentina at the WTO General Council Meeting of 2 November 2000/ WT/GC/M/60, 23 January 2001 are based on this notion. Also debated is the fact that *amicus curiae* briefs might bring greater legitimacy to judicial proceedings. Those who are on the affirmative state that *amici*'s participation to protect community interests can be perceived by the public at large as a means to ensure greater legitimacy to judicial proceeding. Still, others note,[52] the increasing involvement of

[49] On the concept of legality and its evolutions See P.S. REINSCH, "The Concept of Legality in International Arbitration" (1911) 5 *American Journal of International Law* 604; E. BLANKENBURG, "The Waning of Legality in the Concept of Policy Implementation" (1985) 4 *Law & Policy* 481; M. BENNETT, "The Rule of Law" Means Literally What it Says: The Rule of the Law: Fuller and Raz on Formal Legality and the Concept of Law" (2007) 32 *Australian Journal of Legal Philosophy* 90.

[50] A comprehensive analysis of *amicus curiae* in international courts is provided by D. Shelton but see also N. Leroux, "NGOs at the World Court" (2006) 8 *International Community Law Review* 203.

[51] See D. Shelton, *The Participation of Nongovernmental Organizations*, see text in this section.

[52] See for instance A. Bianchi, *Non state Actors in International Law*, see chapter 1 n 72 and chapter 3 n 31.

civil society groups and professional associations can be perceived by those who are directly concerned with judicial mechanisms as an undue interference and, potentially, a disruptive element in the complex process of interest-accommodation that third party settlement inevitably entails.

A look at history can give us greater purchase on this topic. Among the cases in which supranational courts have acknowledged the role of non-state actors in judicial proceedings one might consider the following six. In *Soering v United Kingdom* case (Series A, No. 161, 1989), submitting NGOs succeeded in influencing the European Court of Human Rights' final decision. In the *Shrimps/Turtle*, *Asbestos*, and *Sardines* cases, already mentioned in Chap. 1 of this book, the AB of the WTO formally acknowledged the admissibility of *amicus curiae* submissions and explained its legal authority to accept such submissions.[53] The AB's jurisprudence on the role of non-state actors is one of particular interest. The US government was the first – and so far the only – state that presented NGOs briefs as an integral part of its brief against the complaint of India, Malaysia, Pakistan and Thailand. Drawing from this position, the AB decided it had the authority to accept NGO briefs in the 1998 *Shrimps-Turtle* dispute. The AB explained this decision by addressing the fact that the Working Procedures allow it "to accept and consider submissions or briefs from sources other than the participants and the third parties in an appeal" (further analysis of the merits of this decision is provided in Chap. 2). In *Asbestos* the AB went even further. In the midst of hearings, it invited "any person" to file applications for leave to file briefs concerning the dispute at hand. The invitation, setting highly rigorous conditions for eligibility to file briefs, was posted on the WTO website on November 8, 2000. Eleven applications for leave to file a written brief were submitted within the time limits specified. The AB subsequently reviewed the applications and decided on a case-by-case analysis who was permitted or denied the right to file a written brief. The disruptive nature of this approach is demonstrated by the fact that the AB's invitation for briefs from "any person" sparked angry protest. A number of member states – reportedly Pakistan, Egypt, India and Malaysia – reacted by requesting the Chair of the WTO General Council to convene a special meeting to discuss this issue. The meeting was held on November 22, 2000 and, according to the AB report of the case, several members expressed strong

[53] See, respectively, United States – Import Prohibition of Certain Shrimp Products, No. WT/DS58/AB/R; European Communities – Measures Affecting the Prohibition of Asbestos and Asbestos Products, No. WT/DS1135/AB/R; European Communities – Trade Description of Sardines, No. WT/DS231/AB/R. On the submission of *amicus curiae* briefs before the WTO DSU, See A. Appleton, "Amicus curiae Submissions in the Carbon Steel Case: Another Rabbit From the Appellate Body's Hat?" (2000) 3 *Journal of International Economic Law* 91; S. Dinah, "The Participation of Non-governmental Organizations in International Judicial Proceedings" (1994) 88 *American Journal of International Law* 611; A.K. Schneider, "Unfriendly Actions: The *Amicus* Brief Battle at the WTO" (2001) 7 *Widener Law Symposium Journal* 87; A. Reinisch, C. Irgel, *The participation of non-governmental organisations* see chapter 1 n 51; G. Zonnekeyn, "The Appellate body's Communication on Amicus Curiae Briefs in the Asbestos Case: An Echternach Procession?" (2001) 35 *Journal of World Trade* 553; P.C. Mavroidis, "*Amicus Curiae* Briefs Before the WTO: Much Ado About Nothing" (2001) *Jean Monnet* Working Paper 2, available at www.centers.law.nyu.edu/jeanmonnet.

criticism, arguing that the AB had exceeded its authority. Other examples include the Centre for the Settlement of Investment Disputes' 2005 award on the *Aguas Argentina* dispute allowed submissions by third parties (making explicit reference to the Appellate Body's practice). Finally, it is worth briefly mentioning the decision of the European Court of First Instance in the case *UEAPME v. Council*.[54] The Tribunal asserted that the participation of the social partners in negotiating agreements was equivalent to the participation of the European Parliament in other forms of Community law making. In substance, the court recognized that the role of representation in collective bargaining is closely linked to its role in democratic law making.

4.4.3 Autonomous Initiation of a Case and Creation of Review Mechanisms

In contrast to their participation as *amici*, the opportunity for non-state actors to initiate cases is less extensive. Formal ways of intervention are exemplified by the petition mechanisms that allow civil society actors to bring such cases as complainants. As consistently demonstrated by empirical research, litigation from individuals and groups is often used as a way to change rules and practices through court actions. The collective complaint mechanisms provided by the African Charter of Human and People Rights (which has allowed states, individuals, and NGOs with observer status to submit communications alleging a violation of the African Charter),[55] and the European Social Charter,[56] are cases in point. Article 6 of the complaint procedures of the Aarhus Convention's states that "communications [from the public] may be brought before the Committee by one or more members of the public concerning that Party's compliance with the Convention, unless that Party has notified the Depositary in writing by the end of the applicable period that it is unable to accept, for a period of not more than 4 years, the consideration of such communications by the Committee". In such hypotheses, actions taken in one governmental jurisdiction give rise to grievance by stakeholders living outside that jurisdiction. Thus individuals, NGOs, and other civil society actors (ICs included) are allowed to bring complaints against states that have ratified the concerned agreement.

---

[54] See Case T-135/96, *UEAPME v Council*, 1998.

[55] See C.A. Odinkalu, C. Christenses, "The African Commission on Human and Peoples' Rights: The Development of its Non-State Communication Procedures" (1998) 20 *Human Rights Quarterly* 235.

[56] See H. Cullen, "The Collective Complaints Mechanism of the European Social Charter" (2000) *European Law Review* 25; F. Sudre, "Le protocole additionnel à la charte européenne prévoyant un système de réclamations collectives" (1996) 3 *Revue Générale de Droit International Public* 715.

A third way for the ICs to challenge IOs is to create alternative review mechanisms. This is particularly the case of the UNCAC Coalition. Its primary campaign objective during 2006–2009 was to secure an effective, transparent and participatory monitoring mechanism for the UNCAC. To this end, members engaged in joint advocacy ahead of, and during, key intergovernmental meetings. This phase ended with the adoption, in November 2009, of an UNCAC review mechanism that started operation in July 2010. Currently the UNCAC Coalition is trying to ensure that civil society groups can contribute to the review process while supporting them in making quality submissions. In concomitance, the UNCAC aims to gain government agreement to publish review reports for public scrutiny.

4.5 Informal Implementation by Conflict-Resolution

Informal ways of intervention may include the act of counselling to parties in a dispute, or pressuring parties to initiate proceedings before a court. The possibility of appointing experts (as it is in the case of the Compliance Committee of the Aarhus Convention) can also be considered as an informal source of leverage to influence policy outcomes.[57] Finally, the same holds true for the relationship between the ICs and ombudsmen. The functions of ombudsmen are to provide an independent critical appraisal of the quality of administrative action, and to stimulate its future improvements.

Within this setting of non-state actors' intervention in international judicial proceedings, a related argument needs to be raised. It is unclear whether the participation of a coalition to such proceedings excludes the participation of NGOs that are members of the coalition, and vice-versa. The only historical precedent lies in the International Court of Justice's ancestor, the Permanent Court of International Justice. In the *Union Internationale des Fédérations des Ouvriers et Ouvrières de l'Alimentation* case, the application to present written arguments before the Court from a NGO was rejected on the basis of its belonging to an umbrella organization which had already been invited to submit an argument to the case.[58] The Court followed a logical path and rejected the application on the grounds that the interest had already been represented.

[57] See S. Kravchenko, "The Aarhus Convention and Innovations in Compliance with Multilateral Environmental Agreements" (2007) 1 *Colorado Journal of International Environmental Law and Policy* 7; M. Stallworthy, "Whither Environmental Human Rights?" (2005) 7 *Environmental Law Review* 14.

[58] See PCIJ Rep Series C No 12, at 261.

4.6 Conclusions

Chapter 2 questioned how GCS coalesce into organized networks, or coalitions. Chapter 3 continued by describing the ICs and its recurrent characteristics and addressed the core elements regarding the ICs' functioning and activities. Having differentiated between internal and external mediation, this chapter has described a large number of strategies and actions from the ICs. However, the arguments posed in Chap. 1 challenging the ability of GCS to influence supranational decision-making remain unanswered, namely: the accountability question, the efficiency question, and indeed the issue of participatory democracy. These questions will continue into the upcoming chapters. Chapter 5 will be devoted to analysis of the problems of accountability, legitimacy and responsiveness. These will be assessed from the perspective of both IOs and the ICs. Chapter 6 will introduce the topic of administrative convergence, as promoted by the interaction between IOs and the ICs. Finally, Chapter 7 will try to respond more directly to the basic questions posed at the outset of this volume.

References

Carpenter, C. 2009. Governing the global agenda: "Gatekeepers" and "Issue Adoption" in transnational advocacy networks. In *Non-state actors as standard setters*, ed. A. Peters, L. Koechlin, T. Forster, and G. Fenner Zinkernagel. Cambridge: Cambridge University Press.

Casini, L. 2013. Down the rabbit hole: The projection of the public/private distinction beyond the State. *Jean Monnet* Working Paper 08.

Green, J. 2010. *Rethinking private authority: Agents and entrepreneurs in global environmental governance*. Princeton: Princeton University Press.

Humphrey, J.P. 1984. *Human rights and the United Nations: A great adventure*. New York: Transnational Publishers.

Knop, K. 2002. *Diversity and self-determination in international law*. Cambridge: Cambridge University Press.

Lake D., and W. Wong. 2006. The politics of networks: Interests, power and human rights norms. Working Paper University of California.

Noveck, B.S.S. 2009. *Wiki government: How technology can make government better, democracy stronger, and citizen more powerful*. Washington: Brookings Institutions Press.

Pincus, J., and J.A. Winters. 2002. *Reinventing the World Bank*. Ithaca: Cornell University Press.

Putnam, R.D. 1988. Diplomacy and domestic politics: The logic of two-level games. *International Organizations* 42: 427.

Reinsch, P.S. 1909. International administrative Law and national sovereignty. *American Journal of International Law* 3: 1.

Riles, A. 2001. *The network inside out, Ann Arbor*. Michigan: University of Michigan Press.

Scharpf, F. 1997. *Games real actors play: Actor-centered institutionalism in policy research*. Boulder: Westview Press.

Schmitt, C. 1932. *Positionen und Bergriffe in Kampf mit Weimar-Genf-Versailles*. Berlin: Duncker and Humblot.

Sell, S.K. 2013. Revenge of the "Nerds": Collective actions against intellectual property maximalist in the global information age. *International Studies Review* 15: 67.
Shelton, D. 1994. The participation of non-governmental organizations in international judicial proceedings. *American Journal of International Law* 88: 611.
Thomas, D.Q. 1993. Holding governments accountable by public pressure. In *Ours by right: Women's right as human rights*, ed. J. Kerr. London: Zed Books.

Chapter 5
Cooperation Between Supranational Regulators and Interlocutory Coalitions. Issues of Accountability and Legitimacy

5.1 The Promises and Problems of Cooperation

In Chap. 2, we discussed how cooperation between GCS and IOs was advantageous for both entities – although for slightly different reasons. Aside from the practical benefits of cooperation outlined in the discussion of PPPs (Chap. 4), i.e. a decrease in time spent and costs incurred in negotiation, IOs and the ICs are motivated by the opportunities that cooperation may bring to their substantive goals, namely: to be perceived as more legitimate and accountable bodies. There is, however, a crucial difference between the objectives of this cooperation. Following in Guillermo O'Donnell's footsteps (1998), it may be argued that IOs, when cooperating with the ICs, aim at gaining vertical accountability, which is basically public accountability. Vertical accountability implies that citizens are placed in the position of monitoring the activities of democratic authorities. When these authorities perform well, they merit the public's support; when citizens' expectations are not met, public authorities owe affected citizens explanations, compensation, and even resignations. However, ICs that cooperate with IOs aim at obtaining a different kind of accountability – i.e. horizontal accountability. O'Donnell describes horizontal accountability as a sort of oversight exercised by public agents towards other public agents or agencies. Horizontal accountability, explains O'Donnell, enhances reliability. Indeed, these divergent expectations regarding cooperation have consequences. The current section will focus on cooperation from the viewpoint of IOs. Section 5.2 will analyse cooperative efforts from the ICs.

To summarize the complex issue of IOs' accountability, it is useful to refer to the opinion of Bhupinder Singh Chimni (2004), one of the most recognized critics of the binomial globalization/democratization.[1] Chimni points out that IOs are

[1] See also, from the same author, "Cooption and Resistance: Two Faces of Global Administrative Law" (2005) *IILJ* Working Paper 16, available at www.iilj.org. On imperialism and international law See E. Jouannet, "Universalism and Imperialism: The True-False Paradox of International

G. Sgueo, *Beyond Networks - Interlocutory Coalitions, the European and Global Legal Orders*, Studies in European Economic Law and Regulation 8,
DOI 10.1007/978-3-319-28875-8_5

becoming more prominent – and exercising increasingly intrusive functions – in the everyday life of domestic public bodies and individuals. Even if they do not dominate major mechanisms of coercion (with infrequent exceptions), the rules they adopt significantly constrain state sovereignty, and affect the well-being and opportunities of tens of millions of people (even if most of them are at best only vaguely aware of their existence and know little of their origins and functions). Despite this, IOs are not constrained by rules or mechanisms that may hold them accountable (unlike other forms of domestic public channels or powers). Thus, the powers exercised by IOs lack any real transparency or "democratic" participation. Even when IOs are concerned with the exportation of "good governance" across the world – stresses Chimni – in reality they appear to be motivated by the need to facilitate the operation of transnational capital and to favour the interests of multinationals from Western countries. This crisis of legitimacy is exacerbated by two other crises: one of efficiency (to be addressed in Sect. 5.2), and one of identity (citizens perceive their nation and culture as increasingly disjointed from the supranational mechanisms of political decision-making, and thus wish to reclaim their autonomy from supranational regulators). Given this criticism, IOs that are genuinely concerned with legitimising their decisions have prioritised the modification of decision-making procedures to secure greater attention of the interests of civil society actors. Understood as such, the scope of the involvement of GCS' actors would be, in the telling phrase of Kenneth Prewitt (1998), that of "compensatory mechanisms".

As illustrated in previous chapters, there are numerous examples of IOs showing a commitment to encouraging increased GCS involvement in supra-national decision-making. Further examples include the WBG, the WTO, the UN, and indeed the EU institutions. Since the 1970s, the WBG has consulted and collaborated with thousands of members of civil society organizations throughout the world. In 1990, only 21 % of all projects funded by the WB involved civil society participation. In 2006, this figure had risen to 72 %.[2] An increment so dramatic that Robert Zoellick, a former president of the WB, in 2010 declared that organisations like the WB should put all efforts to connect "more and more countries, companies, individuals, and NGOs" in order to become legitimate. This co-operation has brought crucial change to the policies of the WBG, including the encouragement of greater community participation, increased transparency and publicity, and the creation of review mechanisms.[3] As discussed in Chap. 1, the IP was created in

Law?" (2007) 3 *European Journal of International Law* 379. More generally on the problem of accountability in IOs See J.M. Coicaud, V. Heiskanen (eds.), *The Legitimacy of International Organizations* (New York, United Nations University Press, 2001); R. Mulgan, *Holding Power to Account, Accountability in Modern Democracies* (London, Palgrave Publisher, 2003); C. Harlow, R. Rawlings, "Promoting Accountability in Multi-level Governance: A Network Approach" (2007) 4 *European Law Journal* 542; K. Heede, "Enhancing the Accountability of Community Institutions and Bodies: The Role of the European Ombudsman" (1994) 4 *European Public Law* 587.

[2] See World Bank, *Civil Society-Backgrounds* (Washington D.C., 2009).

[3] Following pressure from environmental organizations, in 1987 the WB reorganized its internal structure: a central environmental department was created, and each of the four regional offices of the WB was sided by an environmental unit. In 1992 the WB added a central vice presidency for

response to civil society demands regarding bank policies and procedures. Following the creation of the IP, a wide range of WBG's documents were declassified and made available for public scrutiny. In recent years, the WBG has established cooperative efforts with a number of ICs, including the CAN, the GCAP and CIVICUS. Like the WBG, the WTO has also put considerable efforts in enhancing cooperation with GCS. As early as 1996, the "WTO Guidelines for arrangements on relations with NGOs" recognized the role of NGOs in improving transparency. Since the Ministerial Conference held at Doha in 2001, the WTO has adopted a new approach towards the engagement of non-state actors in the formulation of its policies. More recently, the WTO has emphasized the importance of open *fora* for communicative interaction and negotiation with NGOs in the formulation of policies.[4] The Informal Council, the NGO Advisory Body, and the Consultative Board on the Future of the WTO are all examples of cooperative efforts with ICs. Within the UN, the involvement of civil society actors has also gained importance over the years. The CONGO was established in 1948, however it was only after 1994 that the participation of GCS was conceived as a way to guarantee political legitimacy to the UN system. At that time, the former UN Secretary General Boutros-Ghali stated that NGOs had become "a basic form of popular participation and representation in the present-day world". Five years later, the successor of Boutros-Ghali, Kofi Annan, proposed a "Global Compact" between the UN, businesses and civil society during an official speech at the World Economic Forum in Davos.[5] Secretary

---

environmentally sustainable development, and in 1993 created the IP. See A. Fox, L.D. Brown (eds.), *The Struggle for Accountability: The World Bank, NGOs, and Grassroots Movements* (Cambridge MA, MIT Press, 1998); C. Caufield, *Masters of Illusion: The World Bank and the Poverty of Nations* (New York, Henry Holt & Co, 1997); F.R. Mikesell, L. Williams (eds.), *International Banks and the Environment: From Growth to Sustainability, an Unfinished Agenda* (San Francisco, Sierra Club Books, 1992). More generally, on global institutions and democracy See J.S. Nye, "Globalization's Democratic Deficit. How to Make International Institutions More Accountable" (2001) 8 *Foreign Affairs* 1; T. Franck, *Fairness in International Law and Institutions* (Oxford, Oxford University Press, 1994).

[4] As an example, one may regard the new "adaptive governance" developed by the WTO in certain areas. Adaptive governance responds as far as possible to the values, interests, and concerns of all stakeholders in order to produce better outcomes. See R. Cooney, A.T.G. Lang, "Taking Uncertainty Seriously: Adaptive Governance and International Trade" (2007) 3 *European Journal of International Law* 523; S.C. Schreck, *The Role of Non-governmental Organizations* see chapter 4 n 2. More generally on NGOs and WTO See A.L. Perrotti, "WTO Relations with Non-State Actors: Captive to Its Own Web?" (2006) 6 *Global Jurist Advances* article 3; R. Buchanan, "Perpetual Peace or Perpetual Process: Global Civil Society and cosmopolitan Legality at the World Trade Organization" (2003) 16 *Leiden Journal of International Law* 673; R.B. Stewart, M. Ratton Sanchez, "The World Trade Organization and Global Administrative Law" (2009) *IILJ* Working Paper 7, available at www.iilj.org. The evolution of the debate on non-state actors participation found explicit acknowledgement in the 2007 World Trade Report (available at: www.wto.org/english/res_e/booksp_e/anrep_e/world_trade_report07_e.pdf). The report recognizes that a more constructive relationship based on mutual cooperation on substantive issues has replaced the previous one-dimensional approach.

[5] The Global Compact aimed at tackling contentious issues such as the protection of the environment, and the protection of human and workers' rights. Albeit designed as a voluntary initiative, the Global Compact invited subscribing companies to make a clear statement of support towards

General Boutros-Ghali also supported the creation of a Commission to analyse the problem of global governance. The final report from the Commission combined wide-ranging proposals for reform, including greater involvement of NGOs.[6] It is not by chance that a number of ICs were established in the aftermath of that report. The UNCAC Coalition is one of those. At the European level, debates about democracy in decision-making processes have spread widely since the mid-1970s. Since then, the Commission, the European Parliament, the Council of Ministers and several executive and independent agencies have placed increasing emphasis on the need for re-conceptualizing governance as enhancing participation of civil society actors. Not only have a number of unofficial documents specifically addressed the necessity of allowing individuals to actively participate in the political life of the Union, but the Consolidated Version of the EU Treaty also gave formal recognition to representative associations and to the civil society in the political dialogue over the EU action.[7] The recent Lisbon Treaty further enshrined and reinforced the

its principles and to publish it on its websites. Failure to comply with such requests within 2 years of becoming a signatory to the Compact resulted in removal from the list of participants. See generally www.unglobalcompact.org.

[6] See Commission on Global Governance, *Our Global Neighbourhood: The Report of the Commission on Global Governance* (1995). For commentary on the report See R. Falk, "Liberalism at the Global Level: The Last of the Independent Commissions" (1995) 24 *Millennium* 563. For more general thoughts about the Global compact and its predecessor, the "Millenium Report", See J.D. Aston, "The United Nations Committee on Non-governmental Organizations: Guarding the Entrance to a Politically divided House" (2001) 5 *European Journal of International Law* 943. More generally on NGOs' involvement in the UN system See T.G. Weiss, L. Gordenker (eds.), *NGOs the UN, and Global governance*, see chapter 2 at section 2.3; D. Otto, "Non-governmental Organizations in the United Nations System: The Emerging Role of International Civil Society" (1996) 18 *Human Rights Quarterly* 107.

[7] See, for instance, the Commission Communication SEC 92 2272 def. (1992), titling "An Open Structured Dialogue between the Commission and Special Interest Groups; the Commission Discussion Paper COM (2000) 11 Final, titling "The Commission and Non-Governmental Organisations, Building Stronger Partnerships", the Commission Communication COM (2002) 704 Final, titling "Towards a Reinforced Culture of Consultation and Dialogue – General Principles and Minimum Standards for Consultation of Interested Parties by the Commission", and the Commission White Paper COM (2001) 428, titling "European Governance: A White Paper". For general discourse on non-governmental participation in European governance See I. de Jesus Butler, "Non-governmental Organisation Participation in the EU Law-making Process: The Example of Social Non-governmental Organisations at the Commission, Parliament and Council" (2008) 5 *European Law Journal* 558; S. Mazey, J. Richardson, *Lobbying in the European Community* (Oxford, Oxford University Press, 1993); R. Geyer, "Can European Union (EU) Social NGOs Co-operate to Promote EU Social Policy?" (2001) 30 *Journal of Social Policy* 477; M. Cowles, "Non-State Actors and False Dichotomies: Reviewing IR/IPE Approaches to European Integration" (2003) 10 *Journal of European Public Policy* 102; R. Bennett, "Business Routes of Influence in Brussels: Exploring the Choice of Direct Representation" (1990) 47 *Political Studies* 240. For academic debate on democracy and the EU See A.G. Menéndez, "The European Democratic Challenge: The forging of a Supranational *Volonté Générale*" (2009) 15 *European Law Journal* 277; C. Scott, "Governing Without Law or Governing Without Government? Newish Governance and the Legitimacy of the EU" (2009) 15 *European Law Journal* 160; A. Reale, "Representation of Interests, Participatory Democracy and Law-making in the European Union: Which Role and Which Rules for the Social Partners?" (2003) *Jean Monnet* Working Paper 15,

participatory dimension of the European model of governance. The Treaty introduced new powers to the Parliament; it initiated the "internalization" of the European Council; it delegated considerable rulemaking authority to the Commission; and it promulgated the Charter of Rights. Most of all, the Treaty of Lisbon introduced the European citizen's initiative, enabling European citizens to directly call upon the European Commission to bring forward policies in areas of interest to them. Although most of the ICs discussed in this book were founded between 1990 and 2000, only in the last decade or so they benefited from such efforts by the EU institutions and become more relevant.

5.2 Horizontal and Vertical Accountability

The same line of reasoning – i.e. the search for accountability and legitimation through cooperation – also works in the opposite direction: from IOs to the ICs. The desire to "legitimise" their activities – and by association that of their members – is a key reason driving the ICs to establish working relations with IOs. Differently from IOs, the ICs are motivated by the search of a horizontal, rather than vertical, form of accountability. What induces the ICs to look for horizontal accountability? The answer is linked to their very nature. The ICs do not hold direct functions of interest representation. Rather, they can be described as a medium between private interests and supranational public bodies. Hence, the ICs are not interested in being publicly accountable in the same way as IOs. On the contrary, they base their existence on reliability, i.e. accountability provided through multilateral checks and balances. The more the ICs are considered reliable and have a positive reputation, the more they improve their leverage in the supranational arena. Reliability, for instance, enhances the possibility for the ICs to attract new members. Given that the ICs mobilise people and resources primarily through a commitment to values, their reputation is representative of those values and thus vital in recruiting new allies to their causes. Reputation also increases the opportunities to acquire additional funds from donors. In Chap. 2, for instance, it was noted that pursuing advocacy and applying pressure implies the use of significant economic resources from GCS' actors. Thus, having a good reputation may indirectly help the ICs (and their members) to sustain these costs.

Given that the ICs make a strong effort to be regarded as reliable actors, it could be asked whether they could be considered as reliable actors in the supranational legal arena. A straightforward answer requires an overall evaluation of the ICs that

available at www.centers.law.nyu.edu/jeanmonnet; K.A. Armstrong, "Civil Society and the White Paper – Bridging or Jumping the Gaps?" (2001) *Jean Monnet* Working Paper 6, available at www.centers.law.nyu.edu/jeanmonnet. On problems related to civil society participation in European decision-making processes See R. Bellamy, "Still in Deficit: Rights, Regulation and Democracy in the EU" (2006) 6 *European Law Journal* 725; G. Majone, "Europe's Democratic Deficit: The Question of Standards" (1998) 4 *European Law Journal* 5; A. Moravcsik, *In Defence of the "Democratic Deficit*", see chapter 1 at section 7.2.

will only be possible in the last chapter of this volume. However, a second – perhaps more topical – question may be explored now: are the ICs effective in enhancing vertical accountability of IOs? In other words, are IOs being put in the condition to fill gaps in their accountability and legitimacy when collaborating with the ICs? The concerns introduced in Chap. 1 seem to challenge the effectiveness of cooperation between IOs and the ICs. A preliminary concern is that GCS' actors are not themselves considered accountable. In the first instance, their accountability (and reliability) is challenged by occasional problematic behaviour. A famous example is that of the mistaken analysis made by Greenpeace on the proposed Brent Spar oilrig disposal in the North Sea. In 1995, Greenpeace launched a campaign against the sinking of the oil platform in the Atlantic Ocean by Shell. In an attempt to fight the use of the oceans by companies as Shell, Greenpeace released an estimate of the amount of oil left on the Brent Spar. It was later revealed that this estimate exaggerated the actual amount tenfold. A second, more important, concern is the absence of independent controls on the finances and operations of GCS' actors. Critics point out that many civil society actors do not appear to be particularly concerned by this issue. At best, they use loose oversight procedures by external boards, or offer minimalist reports of their activities.[8] Many civil society practitioners have even expressed scepticism about the need to develop their accountability.[9] Not accidentally, civil society actors have been cynically labelled with the acronyms of MONGOs ("My Own NGOs", to point at the fact that many NGOs' leadership is self-elected and stays in office indefinitely) or BRINGOs ("Briefcase NGOs"). According to the critics, GCS do not increase the accountability of other supranational actors, including the IOs with whom they collaborate.[10] A third – related – concern

[8] Exemplary is the case of the NGO Steering Committee of the UN Commission on Sustainable Development. The Committee created an elaborate self-regulatory framework for promoting civil society involvement in UN work on environment and development. The process, however, become increasingly burdensome and collapsed in 2001.

[9] See also R. Dahl, *Can International Organizations be Democratic*, see chapter 1 at section 7.3; E.B. Bluemel, "Overcoming NGO Accountability Concerns in International Governance" (2005–2006) 31 *Brooklyn Journal of International Law* 139. A. Ebrahim, E. Weisband (eds.), *Global Accountabilities: Participation, Pluralism, and Public Ethics* (Cambridge, Cambridge University Press, 2007). Alnoor Ebrahim criticizes the "audit model" culture of accountability and favours a system of reflective accountability. This, according to Ebrahim, should focus on organization's mission and capacity to respond to the needs of communities.

[10] There is vast literature on the accountability problem in civil society actors. See M. Edwards, D. Hulme, *Beyond the Magic Bullet: NGO Performance and Accountability in the Post-Cold War World* (London, Kumarian Press, 1996); A. Fowler, *Striking a Balance: A Guide to Enhancing the Effectiveness of Non-Governmental Organisations in International Development* (London, Routledge, 1997); D. Lewis, *The Management of Non-Governmental Development Organisations: An Introduction* (London, Routledge, 2001); L. Jordan, P. Van Tuijl, *NGO Accountability: Politics, Principles & Innovations* (London, Routledge, 2006); M. Kaldor, "Civil Society and Accountability" (2003) 4 *Journal of Human Development* 5; R.E. Goodin, "Democratic Accountability: The Third Sector and All" (2003) *John F. Kennedy School of Government*, Working Paper no. 19. On the concept of accountability in global governance See P.B. Stephan, "The New International Law-Legitimacy, Accountability, Authority, and Freedom in the New Global Legal Order" (1999) 70 *University of Colorado Law Review* 1555; J. McGann, M. Johnstone,

is linked to efficiency. Scholars argue that the more IOs include civil society actors into decision-making processes in order to be legitimate, the less they are effective. The finding that a smaller number of participants in IOs' decision-making processes would guarantee faster and less expensive decisions have led some observers to express concerns about the active involvement of civil society groups in IOs' decision-making. Others observed that informality and flexibility may perhaps result into more IOs' effectiveness, but they could eventually hamper the legitimacy of IOs' conducts.

To address such concerns, this chapter proceeds in the following two steps. It sets out to review shortcomings of accountability and legitimacy in the GCS' actors, and to discuss the extent to which the ICs – i.e. coalitions rather than single actors – may be considered as a remedy to these problems. The first part of this chapter highlights the concept of accountability. Of course, a full analysis of the accountability problem is far beyond the scope of this book. Therefore, this chapter will touch upon the problem only to the extent necessary to analyse whether, and to what extent, the ICs represent a solution to the problem of GCS' accountability. In order to do so, in Sect. 5.2.1 the concept of accountability is defined by pointing at its diverse aspects, and a distinction between two forms of accountability – namely: functional and strategic – is made. Functional accountability is the focus of Sects. 5.2.1, 5.2.2, 5.2.3. The former describes the policies adopted in the ICs to limit the exposure to donors' influence; whereas Sect. 5.2.2 emphasizes the use of self-monitoring initiatives, and Sect. 5.2.3 looks at the use of codes of conduct as a strategy from the ICs to be functionally accountable. The following Sections turn to strategic accountability. Section 5.2.4 introduces the concept of "participation overkill" (described as the choice from smaller GCS' actors not to participate in negotiating processes despite being invited to do so) and explicates why the ICs may offer a viable solution to these issues. Following this line of thought, Sect. 5.2.5 elucidates the use of accreditation standards by the ICs as a further solution to be strategically accountable. The second part of this chapter discusses the issue of legitimacy. The essential aspects of legitimacy will only be touched upon briefly. Thus, Sect. 5.3 attempts to counter the opinion that IOs' illegitimacy is due to the absence of democratic mandate by GCS. In this respect, Sect. 5.4 briefly introduces the "Global Reflexive Interactive Democracy" (GRID) model, theorized by Dario Bevilacqua and Jessica Duncan. The GRID model attempts to provide a solution, albeit not a definitive one, to the issue of GCS' legitimacy. The GRID model is considered only

"The Power Shift and the NGO Credibility Crisis" (2004–2005) 11 *Brown Journal of World Affairs* 159; K. Anderson, "The Ottawa Convention Banning Landmines, the Role of International Non-Governmental Organisations and the Idea of International Civil Society" (2000) 11 *European Journal of International Law* 91; P. Kilby, "Non-governmental Organizations and Accountability in an Era of Global Anxiety" (2004) 5 *Seton Hall Journal of Diplomacy and International Relations* 67; R.C. Blitt, "Who Will Watch the Watchdogs? Human Rights Non-governmental Organizations and the Case for Regulation" (2007) 5 *International Journal of Civil Society Law* 8. For discourse on indicators for measuring NGOs, IOs and governments' policies See D.H. Lempert, "A Dependency in Development Indicator for NGOs and International Organizations" (2009) 9 *Global Jurist Advances* article 6.

to the extent necessary to understand how it may anticipate the role played by the ICs in supporting IOs legitimacy. In this sense, Sect. 5.4 explains how the ICs may be conceived as a structural evolution of the GRID model. The conclusive remarks of the current chapter recollect the issues that are left unresolved by the attempts to enhance accountability and legitimacy through cooperation between IOs and the ICs. On the one hand, the opinion that coalitions of GCS' actors only translate these issues to a different level may have some basis; on the other hand, however, such coalitions thus far provide the best, and perhaps the only, answer to the problems of accountability and legitimacy.

5.2.1 Functional Accountability and the Exposure to the Influence of Donors

There are as many generically descriptive doctrinal labels of accountability as there are scholars who have studied it. The standard definition of accountability refers to the process of being called to account to some authority for one's action. Yet, having broadened its original application to financial accounting practices and being currently understood as an all-encompassing concept that includes all the attributes of an ideal governance structure, accountability has become an ever-present mantra in debates on globalization. While a first generation of scholarly debate was often framed in the language of "decision-maker" (commonly referred to as the "power-holder") and a "decision-taker" (the "account-holder"), and focused on the key principles of accountability[11]; the second generation's perspective moved from

[11] See R. Baldwin, M. Cave, *Understanding Regulation: Theory, Strategy, and Practice* (Oxford, Oxford University Press, 1999). The authors explicate accountability by presenting five key principles to sound regulation. These are: a legislator acting under a sufficient mandate; the acknowledgement of participatory rights to the affected parties; the possession of sufficient technical knowledge by the decision-maker; the presence of a flexible regulatory framework that allows a flexible response on certain issues, and thus permit to allocate efficiency; and, of course, accountability towards the community. See also A. Buchanan, R.O. Keohane, "The Legitimacy of Global Governance Institutions" (2006) 20 *Ethics & International Affairs* 405. Keohane and Buchanan distinguish between a narrow and a broad accountability. While narrow means that accountability is considered only in its formal context, broad accountability encompasses those who presently receive the accounts, such as states, and those who might wish to contest accountability, such as NGOs and populations. Narrow accountability does not ensure meaningful participation by those affected by IOs' rules or due consideration of their legitimate interests. Broad accountability, on the contrary, contains effective provisions for holding institutional agents accountable. The difference between the two forms of accountability described by Buchanan and Keohane can be tested against the concept of transparency. If transparency means merely the availability of accurate information about how IOs work, it is insufficient even for narrow accountability. The ends of narrow accountability is served by transparency only when information about how IOs operate are accessible at reasonable cost, properly integrated and interpreted, directed to the accountability-holders, and the latter are adequately motivated to use it properly in evaluating the performance of the relevant institutional agents. Yet, broad accountability is present only in the moment in which the IO sets institutional practices and normative principles that can be revised in the light of critical reflection and discussion with actors in transnational civil society.

such rationalistic understanding to explore the application of accountability in multi-levelled systems of governance,[12] to expound its relationship with globalization,[13] and eventually to expand further the concept.[14] These efforts notwithstanding, the concept of accountability is still far from being neatly defined. As Mark Bovens (2007) put it, accountability may sometime "resemble a garbage can filled with good intentions, loosely defined concepts and vague images of good governance".

This book teases apart some of the complexities of the scientific debate on accountability and settles upon a narrower description of it. Focus is put on its internal and external aspects. The former is described in terms of functional accountability, and relates to internal management practices and financial responsibility

[12] See D. Curtin, A. Nollkaemper, "Conceptualizing Accountability in International and European Law" (2005) 36 *Netherlands Yearbook of International Law* 3. The two authors draw from existing literature on the theme by pointing at retrospective accountability (accountability as giving account) and, on the other side, prospective accountability (accountability as holding to account). The former is the act of disclosing information and justifying behaviour. The latter, in addition to the disclosure of information and the justification of behaviour, also requires the establishment of a mechanism by which account can be rendered. In Curtin's and Nollkaemper's opinion, current accountability must be measured against multi-levelled systems of governance. The discussion on accountability in the EU, for instance, may be inspiration for the emerging debate on accountability in the international legal order.

[13] See R.W. Grant, R.O. Kehoane, "Accountability and Abuses of Power in World Politics" (2005) 2 *American Political Science Review* 1. The authors distinguish between two models of accountability: participation and delegation. In the participation mode, people with power ought to be accountable to those who are affected by their decisions. In the delegation model, people with power ought to be accountable to those who have entrusted them with it. Most importantly, Grant and Keohane seek to develop a concept of accountability at the global level that is capable of overcoming the limitations deriving from a conception based on domestic models. Global accountability, in their reasoning, includes forms of hierarchical, supervisory, and legal accountability, backed by pressures from markets and from peers, by financial controls, and by public reputational dynamics. Global accountability, Grant and Keohane posit, can also be applied to private actors (NGOs or firms, to make an example).

[14] Both the 2004 "Accountability of International Organisations" Report from the International Law's Association (See International Law Association, Berlin Conference – 2004): Accountability of International Organisations, available at www.ila-hq.org/en/committees/index.cfm/cid/9) and the Global Accountability Project (GAP) of the One World Trust look towards a more expansive view of accountability. The latter in particular was the first initiative aimed at measuring and comparing the accountability of 30 transnational actors from the intergovernmental, the non-governmental and the corporate sectors. The GAP defines accountability as a process "through which an organisation makes a commitment to respond and balance the needs of stakeholders in its decision-making processes and activities, and delivers against this commitment". A definition that emphasises the need to balance among different accountability claims from both internal and external stakeholders. The GAP identifies four dimensions for accountability: transparency, i.e. the provision of accessible and timely information to stakeholders; participation, i.e. the active engagement of stakeholders (internal and external) in the decisions that affect them; evaluation, i.e. the monitoring and review of the organization's goals and objectives; and complaint, i.e. the opportunity for stakeholders to file complaints on the organization's decisions and actions. See also D.H. Rached, "Doomed Aspiration of Pure Instrumentality: Global Administrative Law and Accountability" (2014) 3 *Global constitutionalism* 338.

towards the members of an organization. The latter is termed strategic accountability, and relates to the relationship between the organization and its beneficiaries, and more generally to the international community. When applying this discourse to non-state actors, both forms of accountability are countered by a number of key-issues. As far as functional accountability is concerned, the main criticism relates to the lack in experience and capability suffered by many non-state actors in monitoring and evaluating their own activities. In the 2010 Blackbaud Survey, non-profits responded to the question of whether they had accountability measures in place to allow donors to verify their claims. Only in ten countries did a majority of the respondents say that they either had an audit process or a communication plan in place. Even smaller was the number of countries where, aside from having an audit process in place, non-profits also adopted privacy policies regarding donor information and staff confidentiality. The survey evidenced how not-for-profit actors tend to operate with very limited resources on accountability initiatives. Monitoring and evaluation are not always prioritized, and when they are, documentation presents additional costs and hurdles. In "State of Evaluation 2012", a survey conducted by the Innovation Network,[15] it was reported that the vast majority (90 %) of non-profit organizations surveyed did engage in evaluation in 2012, and that 100 % of respondents reported using their evaluation findings. Yet, more than two-thirds of the respondent organizations declared they did not have the resources nor internal mechanisms in place to meaningfully engage in evaluation processes. According to the survey, 47 % of the organizations with annual budgets greater than five million dollars did not have at least one full-time employee dedicated to evaluation. The survey pointed to limited staff time, insufficient financial resources, and limited staff expertise as the most significant barriers to evaluation across the non-profit sector. A recent example of missed evaluation is the public dispute over the distribution of donations to the Haiti earthquake of 2010. A Public Broadcasting Service (PBS) documentary placed the responsibility for the still abhorrent living conditions of many Haitians on the international NGOs who had received funds and were operating on the ground.[16]

To overcome criticism of the failings in their monitoring and evaluation capabilities, a number of non-state actors have developed specific policies. Three are particularly interesting. The first policy is that of not soliciting any funds from potential adversaries in business or government in order to limit the exposure to donors' influence. The influence of donors may materialise in various forms; however, it mostly stems from the so-called "paymaster principle". Basically, the paymaster principle regards the reluctance of donors who contribute the largest amounts to projects and/or institutions to share control of their contributed resources with those who contribute less, or do not donate at all (as it is normally the case of non-state actors). There are NGOs that fiercely emphasize their impartiality.

[15] See State of the Evaluation, available at www.innonet.org/resources/files/innonet-state-of-evaluation-2012.pdf.

[16] See Haiti: Where did the Money Go? Available at www.filmat11.tv/projects/haiti-where-did-the-money-go/.

Typical examples include Greenpeace, Amnesty International, Human Rights Watch and Médecins Sans Frontières, who consider independence from state sponsorship a crucial element in their organizations. Policies to protect NGOs from the influence of donors become more important with the emergence of the global financial crisis in 2008. International austerity led to increased pressure on bilateral and multilateral donors, often translating into repeated calls to demonstrate if, and under what conditions, the financed projects could contribute to real social and political change. Non-state actors consequently increased efforts in defending their independence from what they soon began to call "pressure to measure".[17]

Differently from single GCS' actors, ICs are less accustomed to adopting specific policies on donations. To explicate this difference one may regard the management practices of fundraising activities. There is nothing excluding – in principle at least – ICs being the beneficiary of donations. Yet, as a general rule, the ICs' members conduct fundraising activities independently, and are directly responsible for the funded projects. Inevitably, donors tend to consider them, rather than the ICs to whom they enjoy membership status, as direct targets of pressure. Thus in their funding contracts, donors can (and actually do) take steps to make members of the ICs more accountable. Sponsors and contributors may also decide to interrupt their donations if the recipients do not perform efficiently.[18] As Sophye Smith (2012) notes with regard to NGOs operating in the field of international development, "donors can turn off the spigot at any time". In such cases, the ICs may indirectly increase (or decrease, if this is the case) their accountability, in response to the behaviour of their members.

There is, however, a number of ICs that explicitly declare their independence from external funding, or commit to accountability standards in receiving and managing funds. These include Alter-EU, CAN and the Euclid Network. Alter-EU comprises among its priorities the commitment to be transparent about financing sources. To this end, Alter-EU provides direct links to its members' financial webpages, as well as information about any direct founding sources. Most importantly, Alter-EU considers economical support provided by the groups represented in the Steering Committee as the general rule, being external funding considered as the exception to this rule. For the years 2013–2014, for instance, Alter-EU reports that a number of foundations (the Isvara Foundation, the Open Society Foundations, AK Europa, and the OGB Europaburo) covered the salaries and office expenses, as well as some organisational costs. Second is the example of CAN. Points 87–96 of the CAN Charter are dedicated to fundraising policies. These establish that all funds (even those funds raised by local and regional nodes of CAN) are subject to the approval of the Board. The Board, in turn, commits to full disclosure about the use of funding. Point 96 of the CAN Charter is particularly important, in that it states that: "All funds raised through CAN International shall, to the extent that funding

---

[17] See the report from WeGov and The Engine Room, "Measuring Impact On-The-Go", available at www.theengineroom.org/wp-content/uploads/engnroom_monitoringguide_finalmay14.pdf.

[18] See more generally B. Yontcheva, "Hierarchy and Authority in a Dynamic Perspective: A Model Applied to Donor Financing NGO Proposals" (2003) *IMF* Working Paper n. WP/03/157.

and resources allow, be subject to an annual audit based on generally accepted accounting principles". Differently from the CAN and Alter-EU, the Euclid Network adopts a more liberal approach. This IC recognizes that the ability to successfully access EU funding can play a fundamental role in the sustainability of many civil society organizations. It therefore dedicates a section on its website to pool useful resources, links and information about funding opportunities to further support civil society organizations. A beginner's guide is included among the documents published in this section. This guide contains information on transparency and accountability in fundraising activities. Finally, in other cases the ICs seem to adapt the rules of the IOs with whom they cooperate. Examples of this include the CINGO and the CONGO. The CINGO created a complementary association, named "INGO-Service", and tasked it with managing all financial resources of the coalition. Such rules are established in accordance with the COE standards. Similarly, the CONGO established a financial committee to support the Board in all financial matters. Most importantly, point 59 of the Rules of procedure of the CONGO states that the Board may take steps to facilitate the raising of funds, including support for the establishment, "in accordance with national laws applicable at UN centres, or elsewhere as appropriate, of foundations or trust funds".

5.2.2 Functional Accountability and Monitoring

To overcome the critiques regarding their accountability (or lack thereof), GCS' actors also adopt self-promoted monitoring and codes of conduct. The current section will introduce and briefly illustrate initiatives of self-monitoring, while Sect. 5.2.3 will discuss codes of conduct. Self-monitoring, as the definition suggests, consists of the voluntary adoption of standards of transparency and responsiveness, as well as the commitment to respect evaluations made according to such standards. Efforts to incorporate accountability mechanisms to monitor policy solutions have existed since a long time, although they have increased in prominence in the last decade. Not only NGOs, but also for-profit actors, and particularly TNCs, have introduced self-monitoring standards to improve their accountability. When they first emerged, these accountability systems were mostly unilateral and company-based. Virtually all companies had their own internal management system to drive the accountability standards and many established board committees to oversee them. In 2002, the Royal Dutch and Shell group combined their social and financial reports for the first time. Over time, however, internal accountability mechanisms have grown and gradually evolved into multi-stakeholder initiatives. Among the best-known initiatives is the NGO monitor. This is a coalition aimed at targeting progressive advocacy NGOs and their participation in global governance arenas. More precisely, NGO Monitor aims to publicize distortions of human rights issues in the Arab-Israeli conflict, and to provide information and context for the benefit of NGOs working in the Middle East. Thus, the scope of increasing accountability is pursued through indirect means. In fact, as outlined in its mission statement, NGO Monitor's main goal is to lead to an informed public debate on the role of humanitarian NGOs. The publishing of reports, factsheets, monograph series, and other documents concerned with topics of interest of this coalition, constitutes the most important part of its activity. Similar in aims and form to NGO monitor are the Active Learning Network for Accountability and Performance in Humanitarian Action (ALNAP)[19] and the Global Accountability Report Project (GAP).[20] The former consists of an international interagency forum that promotes standardization of evaluation. There is a wide number of leading international NGOs participating in ALNAP. The GAP Report compares the performances of international NGOs with that of national public bodies and IOs.

Of interest is also the case of the HAP. In 2006 the HAP launched the NGOs Accountability Charter, supported by a number of leading international NGOs as Amnesty International and Oxfam International, in an effort to ensure greater accountability through the promotion of a common standard on quality and accountability. Among the aims of this Charter is the establishment of a Core Humanitarian Standard. The final version of the Core Humanitarian Standard was made available at the end of 2014, following a 3-year consultation process across the humanitarian sector, combined with the effort to draw together key elements of the existing humanitarian standards and commitments (including the Code of Conduct of the International Red Cross, and the OECD DAC criteria for evaluating development and humanitarian assistance).

One last point before moving to codes of conduct: the examples reported (and the many other accountability mechanisms in place) might help functional accountability of GCS, however it should be noted that this is not a solution without its critics. Benjamin Cashore (2002), for instance, stresses that these initiatives derive their authority from manipulation of global markets and attention to customer preferences.

5.2.3 Functional Accountability and Codes of Conduct

Codes of Conduct are a third strategy used within the GCS to increase accountability. These codes are very common among non-state actors. Almost all the major GCS' organizations adopt a code to regulate the conduct of their workers and volunteers, and to assess ethical standards. While there is no direct evidence of a members' code of conduct being incorporated into the rules of the ICs, it is a common practice for the ICs to develop their own codes of practice. Not only are these codes aimed at providing an immediate response to the call to improve accountability, but they also reinforce peer controls within the ICs.

---

[19] See generally www.alnap.org.

[20] See generally www.oneworldtrust.org/publications/cat_view/65-global-accountability-project.

There are at least two types of ICs' codes of conduct. Some are merely functional statements of best practices, as in the case of CIVICUS. In 2008, this coalition established an "INGO Accountability Charter" – addressed to both members of the coalition and external non-state actors – and publishes a yearly report of the progresses made towards the aim of increase its accountability rate.[21] The CINGO is another case in point. CINGO adopts the COE Recommendation CM/Rec(2007)14 of the Committee of Ministers to member states concerning "The legal status of non-governmental organisations in Europe".[22] This Recommendation defines the minimum standards concerning the creation, management and the general activities of NGOs in member states of COE. Section VII of the Recommendation titles "accountability" and contains a number of obligations for NGOs, including transparency, liability and participation. Other codes of conduct are narrower, and focus on specific aspects of the life of the ICs. Take the case of CONGO, which has drafted a voluntary "code of conduct" for NGOs wishing to apply for membership status. Similarly to CONGO, the CAN adopts a code of conduct for attendees to its meetings and establishes that breaches of the codes' criteria will lead to the expulsion from the meeting.

As mentioned before, codes of conduct of the ICs are an important mechanism in reinforcing peer controls. It is not enough that the members of an IC agree that some coordination into a network is needed; they must agree upon the fact that the coalition in which they are members is worthy of their full support. Thus, members who delegated authority to a specific IC may withdraw such authority when that coalition no longer respects certain perspectives and values. Once they become constituents of an IC, non-state actors are eager to monitor their colleagues' adherence to the agreed standards, since their own reputation might be affected by it. Having said that, it is also worth noting that the length and depth of peer controls may vary depending on two factors: first is the typology of agreement that governs the ICs; second is the accession policy. Type A agreements favour closer control by the ICs' members. However, in coalitions governed by types B and C agreements, peer control may be less interfering, since it is assumed that members enjoy a greater degree of freedom. As far as the accession policy adopted by the ICs is concerned, this closely relates to accreditation standards, a topic to be dealt with in Sect. 5.2.6. For the moment it suffices to recall that the ICs may settle on different standards for accepting new members (as Chap. 4 explicated). The greater the number of members in an IC, the stronger its advocacy network is likely to be. A larger network may also influence the quality and quantity of peer controls. However, more members also mean lengthier procedures to reach consensus, and may therefore result in weaker advocacy.

[21] See generally www.ingoaccountabilitycharter.org/home/charter-members/civicus/.

[22] See generally www.wcd.coe.int/ViewDoc.jsp?id=1194609&Site=CM&BackColorInternet=9999CC&BackColorIntranet=FFBB55&BackColorLogged=FFAC75.

5.2.4 The Participation Overkill

To address the discourse of strategic accountability, it is worth evoking the critiques raised by scholars regarding the acknowledgement of participatory rights to GCS' actors. These may be summarized in two main arguments. First and foremost is the assumption that the vaster the number of transnational civil society groups is, and the broader is their geographical provenience, the harder is for IOs to deal efficiently with them. The exercise of participatory rights from an increasing number of GCS' actors may in fact delay and distort IOs' decision-making. Critics argue that a greater use of human resources would diminish the feasibility of rapid substantive results, and because of the longer time schedule needed to process the amount of information provided by a large number of participants, would increment the overall costs of decision-making processes. Linked to this problem is a second area of concern. Studies on civil society's participation in international policy-making have pointed out the difficulties for smaller NGOs to keep up with the huge number of meetings that inevitably characterize dealings in the international community. The LSE Yearbook on GCS calculated, for the year 2012, 392,588 official meetings, held in 167 countries and 1,374 cities across the globe. Because of the limited finances and staff resources of small GCS' actors, they may choose to avoid participation – and therefore voluntarily reduce their influence in negotiations. Martin Kaiser has conceptualized this phenomenon in terms of "participation overkill". In Kaiser's opinion, many NGOs choose not to participate in negotiating processes, even when these are of considerable importance, despite being invited to do so.[23] Both the above critiques seem to suggest that inclusiveness is more a theoretical concept than a realistic one. The obvious conclusion would be that the participation of civil society's groups to IO's policy-making should be constrained by more formal rules, and circumscribed to a few selected actors.

This volume does not address this claim directly. It attempts, however, to raise attention to two facts that appear to be of some relevance to it. The first is that the objections made towards GCS' participation in the supranational legal arena have been formulated almost exclusively in relation to the framework of cooperation between IOs and single non-state actors. Here an attempt is made to reformulate this issue taking into account the fact that a number of IOs now cooperate with ICs. In essence, it is argued that formalized networks of GCS' actors, as the ICs can be described, may offer a viable solution to the issue of the effectiveness as well as to the actual exercise of participatory rights from smaller actors. Of course, while attempting to reformulate the answers to the above objections, consideration is given to the fact that the ICs face a similar problem of IOs, in that they are requested to deal with a large quantity and variety of actors. Yet, it is argued that the strategies they adopt to deal with these issues appear to move a step further toward the solution

[23] See M. Kaiser, National Forest Programmes and Environmental Non-Governmental Organisations: Participatory Overkill or Real Opportunity for Strengthening Ecological Needs of Forest Related Policies, available at www.greenpeace.com.

of the problem of efficiency in IOs' decision-making. While, in fact, IOs have been inherently incapable to "filter" all GCS' instances that are interested in taking part in their policy-making, partnerships with ICs opened to a new opportunity: i.e. to transfer to the ICs the problem of efficiency. This implies that the ICs are supposed to filter the large spectrum of interests and points of view pertaining to the myriad of groups and actors operating at the supranational level. In other words, the ICs are considered a second-level filter of civil society's interests (being the NGOs and other civil society actors a first level filter). Thus, all things being equal, the key question would not be whether IOs could set on decision-making procedures that are inclusive and efficient at the same time; but rather how the ICs can be strategically accountable (in the sense that they could provide sufficient proof to be able to deal with the quantity and variety of GCS' actors).

Issues related to the quantitative and qualitative variations of actors from the perspective of the ICs will now be discussed. The sections that follow will then discuss how the ICs face both issues. In terms of quantity, we may assume that the ICs are exposed to what Jonathan Koppell (2005) describes as "multiple accountability disorder". This occurs when an organization attempts to respond to multiple accountability demands. As a consequence of this disorder, explains Koppell, the organization may diminish its chances of survival. Similarly to Koppell, Michael Edwards (1999) notes that increasing demands on civil society actors to develop the accountability trapping of financial/participatory/transparency audits could result in excessive bureaucratisation and increase the distance from the communities they represent. The ICs are required to respond to almost as many accountability demands as are their members. Which, as a further consequence, may lead to the shortcomings described by Edwards.

Closely related to this issue is the problem of the variety of types of GCS actors operating in the international sphere. Chapter 1 explained that the GCS encompasses an enormous diversity of actors and motives, and that – because of such diversity – GCS is challenged by conceptual and practical problems. In this sense, the ICs are confronted with the fact that the current supranational arena is dominated by NNGOs, as opposed to SNGOs. Critics claim that this situation amplifies certain political views that are not reflective of the views of developing countries. NNGOs could claim legitimacy for representing SNGOs and tend to speak on their behalf, without proper consultation.[24] Does the world of INGOs represent GCS, asks Paul Wapner (1996), or does it merely reproduce a "world culture" dominated

---

[24] See A. Contu, E. Girei, "NGOs Management and the value of "partnership" for equality in international development: What's in a name?" (2014) 67 *Human Relations* 216. Contu and Girei illustrate the relationship between NNGOs and SNGOs in terms of imposition and influence. Imposition means that NNGOs have more experience and more technical means than its Southern partners, which puts it in a superior, even though non-hierarchical, position. Influence, in turn, means that NNGOs influence and redesign the Southern partners projects in order to fit with what the donor's priorities are or what the funding market needs. Other authors have described the civil society North-South divide through the lens of IOs. Phillip Jones and David Coleman for instance, observed how the replacement of the NGO-WB Committee with the WB-Civil Society Forum, has pitted northern and southern NGOs against one another, and ultimately reduced the influence of

by Western liberal hegemony? According to the data collected by Keck and Sikkink, in 1963 approximately 77 % of the secretariats of INGOs with social change objectives were located in Europe, while only 6 % was located in a Southern country of the world (in 1983, Keck and Sikkink reported that these proportions had slightly changed to 68 % and 17 %, respectively). In her study on the North-South divide, Jackie Smith (2005) notes that before the 1980s most of the TSMOs were organized across the North-South divide. Since then they have began to be organized exclusively within either the global North or the global South. In 2004 Peter Uvin (2004) estimated that about 50 of the roughly 2,000 humanitarian NGOs he had examined in his study controlled as much as 80 % of available financial resources. An estimate later confirmed by a study presented at the 2009 Annual Meeting of the American Political Science Association in Toronto. This study showed that even in the EU, grants and funds are given to the oldest and wealthiest NGOs instead of being distributed across civil society groups of the new member states, as one could legitimately expect.[25] A few international NGOs have even experimented with moving their headquarters from Northern countries to the South, in an attempt to differentiate themselves from typical NNGOs. A case in point is that of ActionAid (who moved their headquarters from the United Kingdom to South Africa).

If these critical views are true, then ICs are at risk of domination by powerful members (e.g. Northern international NGOs) while weaker members (e.g. Southern NGOs) suffer serious costs by not participating. Insofar as these conditions exist, two further consequences occur. To begin with, it may be assumed that the consent of weaker members is not genuinely voluntary, as their choice of joining a coalition is only made in the absence of acceptable alternatives. Becoming members of an IC, in fact, could be the only viable option to get funding and have some leverage at the supranational scene for smaller GCS' actors. Indeed, this would delegitimize the ICs itself. These would be presumptively illegitimate since their practices and procedures would predictably thwart the credible pursuit of the very goals upon which they justify their existence.

5.2.5 *Strategic Accountability and the Rules Governing the Interlocutory Coalitions*

ICs have adopted two strategies to confront these problems and be considered strategically accountable. The first consists of introducing 'rules of procedure' aimed at avoiding issues of effectiveness within internal decision-making processes/ mechanisms. The second consists of the adoption of accreditation standards.

---

civil society on WB's policies. For further details See P.W. Jones, D. Coleman, *The United Nations and Education: Multilateralism, Development and Globalisation* (Abingdon, Routledge, 2005).

[25] See C. Mahoney, J. Beckstrand, *Following the Money: EU Funding of Civil Society Organizations*, paper prepared for presentation at the 2009 Annual Meeting of the American Political Science Association in Toronto, 2009.

This section will describe a few cases in which rules have been introduced to boost efficiency. Section 5.2.6 will move to discussion of accreditation standards.

The agreements governing the ICs, of both types A and B, often contain provisions specifically designed to avoid issues of effectiveness. In the ICs governed by agreements of type A, the conditions for the accession to the network and for participating to the organization of its activities are aimed – *inter alia* – at favouring an effective dialogue with IOs' representatives. Consider, for instance, the Consultative Platform's Terms of Reference. The criteria that govern the number of participants, the frequency, and the location of meetings are all aimed at improving effectiveness. The same applies for the rules regarding the appointment of Chairs, Vice-Chairs and the mandate of the Platform. The CINGO's rules of procedure distribute the coalitions' functions among its internal organs, in an effort to ensure its actions are as efficient as possible. The Conference identifies the general actions needed to organize its participation in the COE Quadrilogue, and ensures the correct functioning of the participatory status. The Bureau implements the internal and external communication policy of the CINGO, particularly at the EU level. Finally, the Committees' and Transversal Groups' purpose is to facilitate the co-ordination between single members NGOs, and also to serve as common interlocutors for all COE bodies. In addition, the rules of procedure regulate the organization, the frequency and the time-schedule of the CINGO's official meetings. Also in coalitions governed by agreements of type B, a regulatory framework provides for the better co-ordination of coalitions' activities. The NGO Forum's by-laws contain provisions on the organization of the coalition's activities, including the provision of timelines for the organization of a meeting and the adoption of decisions. The Pan-European ECO Forum appoints a Coordination Board in order to represent the coalition in the EFSA's official processes.

5.2.6 The Use of Accreditation Standards

Accreditation standards are a second solution to overcome issues of effectiveness. Accreditation criteria may be imposed by the IOs,[26] or they may be adopted by the ICs. To make the former case in more detail a quick summary of the following ICs will now be illustrated: the Transport Forum, the Consultative Platform, the CINGO, the Better Aid Network, the CONGO and the UNCAC Coalition. In such ICs the number and quality of the members is subject to constant monitoring from the concerned IO. In the case of CINGO, for instance, participatory status is granted by the COE to international NGOs that are particularly representative at European level

[26] These accountability standards have been theorized for single NGOs by R.O. Kehoane, J.S. Nye, "Democracy, Accountability and Global Governance" (2001) *Harvard University Politics Research Group* Working Paper No. 01-4, available at www.ksg.harvard.edu/prg/nye/ggajune.pdf. See also R.O. Kehoane, J.S. Nye, *Transnational Relations in World Politics*, see chapter 1 at section 6.1.

and in the fields of their competence. In addition, NGOs with participatory status have to demonstrate capability of supporting the achievement of the COE's goals by contributing to its activities and by making its work known among the European public. Additional criteria upon satisfaction of which applicants ascend to the rank of accredited members may concern the possession of an established headquarters with executive officers, a democratically adopted constitution, or the fact that the member has existed for a number of years at the date of receipt of its application for accreditation. The Transport Forum selects its members following a call for applications published in the Official Journal of the European Union. Members representing trade unions are an exception, since it is the Commission that calls upon the European Trade Union Confederation to appoint six members to represent the fields of energy and transport. Not to mention the case in which accreditation standards are imposed indirectly, as in the case (reported in Chap. 1) of the European Commission using the criterion of representativeness to indicate which civil society groups are worth to being consulted with respect to others.

Commentators have discussed whether the imposition of accreditation standards by IOs should be considered as an exception rather than a recurrent option. According to Peter Van Den Bossche (2005), the large part of IOs do not dispose of elaborate procedures for accreditation of NGOs within both decision-making processes and for the review of accreditation decisions. Van Den Bossche argues that the absence of detailed accreditation requirements may be due to the fact that the involvement of NGOs in the deliberations and processes of the IOs is very limited and the need for selecting NGOs, therefore, small. Other authors disagree that criteria for accreditation offer a solution to the accountability problem: according to Seema Sapra accreditation potentially creates barriers of access to supranational policy-making for most NGOs, and could impair the free competition between NGOs.[27]

More common is the case in which the ICs independently adopt accreditation standards for their members. Chapter 4 observed that these standards might provide a solution to speediness in internal decision-making. Here a different scope of the same standards is discussed: how they may serve to the scope of promoting strategic accountability. To put it simply, applicants to a IC may be asked to fulfil specific criteria to become part of the coalition, including the possession of an executive organization, financial independence from governmental bodies, international standing, independent governance, geographical affiliation, adherence to behavioural standards, and commitment to common goals.[28] There are two possible variants. The first, and primary, regards the adherence to accreditation standards directly imposed on eligible members. In order to become members of the Consultative

[27] See S. Sapra, *The WTO System of Trade Governance*, see chapter 1 at section 6.3.

[28] Arthur Benz and Yannis Papadopoulos have pointed out that governance through networks is based on the acceptation of rules from its participant. See A. Benz, Y. Papadopoulos, "Is Network Governance Democratic? Different Assessments for the National and International Level" (2003) *Centre for Democratic Governance* Working Paper available at www.demnetgov.ruc.dk/conference/papers/HelsingoerAB-YPI.pdf.

Platform, for instance, the representative organizations have to receive the formal permission from the EU's Member State in which they operate. Then both the EFSA's Executive Director and the MB, on the basis of conditions devised to verify that the candidates are qualified in the relevant field, scrutinize their candidatures. Participation in the HRDN coalition is open to NGOs that engage at EU level in the promotion of human rights, democracy, and conflict prevention in and outside of the EU. Applicants are admitted to the network if none of the current members object. Also in the case of CAN, all non-government/community based non-profit organizations – "that do not represent industry and which have an interest in the promotion of sustainable development and are active in, have a focus on, or interest in climate change issues" – are eligible to become members. Membership is formally requested through the signature of a standardized questionnaire, and its acceptance is submitted to the approval of the competent Regional Node of the coalition. The necessity to put accreditation standards and, at the same time, that of not missing too many eligible participants is solved by dividing different classes of membership (a solution widely adopted in the ICs, like in the case of CONGO, as shown by Chap. 3). In the CAN, the status of observer can be granted to three classes of applicants: first, non-profit organizations and individuals that qualify for membership of CAN but wish to have observer status only; or, alternatively, applicants that do not qualify as members but wish to have observer status; and, finally, applicants that qualify for CAN membership but not for membership to a Node to which they belong. Once admitted as observers, members with observer status are permitted to observe CAN meetings and have access to CAN materials. However, they have no rights to influence the decision-making process of CAN. They are also required to respect the confidential nature of internal CAN meetings, and may also be excluded from attending a meeting at the request of full members. The facilitator/chairperson or CAN Board members may exclude such members/observers from CAN meetings at the request of CAN full members. Also the rules for resignation and expulsion take into account the necessity to provide the CAN accountable.[29]

[29] In terms of resignation, the Charter governing the coalition limits its validity to the fact that "all the obligations to CAN or to a (Regional) Node have been fulfilled". This is meant to avoid the possibility that members could join and then operate in absolute freedom, against the goals of the coalition. Rules on expulsion are particularly interesting. To begin with, expulsion is provided when a member violates the Code of Conduct of the coalition. In order to finalize the expulsion, however, at least three members of CAN, or the National or Regional Nodes, have to apply for it to the Secretariat, indicating the motivations of the requested expulsion. The Secretariat transfers the request to the CAN board, which in turn appoint an Ethic Committee to hear the matter of expulsion. Not only must the Ethics Committee provide the member whose expulsion is in discussion the opportunity to be heard or to remedy any actions complained of in the application – and, to this extent, it has to determine the procedure to be followed based on the rules of natural justice and fairness – but, also, an expelled member may appeal to the CAN Board. In the event of an appeal, the CAN Board is convened to hear the appeal. As for the Ethics Committee, the CAN Board has to provide the respect of the principles of natural justice and fairness. Besides that, is not the CAN Board, but the General Assembly, to which the final decision is referred, that formally approve the expulsion. The procedure may seem a bit complicated and time-consuming. Yet, if seen from a different perspective, it also shows a strong commitment of the coalition to the basic principles of democratic governance.

A second, less effective, variant of accreditation standards occurs in the case in which the IC relies on the functional accountability of its members. However, shifting the focus of the accountability to the members, in the place of the coalition, only transfers the issue of accountability. This is even more so for the ICs composed of hundreds of members. For this reason, some ICs opt for restricting the range of members with a mandate to be accountable. Alter-EU is a case in point. As described in Chap. 4, Alter-EU is politically coordinated by a restricted number of members: those who sit in the Steering Committee. All the members of the Steering Committee contribute to the expenses of the coalition in exchange of the position they hold. As a consequence, these members are also requested to indicate their budgets and to be transparent in their activities (which, in the case of Alter-EU, also implies that they are registered to the European register for transparency).

These examples may hint that formal and informal ways of interaction between the ICs and IOs are more likely to guarantee a better balance between diverging civil society's and governmental interests at the supranational level as well as to improve the quality of IOs' policy-making. Given the complexity of what is being regulated by IOs (which makes their regulations necessarily complex), the attainment of regulatory goals seems to depend heavily on the main and continuous mediation pursued by the ICs.

5.3 The Issue of Legitimacy

Legitimacy is closely linked to the question of accountability, although they do not overlap. In practice, all legitimate power is also accountable, whereas not all accountable power is legitimate. In the most common acceptance of the term, legitimacy consists of the diffuse belief in a community of an appropriate use of power by a legally constituted authority following correct decisions on making policies.[30] This is what scholars generally define as "formal", "legal" or "normative legitimacy". Until the recent past, normative legitimacy was foremost connected to the nation-state. It is now acknowledged that legitimacy crosses national boundaries and applies to IOs: obviously, notes Graham Long (2008), legitimacy is a problem in practice only to the extent that some institutions wield power in world politics. More broadly, legitimacy is described as the ability of rule-makers to assess its rules on stakeholders' needs (and in this sense it is called "social legitimacy").[31]

[30] Scientific literature on legitimacy is vast. For a general discourse on legitimacy in international organizations See M. Suchman, "Managing Legitimacy: Strategic and Institutionals Approaches (1995) 20 *Academy of Management Review* 571.

[31] There is also an "ethical legitimacy", i.e. a standard of moral rightness applied to make moral claims about law and the exercise of power. Indeed, all dimensions of legitimacy play a role in the context of GCS' actors. Anne Peters mentions the case of a given NGO (See A. Peters, L. Koechlin, T. Forster, G Fenner Zinkernagel (eds.), *Non-state Actors as Standard Setters*, see chapter 3 n 18, chapter 4 n 11 and n 32, at 19. This may be socially legitimate because it enjoys popular support; it may be ethically legitimate because it commits to global values such as the protection of the environment; and, finally, it may possess a legal legitimacy because of it accredited status towards some IO.

Participation is therefore essential to legitimacy, and particularly to social legitimacy, in the sense that people agree on the existence of a particular rule-maker and participate in its activity, because of their belief to influence its results. It is because of this trust that a relationship of social legitimation is established. As put by Daniel Esty (2006), a decision-making process that is transparent and provides opportunities for inclusion of a broad range of views "is key to legitimacy, substituting for the missing democratic legitimacy and accountability that elections provide".

Albeit with some divergences,[32] legitimacy is generally assumed to be of importance to IOs. Scholars have suggested many ways to increase legitimacy in supranational governance. Authors generally state that IOs' legitimacy may be achieved in two ways: through indirect representation; or through procedural mechanisms resembling the typical structure of an administrative process of law. The first narrative understands IOs' rule-making as a system of multi-level governance, involving representation of constituents' concerns across the spectrum of political matters through non-hierarchical steering and management of networks of public and private actors. This narrative postulates that the inadequacy of IOs to develop close contacts with civil society guides stakeholders' participation at the domestic level. The processes held at the domestic level influence the supranational outcomes.[33] The second narrative acknowledges and insists upon civil society's direct engagement within IOs' regulatory processes. On this point, Allen Buchanan and Robert Keohane argue that IOs' legitimacy ought to be dynamic and relational.[34] Dynamic because legitimacy for IOs requires the capacity for on-going, increasingly inclusive public deliberation about their proper goals and about the role IOs ought to play

[32] Ulrick Beck (See U. Beck, *La società cosmopolita, Prospettive dell'epoca post-nazionale* – Bologna, 2003) describes globalization as a social experience, where the territorial identity of societies fades and a new sense of cosmopolitanism emerges. By contrast, Saskia Sassen (See S. Sassen, *Territory, Authority, Rights. From Medieval to Global Assemblages* – Princeton, Princeton University Press, 2006); "The State and Globalization: Denationalized Participation" (2004) 25 *Michigan Journal of International Law* 1158) understands globalization mostly as a vehicle for de-nationalization. Thus, under the conceptual construct of Sassen, globalization signifies the departure from the traditional conception of legitimacy based on compliance with national laws and rules. On the contrary, Beck's assumption is that globalization magnifies the process of achieving legitimacy because it relies on universalistic standards shared among regimes.

[33] On multi-level governance See, *ex multis*, B.G. Peters, "Governance: A Garbage Can Perspective", in E. Grande, L.W. Paul (eds.), *Complex Sovereignty: Reconstituting Political Authority in the Twenty-first Century* (Toronto, University of Toronto Press, 2005), at 68; H. Yanacopulos, "Patterns of Governance: The Rise of Transnational Coalitions of NGOs" (2005) 19 *Global Society* 247. See also the 1995 Report of the Commission on Global Governance, available at www.libertymatters.org/chap1.htm. See also F.E. Johns, "Global Governance: An Heretical History Play" (2004) 4 *Global Jurist Advances* article 3. The author's claim is that modern systems of governance might be compared and understood in confrontation with sixteenth century Venice. On post-modern governance See A. Negri, "Postmodern Global Governance and The Critical Legal Project" (2001) 1 *Global Jurist Advances* article 2.

[34] See A. Buchanan, R.O. Keohane, *The Legitimacy of Global Governance Institutions*, see text n 11, at 407.

in the global arena; relational because the needed on-going public deliberation depends not only upon the characteristics of the institutions themselves but also upon connections between the IOs and agents and institutions outside of them.

5.4 The GRID Model

In particular, it is this second concern that Dario Bevilacqua and Jessica Duncan's (2010) GRID model aims to overcome.[35] Bevilacqua and Duncan apply the GRID to the agro-food regulatory framework, given its sensibility to the problem of public participation. However the same model may be applied in other regulatory sectors. GRID seeks to enhance participation by framing an approach based on reflexive democracy and interactivity. Regarding the former, focus is directed towards co-operation and mutual understanding. Described as "democracy-enhancing links" between decision-makers and civil society, civil society actors are obliged to deliver information to the general public and transform their preferences into propositions to be used to influence IOs' decision-making processes. Interactivity, as conceptualized in the GRID model, refers to the development of policies through the cooperation of stakeholders' networks.

GRID, this argument goes, seeks to develop an innovative system of civil society involvement in supranational decision-making, and thus to possibly overcome the problem of GCS' actors legitimacy. In order to do so, it involves a horizontal and a vertical phase. The horizontal phase includes cooperative exchange between all the organizations and actors inside a specific regulatory framework. This phase is aimed at informing civil society about regulatory acts originating from institutional regulators, and developing common platforms to influence those regulations. The vertical phase comprises the action of influencing supranational regulators through proposals, reports and surveys, and indeed the explanation to the members of the network of how global institutions act and respond to networks solicitation.

5.5 Conclusions

The purpose of this chapter was not to resolve questions of how to improve the accountability and legitimacy of GCS, and how to improve IOs' accountability and legitimacy through collaboration with the ICs. However, this chapter has cleared a path to answering to those questions. To begin with, the issues of GCS' accountability and legitimacy have been addressed. When the issue of legitimacy was discussed in Chap. 1, it addressed criticisms that actors in the GCS are illegitimate

[35] See also D. Bevilacqua, "La regolazione degli OGM. La multidimensionalità dei problemi e le soluzioni della democrazia amministrativa" (2007) 15 *I frutti di Demetra* 59.

because they do not enjoy any democratic mandate by the global citizens. Upon closer scrutiny, however, this position appears unpersuasive on three grounds. First, for practical reasons. Many governments participate in international policy-making, despite the fact that are undemocratic and illegitimate. There are also non-state actors that wield global power, but nobody calls into question their legitimacy. This is particularly the case of big corporations. The fact that rulemaking by GCS actors generally translates into soft law is another argument against opinions that GCS wield illegitimate power. Chapter 4 explained how this soft law leverages the role of GCS on the international scene. However, as this law is unenforceable, it has a lesser impact with respect to hard law. It therefore implicitly demands minor democratic credentials. Third, the lack of formal democratic credentials from non-state actors is counterweighted by the fact that GCS' representatives have a voice but not a vote, in supranational policy-making. In other words, the democratic function of non-state actors is not to be representatives in a parliamentary sense. This means that the lack of formal democratic credentials does not constitute an absolute factor of illegitimacy. To the contrary, having a supposedly democratic mandate by a global citizenry would counter the function to represent and give voice to specific minorities towards IOs. It may be even argued that – differently from state actors – GCS' actors stakeholders are not citizens, but a complex group in which financial sponsors, supporters and aid recipients are included.

On the basis of these arguments, the current chapter discussed a number of hypotheses on how the ICs are contributing to the legitimacy of GCS. Legitimacy can be attributed to the ICs moving from the argument that they offer a valuable expertise in policy arenas where governments lack resources or specific knowledge. Legitimacy is also awarded through transparency and procedural accountability. According to this mode, members of the ICs gain legitimacy if they adhere to standards of professional and ethical conduct imposed by the ICs. The discourse on the ICs' legitimacy is crucial to that of IOs. It glimpses the dynamics of convergence in supranational governance. As a medium between IOs and GCS, the ICs become part of supranational governance. Not by chance, the starting point in the next chapter will be that of administrative convergence. At the same time, the linkage between the legitimacy of the ICs and that of IOs bring into question a problem of uniformity. Since the ICs may cooperate with different IOs, it is possible that they could be forced to reconcile different demands of legitimacy. Different IOs may in fact value different sources of legitimacy in different ways. This problem will be addresses in more details in the final chapter of this book.

References

Bevilacqua, D., and J. Duncan. 2010. Towards a new cosmopolitanism: Global reflexive interactive democracy as a new mechanism for civil society participation in agri-food governance. *Global Jurist Advances* 10: 2.

Bovens, M. 2007. Analysing and assessing public accountability: A conceptual framework. *European Law Review* 13: 447.

Cashore, B. 2002. Legitimacy and the privatization of environmental governance: How non-state market-driven governance systems gain rule-making authority. *Governance: An International Journal of Policy, Administration, and Institutions* 15: 503.
Chimni, B.S. 2004. International institutions today: An imperial global state in the making. *European Journal of International Law* 1: 1.
Edwards, M. 1999. *Future positive: International co-operation in the 21st century*. London: Earthscan.
Esty, D. 2006. Good governance at the supranational scale: Globalizing administrative law. *Yale Law Journal* 115: 1490.
Koppell, J. 2005. Pathologies and accountability: ICANN and the challenge of "Multiple Accountability Disorder". *Public Administration Review* 65: 94.
Long, G. 2008. Justification and legitimacy in global civil society. *Journal of Global Ethics* 4: 51.
O'Donnell, G. 1998. Horizontal accountability in new democracies. *Journal of Democracy* 9: 112.
Prewitt, K. ed. 1998. *Networks in international capacity building: Cases from Sub-Saharan Africa*. SSRC Working Paper, New York Social Science Research Council.
Smith, J. 2005. Building bridges or building walls? Explaining regionalisation among transnational social movement organizations. *Mobilization: An International Quarterly* 10: 251.
Smith, S. 2012. NGOs and legitimacy in international development. *Kansas Law Review* 61: 377.
Uvin, P. 2004. *Human rights and development*. Bloomfield: Kumarian Press.
Van Den Bossche P. 2005. Rules on NGO accreditation. Do existing legal arrangements facilitate the legitimization of the role of NGOs in International Organizations?. *Maastricht Faculty of Law* Working Paper Series n. 10.
Wapner, P. 1996. *Environmental activism and world civic politics*. New York: Suny Press.

Chapter 6
Interlocutory Coalitions and Policy Convergence

6.1 Global Civil Society and Advocacy

Previous chapters discussed why ICs exist and the scopes of their objectives. In Chap. 2 the ICs were described as the natural consequence of a number of concurring factors. These include: the increase in cooperative efforts from GCS' actors in transnational issues, the widespread diffusion of technology, the globalization of media outlets, and, decisively, the potential benefits offered by networks. Chapter 4 described these benefits. It maintained that ICs are formed out of the efforts to promote productive discourse and confrontation among actors of the GCS. Hence, in Chap. 4 the ICs were described as structures for mediation among GCS' actors, where uniform strategies are elaborated before being advocated towards IOs. Chapter 5 moved a step forward in exploring the relationship between the ICs and IOs. The ICs were compared to mechanisms that compensate the gaps in IOs' accountability and legitimacy while providing a solution to the problem of GCS' accountability and legitimacy.

This chapter resumes discussion from this point. It attempts to validate the hypothesis that the ICs are meaningful tools to promote the democratization of supranational administrative governance. To do this, two questions will be posed. The first is more topical, in that it speculates on how the ICs may be considered "policy entrepreneurs", "transfer agents" or – to borrow from the political sciences' terminology – "idea brokers" – to describe actors who concretely contribute to influencing the interactions between policy makers or, as in our case, between global and European decision-making processes. A second (more abstract) question seeks to determine whether the growing networking among GCS' actors is forming a "bridge" between the global and the European administrative systems. To really appreciate the extent to which the ICs may be drivers of the convergence of administrative policies and principles at the supranational level, the current section is organized as follows: a preliminary distinction will be made between the contribution

G. Sgueo, *Beyond Networks - Interlocutory Coalitions, the European and Global Legal Orders*, Studies in European Economic Law and Regulation 8,
DOI 10.1007/978-3-319-28875-8_6

to the shaping of principles of administrative governance at the supranational level given by single civil society actors (and particularly by NGOs) and the ICs, respectively. Rather than focusing on the strategies used by the ICs to influence IOs' decisions (as Chap. 4 did), the current chapter will assess the differences between single GCS' actors and organized networks of GCS' actors. It will be suggested that the ICs are a significant factor in spreading interaction and convergence between the EAS and GAL. This claim builds on two subsidiary arguments, one relating to the notion of administrative convergence, the other concerned with future scenarios in supranational civil society's networks. Administrative convergence will be addressed from Sect. 6.1.1 onward. Two types of convergence will be analysed. The first is convergence through attraction, whereas the second is described as convergence through imposition. These two forms of convergence are self-completing. Convergence as pursued through the influence of the ICs on GAL and European Administrative Law (EAL) follows from attractiveness and imposition, or combinations thereof. Having this in mind, and the nature of the ICs, Sect. 6.2 will attempt to re-assess the famous "boomerang effect" theorised by Keck and Sikkink. Five differences will be sketched between the original boomerang model and the convergence promoted by the ICs. One of these differences is particularly important. Given the description of the ICs as drivers of administrative convergence at the supranational level, it may be argued that the ICs themselves are likely to converge over time by adapting their organizational structures and activities in order to deal rationally with the task of influencing supranational policy-making. A new question concerning the existence of a link between the growing networking among GCS' and the global and the European administrative systems will then be introduced. However, as this topic concerns the discourse on future scenarios of supranational civil society's networks, and their challenges, it will be further analysed in the conclusive chapter of this volume (Chap. 7). Coming back to the current chapter, Sect. 6.3 is dedicated to the analysis of administrative convergence in the framework of EAS and GAL. This section endeavours to assess the challenges that face administrative convergence. These include institutional inertia and cultural preferences. Institutional inertia occurs when efforts towards convergence are little more than symbolic behaviour. Cultural preferences, instead, may render particular solutions unattractive in particular polities.

Let us begin by distinguishing between the contribution made by individual actors in the GCS and the ICs to the shaping of principles of administrative governance at the supranational level, and why a separation may be drawn between their respective contributions. Hypothetically, both contribute to fostering stakeholders' participation, access to documents, clarity of procedures and clear drafting, judicial review, as well as consistency in the interpretation and application of the law within the European and global institutions' rule-making. Thus, at least at first glance, it might be argued that policy transfers across European and global administrative systems benefit from the presence of single non-state actors as well as of the ICs. However, on a closer inspection, an important difference is evident. The influence of single non-state actors on IO's decision-making is fundamentally erratic. The rhetoric about the democratization of the supranational legal space through the involvement of GCS has run far beyond real achievements. The reasons of this substantial failure have been analysed in previous chapters of this volume and will only be briefly touched upon here. The failure behind the contribution of GCS' actors to the democratization of supranational decision-making is mainly due to two factors, both discussed in Chap. 4. The first involves the excessive number and variety of competing civil society players operating at the supranational level, all at the same time. On the one hand, the polycentric system of supranational governance provides the bedrock for civil society's presence in the supranational sphere. However, on the other hand, it challenges the formation of a homogeneous civil society with a shared identity of its constituency. To prove this, one should consider two phenomena. First, the tendency of NGOs from different parts of the world to advocate for different goals, rather than being united, when given the opportunity to confront governmental representatives; and second, the Kaiser's "participatory overkill", i.e. the excessive costs that may discourage minor non-state actors from participating in supranational decision-making, despite being invited to do so. The second reason explaining the substantial failure of GCS' actors to contribute to the democratization of supranational decision-making involves shortcomings in accountability and legitimacy of single GCS' actors.

Combined, these two factors diminish the capability of GCS actors to influence the democratization of the supranational legal order. Perhaps inevitably, this raises the issue of whether the same the limits constrain the ICs. Although as answered in Chaps. 3 and 4, this is not the case. Firstly, because the ICs are designed to bring non-state actors together into networks for advocacy. They were actually born out of the necessity of championing a sense of communality among their members. Second, the ICs increasingly make use of certification criteria to restrict and regulate the access of new members. Filtering accession to a coalition may provide stronger cohesion (as discussed in Chap. 4), and may guarantee greater accountability (as explained by Chap. 5). Third, in the ICs all topics of interest must be debated and agreed upon amongst coalition members well before they are presented to IOs. This facilitates coherent (and possibly effective) advocacy within supranational decision-making. Fourth, it is worth remembering that membership to the ICs is not exclusive. Non-state actors are free to join more ICs – which, in fact, they often do – as well as to operate autonomously. This helps to overcome the divisions between transnational actors who operate across continents and time zones, and actors who are situated in marginalized locations and operate mainly at the local level. Non-state actors may in fact operate in autonomy, but they are likely to adopt a similar position agreed to within the ICs.

After all, there is wealth of research that focuses on how supranational networking benefits the democratization of legal orders. Barbara Wejnert, Paul Ingram and Magnus Thor Torfason – to name but a few – have analysed the diffusion of democracy through networks. In the opinion of Wejnert (2014), three elements combine to help the spread of democracy: spatial proximity, media communication, and membership in international networks. The last is also the most important. Wejnert explains how membership in international networks exposes governments to the influence of the other members of the same network, and might therefore foster democratization. Ingram and Torfason (2010) also address the role of IOs in the democratization of international networks. These IOs, they explain, provide interpretation and interaction venues for elites, and support a shared identity among the populace of member-states. This increases the likelihood of change consistent with shared norms, and decreases the likelihood of inconsistent change. The most immediate conclusion of these arguments is that, at least in theory, the ICs' have a stronger potential in influencing policy transfer compared with that of single non-state actors.

6.1.1 Administrative Convergence Across Borders

Indeed, the capacity of the ICs to meaningfully drive policy transfers across the European and global systems of administrative law need to be established with facts and examples. To do this, we need to discuss administrative convergence. As in the cases of accountability and legitimacy, the concept of 'administrative convergence' does not have an agreed meaning. At root, administrative convergence is the process that brings administrative systems to grow alike, since they develop similarities in structures, processes, role conceptions and performances. However, some scholars describe administrative convergence as part of the broader notion of "policy transfer", whereas others oppose the idea that convergence equates such a notion, and prefer to describe it as an outcome of policy transfer. Other scholars prefer to focus on measuring, rather than defining, administrative convergence.[1] It is not within the scope of this volume to engage these claims directly. Rather, we will focus on the application of the notion of administrative governance within EAL-GAL relationships. It has been already said that administrative convergence implies both a reduction of variance and uniform enforcement of common principles, rules and regulations. Conceived as such, administrative convergence considers as transferable across legal systems not just legal documents, but also knowledge of policies, administrative arrangements, institutions and even ideas. In their seminal research on policy transfer, David Dolowitz and David Marsh identified eight "objects" of transfer: policy goals, policy content, policy instruments, policy programs, institutions, ideologies, ideas and attitudes and negative lessons.[2] Clearly, this is a phenomenon that not only concerns the interactions occurring across domestic legal systems, but also encompasses other actors and venues, including IOs, epistemic communities and transnational advocacy networks.

The concept of policy convergence expanded between the late 1990s and mid-2000s, broadening into academic disciplines as wide-ranging as law, economics and political sciences. Before 1996, the terms "policy transfer" or "lesson drawing"

---

[1] See for instance M. Kaeding, "Administrative Convergence Actually – An Assessment of the European Commission's Best Practices for Transposition of EU Legislation in France, Germany, Italy, Sweden and Greece" (2007) 29 *Journal of European Integration* 425.

[2] See D.P. Dolowitz, D. Marsh, *Learning From Abroad* see chapter 4 n 35, text n 9 and n 11.

(another label used to describe the same phenomenon) featured in the title or abstract of barely a dozen articles published on Google Scholar; between 1996 and 2000 this number had increased to 20, finally surpassing 30 after 2001.[3] Today, a growing body of literature addresses the topic of policy convergence and its sources. In 2015, a random search on Google Scholar will produce over 15,000 results for "policy transfer" and around 300 results for "administrative convergence". As it is currently understood, policy transfer is shown to occur within horizontal and vertical networks, and to extend across borders. Further, the concept of policy transfer is broad enough as to account for voluntary and coercive transfer, as well as for transfers of wholesale policies or of a more limited number of policy tools. Diane Stone, for instance, conducted extended research on IOs seeking to impose their policies on other actors, as well as on non-state actors promoting transfer through persuasion. She explains that transfer agents may be not based or identified with either the importing or exporting legal systems. In this sense, they can be described as "global policy advocates" – to borrow from Mitchell Orenstein's terminology (2003) – that drive policy diffusion at the supranational level. Paul Di Maggio and Walter Powell (1991) go as far as to suggest that convergence may lead to institutional isomorphism.[4] In a similar vein, some authors suggest that policy transfer should not be limited only to an activity of importing or exporting of policies across legal venues. Rather, it should include the elaboration of new ideas. Named as "cognitive influence", this form of policy transfer includes both the restyling of legal ideas in a way that makes sense for organisations with different interests and/or priorities, and the framing of new policies solutions designed to solve policy problems.[5]

6.1.2 Attractiveness and Imposition

Upon establishing administrative convergence as a phenomenon that occurs at the supranational level, the next step is to introduce the major types of administrative convergence. Jacob Olsen distinguishes between two main hypotheses of administrative convergence.[6] He describes the first in terms of "attractiveness", while the

---

[3] See D. Benson, A. Jordan, "What Have We Learned From Policy Transfer Research? Dolowitz and Marsh Revisited" (2011) 9 *Political Studies Review* 366, at 368.

[4] According to Di Maggio and Powell there are three sources of institutional isomorphic change: coercive, mimetic, and normative. Coercive isomorphism occurs when an organisation becomes similar to other organisations to which is dependent. Uncertainty triggers mimetic isomorphism. Mimesis stems from the need to cope with uncertainty by imitating organisations that are perceived to be more legitimate. Normative isomorphism refers to communities of professionals and the systems in which they are educated and recruited. These common patterns produce a common cognitive base that contributes to make organisational structures similar one to another.

[5] See, for instance, O. Nay, "How Do Policy Ideas Spread Among International Administrations? Policy Entrepreneurs and Bureaucratic Influence in the UN Response to AIDS" (2002) 32 *Journal of Public Policy* 53.

[6] See J.P. Olsen, *Towards a European Administrative Space* see chapter 1 n 8, at 4.

second is traced in terms of "imposition". To simplify a complex argument, Olsen states that attractiveness signifies learning and voluntary imitation of a superior model. Organizational forms are copied because of their perceived functionality, utility, or legitimacy. In light of this, the term "emulation" – used by Colin Bennett (1991) – is perhaps even more appropriate to describe the idea of administrative attractiveness. In fact, regulations and institutions are modified only when a set of beliefs, or ideals, has developed sufficient power to be considered as a superior model. In this case, the driver that promotes convergence is not capital mobility, but rather the need to conform to ideals – and the prestige attached to them.[7] Also used, as a lexical counterpart of attractiveness, is the term "diffusion". Convergence by diffusion embodies the independence of the actors that voluntarily adopt a certain policy innovation and their interdependence, in the sense that they factor in the choices of other actors.[8] There are numerous examples to illustrate attractiveness. Dolowitz and Marsh used the case of welfare-to-work policies transferred from the United States to Britain (and, following its success in reducing level of unemployment, from Britain to other European governments).[9] Miguel Aparicio (1984) illustrates attractiveness having in mind the section of the Spanish constitution dealing with the roles of the Prime Minister and the President. This, explains Aparicio, was modelled on the German constitution. Sandra Lavenex (2013) reports the 1995 Euro-Mediterranean Partnership – also referred as the "Barcelona Process" – between the EU institutions, the Arab states of the southern Mediterranean, and Israel.

However when no single way of organizing administrative governance is seen as functionally or normatively superior, convergence by imposition is likely to happen. As in the case of attractiveness, imposition can also be described with many terminological variances: from "penetration",[10] to "coercive transfer",[11] or "external inducement".[12] All these definitions seem to suggest that, differently from attractiveness, convergence conveyed through imposition does not build upon a cooperative arrangement or voluntariness. Rather, it is based on the use of authority and power that compel actors to conform. With imposition, actors are forced to adopt policy innovations that they would not have adopted otherwise. Not by chance, such type of convergence is driven by the exploitation of economic or political power asymmetries. In the words of Daniel Drezner: "the pressure to modify regulatory

[7] See D.W. Drezner, "Globalization and Policy Convergence" (2001) 3 *International Studies Review*, 53, at 60. See also K.J. Hopt, E. Wymeersch, H. Kanda, H. Baum, *Corporate Governance in Context: Corporations, States, and Markets in Europe, Japan, and the US* (Oxford, Oxford University Press, 2005).

[8] See P.O. Busch, H. Jorgens, "The International Sources of Policy Convergence: Explaining the Spread of Environmental Policy Innovations" (2005) 12 *Journal of European Public Policy* 1.

[9] See D. Dolowitz, D. Marsh, *Learning From Abroad* see chapter 4 n 35, text n 2 and n 11.

[10] See C.J. Bennett, *Review Article* see text at section 2.2.

[11] See D. Dolowitz, D. Marsh, *Learning From Abroad* see chapter 4 n 35, see text n 2 and n 9.

[12] See G.J. Ikenberry, C.A. Kupchan, "Socialization and Hegemonic Power" (1990) 44 *International Organizations* 283.

policies comes from the threat of mobile capital to exit, causing non-converging states to lose their competitiveness in the global economy".[13] Similarly to Drezden, Klaust Hopt, Eddy Wymeersch, Hideki Kanda and Harald Baum consider mobility a primary force behind convergence: rules are borrowed by governors to capture the benefits of economic performance.[14] A typical example of this form of convergence is membership of supranational legal regimes such as the EU. Membership always comes with the imposition of economic and political measures. It should be noted, however, that convergence through imposition may exist in both hierarchical and non-hierarchical relationships. Obviously, in the case of the former there are binding rules and sanctioning tools to avoid policy divergence. However, in the latter case there is no direct prescriptive relationship between the actors involved in convergence. This is imposed by the (perceived) superiority of some actors – the "great powers", in the definition used by Daniel Drezner[15] – over other actors.

Attractiveness and convergence are commonly described as mutually exclusive forms of convergence. Olsen and other scholars suggest that administrative convergence may follow from attractiveness or imposition. Instead, this volume assumes that, especially in the conceptual landscape of EAS/GAL relationship, convergence as pursued through the influence of the ICs follows from attractiveness and imposition, or combinations thereof. In other words, the two forms of convergence are considered as self-completing. This notion rests on the idea that the ICs may mobilize good practices and normative standards from different legal arenas by linking various actors and institutions across borders (which can be sketched as convergence through attractiveness), but they may also construct a web of rules by relying on IOs' leadership and authority (which can be described as convergence through imposition).

The standards produced by the ICs may help to clarify this point. Chapter 4 explained that when the ICs create new standards, these are often merely symbolic, with little or no real effect. In order to gain leverage on the supranational level, standards need "institutional interpretation", i.e. they need to be supported by a well-articulated and organized system of monitoring and enforcement. This support may be provided through attraction and imposition. Attraction is enhanced by the diffusion of standards across various ICs, whereas imposition occurs in the moment in which the IOs decide to implement the concerned standards – and in the latter case imposition may assume various forms: by "reference", when the integral text of a decision is referenced in another legal text from a different IO; by "incorporation" of only few programmatic lines; or by "application", when standards are given direct application.[16] Indeed, the reverse hypothesis is also possible: convergence is initially supported through imposition, and in a second moment through attractiveness. Case in point is that of global financial standards. Normally, financial

---

[13] See D.W. Drezner, *Globalization and Policy Convergence* see text n 7, at 60.

[14] See K.J. Hopt, E. Wymeersch, H. Kanda, H. Baum, *Corporate Governance in Context* see text n 7.

[15] See D.W. Drezner, "Globalization, Harmonization, and Competition: the Different Pathways to Policy Convergence" (2005) 12 *Journal of European Public Policy* 841, at 842.

[16] See M. Conticelli, *The G8 and "The Others"* see chapter 3 n 8, at 8.

standards would be considered exemplary of convergence through imposition (and Sect. 6.1.4 will discuss some). However, argues Maurizia De Bellis (2013), global financial standards may be implemented through methodologies, assessment programmes, or training/technical assistance programs. Thus, even if financial standards were initially spread through imposition, attractiveness would likely perform a role in the phase of implementation.

6.1.3 Convergence Through Attraction

To further elaborate on the concept of convergence by attractiveness: it was posited that this is marshalled by cross-fertilization among the ICs' activities. This assumption implies that the knowledge and experience of the ICs' are likely to be shared in advocacy campaigns towards different IOs. This happens partly because of their international leverage, and partly because members of the ICs may join more coalitions at the same time. The ICs may encourage convergence through attractiveness in three ways. The first is actually linked with the potential of networking among civil society actors. When non-state actors that enjoy membership status in various ICs participate in IOs' decision-making processes, they indirectly contribute to ensuring a degree of coherence in IOs on topics of relevance to administrative governance (e.g. participatory rights and transparency). David Hunter argues that "networks are critical for disseminating lessons learned"[17]; Gauthier De Beco concurs: "Networks cross borders, but, in contrast to international organisations, do not have the capacity to enforce rules through governmental institutions. Instead, to achieve common goals, networks facilitate the sharing of best practices between their members so as to enable them to improve their individual performances".[18] Hence coordination among the members of a coalition – as well as formal and informal contacts between diverse ICs – plays a crucial role in spreading integration in EAS/GAL. In a related manner, exchanges in practices and conducts of participation between the ICs limit IOs' free riding from policies and orientations that are increasingly shared with other IOs. Cases in point include the UNAIDS and the OECD. The UNAIDS – a multilateral initiative to co-ordinate responses to the AIDS pandemic – reflects the institutionalization of epistemic communities and relies on significant contribution from non-state actors. As far as the OECD is concerned, in 1990 it established a public management programme aimed at spreading information on matters such as accounting standards, human resources management and transparency.[19] Admittedly, this programme only involves governments' officials and civil servants. However, the best practices shared during the meetings and official encounters are designed to

[17] See D.B. Hunter, *Civil Society Networks* see chapter 4 n 36.

[18] See also G. de Beco, *Networks of European National Human Rights Institutions* see chapter 3 n 12, at 14.

[19] See generally www.oecd.org/gov/thepublicgovernanceandterritorialdevelopmentdirectorat-egovnetworks.htm.

be shared with national-based civil society actors. As part of the Project, the OECD joined the EU in the SIGMA initiative (Support for Improvement in Governance and Management in Central and Eastern Europe). SIGMA advises national governments on methods to improve public governance. Its key objectives include capacity building in the public sector, enhancing horizontal governance, and improving the design and implementation of public administration reforms.[20]

A second way to spread convergence through attractiveness is through the diffusion of standards, codes of conduct, or informal agreements amongst the ICs. Increasingly, the ICs are drawing upon these tools of soft-law and incorporating them into their own agenda setting mechanisms. Tools of soft law may be recycled when a coalition believes that a standard or agreement adopted by another coalition provided an efficient solution to a given problem. Similarly, a coalition may draw upon tools adopted within other coalitions after their own attempts have failed and they need to adopt solutions that worked well in other situations. In both cases, the ICs adopt soft rules drafted by other coalitions in the belief they will improve their chances of successful engagement and advocacy with other IOs. Chapter 4 already provided a few examples. Civil regulations, for instance, may help the convergence of administrative principles of governance between the GAL and the EAS.

A third, and final, way to enhance convergence by attractiveness relates to the concept of bureaucratic culture. There is a broad consensus in the academic literature that, first, policy goals are shaped on the basis of the environments (the organization's mission, the operating procedures, and the staff) in which bureaucrats work; and, second, that bureaucratic reorganisations are initiated and controlled mainly by administrative elites. Eyal Benvenisti and George Downs (2007) remind that State bureaucracies are the few with the expertise needed to effectively monitor the broad expanse of IOs' activities. Further, it is argued that the more the bureaucratic actions accumulate in a given issue-area, the greater the chances that they will be used in other issue areas, by other administrations. Without aiming to provide a full list, there are a few interesting examples. Max Weber (1978), for instance, identified in the specialisation of knowledge as the major instrument by which bureaucratic administrations build their superiority over citizens and private interests. Elliot Posner (2005) described how civil servants in Brussels created autonomy for themselves from other key actors and crafted the political landscape in which they operate. They did so – according to Posner – "by forging new interests, embedding themselves in supportive coalitions, liberally interpreting Europe-wide laws". Bureaucratic culture may involve civil servants from various administrations, even operating in different legal systems, as the KARLUS programme exemplifies. Between 1993 and 1994, the European Institute for Public Administration ran the KARLUS programme for the EU Commission. The programme aimed at favouring the exchange among member states of officials engaged in the administration of the internal market. Following this experience, in 1998 the EU Commission adopted

[20] On SIGMA and convergence See E.G. Heidbreder, "Structuring the European Administrative Space: Policy Instruments of Multi-Level Administration" (2011) 18 *Journal of European Public Policy* 709, at 717.

the well-known scheme for detached national experts (national civil servants are called to serve for the EU bureaucracy for a number of years before returning to their national administrations). Another case is that of professionals operating as consultants of policy makers that nurture the administrative culture. IOs involved in policy transfer often make recommendations as to the consultants who should be hired for specific project or task. Such experts are part of a transnational community that – note Dolowitz and Marsh – form common patterns of understanding with regard to policy-making. Gregory Shaffer (2014) brings the case of WTO law that enhances the role of technocrats in national public administrations who engage, *inter alia*, in standard setting, the review of patents and the criteria for providing protection based on antidumping. On occasion, members of the judiciary may also be considered as part of the administrative elites that drive policy convergence. Not accidentally, Chap. 1 of this volume described the global judiciary as a driver of an increasingly globalized administrative law.

6.1.4 Convergence Through Imposition

Convergence through imposition builds upon the basic assumption that the leadership position of IOs in specific fields of regulation helps their policies and standards to become important benchmarks for other IOs. In this sense, IOs' leadership can also be described in terms of authority, i.e. the ability to induce deference in others. As Deborah Avant, Martha Finnemore and Susan Kell explain in their volume on global governance, authority is a form of social relationship.[21] It is in fact created by the recognition, even if only tacit or informal, of others. And such deference – explain the authors – confers power. Avant, Finnemore and Kell describe five types of authority for global governors. Institutional authority derives from holding office in some established organizational structure; delegated authority is loaned from some other set of authoritative actors (as in the case of sub-state agencies); experience authority is based on specialized knowledge, epistemic communities being a case in point. The fourth and fifth types of authority are particularly relevant to the discourse of administrative convergence. Principled authority is legitimated by service to some widely accepted set of principles, morals, and values. This is the kind of authority that permeates civil society actors and the ICs. Capacity-base authority involves deference based on perceived competence. This is the kind of authority exercised by IOs over other IOs.

Section 6.1.2 explained how examples of convergence by imposition are especially apparent in the finance sector. The Performance Standards adopted by the IFC, for instance, inspired the 2003 "Equator Principles" initiative. These are a set of principles aimed at developing environmental and social standards among commercial banks. According to the Equator Principles, banks may require the borrowers to comply with when issuing loans for infrastructure development. No institution is

[21] See D.D. Avant, M. Finnemore, S.K. Sell, *Who Governs the Globe* see chapter 1 at section 1.

in charge of issuing, interpreting or amending these principles. The banks themselves carry out the role of regulators. The initiative has spread rapidly among private financial institutions as well as other IOs and today it covers around 80 % of global project finance. The ADB, for instance, introduced several improvements to its policies after having taken inspiration from the WBG's reforms.[22] Similarly, in the field of aides to development, the IMF often requires that a recipient country pursue particular economic policies, mostly cuts in public expenditure and an increase in the use of the market. It is for this reason that the IMF, and more generally all the Bretton Woods institutions, have long been accused of dispensing "one-sits-fits-all" policies coercively imposed through loan conditionality.[23] The model of accession conditionality further exemplifies convergence through imposition. This is the case in which IOs link certain benefits of membership to the requirement of reforms. Take the 1992 Operational Directive 4.02 and the 1999 Comprehensive Development Framework of the WB. The former tool required the preparation of National Environmental Action Plans as a condition for receiving WB's loans. The latter tool allows the WB to impose "structural adjustments" to the internal legal systems of assisted countries as a condition to access new loans or decrease interest rates on existing ones. These structural adjustments often address issues of administrative governance, such as transparency or accountability of public bodies. Most notably, the EU applies this model in the context of its enlargement policy. In 1993 the European Council agreed on the Copenhagen Criteria that made the consolidation of liberal democracy the principal condition for starting accession negotiations. The EU also exercises this form of leverage in the broader context of economic governance. Between 2010 and 2011, for example, governments of technocrats were nominated in Greece and Italy aimed at, *inter alia*, making sure that domestic reforms were fulfilled in accordance with EU's requirements.

6.2 The Effects of Convergence: Re-assessing the Boomerang Effect

Moving beyond the types of administrative convergence, this Paragraph will examine the effects of convergence on EAS/GAL relationships, as well as reassesses the "boomerang effect" described by Keck and Sikkink. This reassessment is useful because of the close relationship between the role of the ICs in promoting administrative convergence and the functioning of the boomerang effect. Since we conceived the ICs as engines of administrative convergence (either through attractiveness or imposition) we may now compare their penetration into global and European

[22] See A. Hardenbrook, "The Equator Principles: The Private Financial Sector's Attempt at Environmental Responsibility" (2007) 40 *Vanderbilt Journal of Transnational Law* 197; E. Suzuki, S, Nanwani, "Responsibility of International Organizations: The Accountability Mechanisms of Multilateral Development Banks" (2005) 27 *Michigan Journal of International Law* 177.

[23] See J. Stiglitz, *Scan Globally, Reinvent Locally* see chapter 3 at section 1.6.

administrative governances to what Keck and Sikkink named the boomerang effect – and Kathrin Zippel (2006) later re-named "ping-pong effect". According to this effect, any appeal made by external actors to the international community bounce back and put pressure on IOs and national governments.[24] In Keck's and Sikkink's view, a boomerang pattern can be sketched when national/local groups operating in a repressive and closed political system circumvent their government by looking for allies on the transnational level to place pressure upon their state from the outside. Via these connections to transnational networks, national NGOs gain access to international public opinion, donor organizations, IOs, and Western governments, which can then be mobilized to put pressure on the norm-violating state. It is thus a "transnational network" of public and private actors that provide national groups with financial resources as well as information and leverage on the international public opinion. In this process, according to Keck and Sikkink, transnational networks serve three purposes. The first is getting the issue on the international agenda and thus shaming the norm-violating state. The second is the attempt to legitimate the claims of domestic groups – which closely relates to the first. Finally, the third purpose of transnational networks is to challenge norm-violating states through a structure operating at the transnational level.

In many respects, the same dynamics appear in the relationship between the ICs and IOs. To begin with, the former supports issues at the supranational level. At the same time, the advocacy from the ICs challenges governments (albeit only indirectly, since the ICs only interact with the IOs). There are, however, five important differences between the dynamics behind the ICs' advocacy and those described by Keck, Sikkink and Zippel. The first concerns the balance between the national and the supranational levels. Differently from the boomerang effect, in which the domestic level plays a significant role, in the case of the ICs national powers are reduced in importance, to the advantage of the supranational level. Undoubtedly, all supranational policy-making is crafted to produce effects at the local level. The leverage from the ICs, however, is organized and developed mostly at the supranational level. Not only are the topics to be advocated agreed upon through the ICs, but these coalitions are also expected to advocate such topics towards the supranational regulators they cooperate with. A second difference from the models of Keck and Sikkink concerns the involvement of both the public and the private sector in pursuing administrative convergence. When the boomerang theory was conceived, there were still doubts as to whether the presence of the private sector in the process of administrative convergence would be beneficial, or whether it would be seriously undermined by the subverted relationship of power between the public and the private sectors. Nowadays, while the public/private distinction is still important, the

[24] See M.E. Keck, K. Sikkink, *Activists Beyond Borders* see chapter 1 at section 1, see chapter 1 n 60 and 68, see chapter 3 n 28, see chapter 4 n 29. See also E. Sorensen, "Governance Network as a Frame for Inter-Demoi Participation and Deliberation" Working paper 2007:1, *Centre for Democratic Network Governance Roskilde University*, available at www.ruc.dk/demnetgov; M.E. Warren, "Governance-Driven Democratization" Working paper 2008:3, *Centre for Democratic Network Governance Roskilde University*, available at www.ruc.dk/demnetgov.

content of each sphere and their interaction with each other is no longer considered an issue. Chapter 4 of this volume explained how the ICs and IOs cooperate through PPPs. It is safe to say that in the current supranational legal domain the indistinct border between the public and the private sphere is now conceived as an opportunity rather than an issue. The third difference relates to the reasons motivating convergence. Closer collaboration between the ICs and IOs signifies that policy transfer is motivated by reasons other than contestation. While the boomerang effect theory postulates that an international network is mobilized to challenge a particular (domestic) policy, in the case of the ICs, the push for reforms may also be the motivation for policy transfers. As an example, economic crises are likely to put pressure on the IOs to enhance engagement from governments to borrow policies from other governments. This brings us to the fourth difference from the original boomerang effect. This difference is concerned with the "degree" of transfer. On this point, Dolowitz and Marsh already noted that policy transfer is not an all-or-nothing process. They distinguished four degrees of transfer: the first is "copying", which involves direct and complete transfer; the second is "emulation", in which ideas – rather that the policies themselves – are the objects of transfer; the third is "combination", in which ideas and policies are combined and transferred together; fourth and final is "inspiration", where policy in another jurisdiction may inspire a policy change. Richard Rose (2005) updated these categories to include: copying, adaptation, hybrid, synthesis, disciplined inspiration and selective imitation. In Keck's and Sikkink's model, discipline inspiration and selective imitation appeared as the main forms of convergence. By contrast, the relationship between the ICs and IOs seems to favour emulation and inspiration. A fifth, and final, difference from the original boomerang effect is linked with the consequences that convergence has for the actors that drive it. In effect, this is a point that Keck and Sikkink leave almost unexplored. However, it is important to understand how advocacy efforts from the ICs produce convergence among the ICs themselves. The ICs, as with any other actor of advocacy, are hinged on a duty to accomplish their tasks. This means that they would likely adapt their organizations and activities in accordance with the changes they want to induce in IOs' policy-making. In the long run, this adaptive process will render the ICs increasingly similar to one another, at least in terms of organizational outlines, procedures and activities they undertake. Without need to go into further details (the conclusions of this volume will take the endeavour to explain this point) it can be noted that this isomorphism is an opportunity, but also a threat to the future of the ICs.

6.3 Administrative Convergence, the EAS and the GAL

With the importance of the ICs for the concept of policy transfer at the supranational level defined, a few additional considerations can be made with regard to administrative convergence within the conceptual landscape of EAS and GAL. Specifically, regarding the forces that may oppose administrative convergence.

While there is an underlying assumption that policies that have been successful in one legal regime will be successful in other regimes, at least two reasons challenge this assumption. The first is institutional inertia, the second relates to cultural divergences. Institutional inertia occurs when policy-makers only formally adopt rules crafted in other legal systems. In particular, this may occur in the imposition of democratic values to national governments in the framework of financial agreements with IOs such as the IMF or the WB. Another force against convergence is that cultural preferences render particular solutions unattractive in particular polities. Given that the issue of cultural divergence, and its impact on the ICs, will be dealt with again in the conclusions of this book, in what follows it will only acknowledged to the extent to which it affects administrative convergence. Administrative law is particularly concerned by the problem of cultural divergence. The scopes and definition of administrative law differs across legal systems. Take the administrative systems of the EU as an example. They are different not only in the rules and regulations applied to society, but also in the rules and regulations that regulators apply to themselves. The obvious consequence of this is that convergence, if applied to administrative law, may not exist, or may be less evident than, say, convergence of private or business law. This objection, however, has fewer grounds in the supranational legal domain. Supranational administrative law, both European or global, is mainly composed of principles that are borrowed from domestic administrative systems. Thus, principles of administrative governance, rather than substantive rules, are conveyed through convergence among supranational regulators. Richard Rose (1987) suggests that legal obligations and political interests may also be included among the causes impeding institutional change. The former consists of the obligations that norms approved by administrations that are placed on succeeding administrations, de facto producing few policy changes. Political interests, in Rose's description, consist of the opposition from pressure groups that have become part of a policy community towards institutional changes.

The consequences of such obstacles to convergence may vary. However, for the sake of simplicity, three are salient. First is uninformed transfer, when the borrowers have insufficient information about the policy that is transferred and how it operates in the lender's legal regime. Second is that of incomplete transfer. In this instance, crucial elements of the policy are missed during the transfer. The obvious consequence is, again, failure in transferring policies. A third case of failure in policy transfer is that of inappropriate transfer. In this case, it is assumed by Dolowitz and Marsh, the borrower did not pay sufficient attention to the differences between contexts.

References

Aparicio, M. 1984. *Introduccion al sistema politico y constitucional espanol*. Barcelona: Ariel.

Bennett, C.J. 1991. Review article: What is policy convergence and what causes it? *British Journal of Political Science* 21: 215.

Benvenisti, E., and G.W. Downs. 2007. The empire new clothes: Political economy and the fragmentation of international law. *Stanford Law Review* 60: 595.

De Bellis, M. 2013. Global financial standards and networks: The global administrative law perspective. *Revista de derecho publico de l'Universidad de los Andes* 30: 1.

Di Maggio, P., and W.W. Powell (eds.). 1991. *The new institutionalism in organizational analysis*. Chicago: University of Chicago Press.

Ingram, P., and M.T. Torfason. 2010. Organising the in-between: The population dynamics of network-weaving organisations in the global interstate network. *Administrative Science Quarterly* 55: 577.

Lavenex, S. 2013. Globalization and horizontal promotion of democracy. In *Democracy in the age of globalization and mediatization*, ed. H. Kriesi, D. Bochsler, J. Matthes, S. Lavenex, M. Bühlmann, and F. Esser. London: Palgrave.

Orenstein, M. 2003. Mapping the diffusion of pension innovation. In *Pension reform in Europe: Process and progress*, ed. R. Holzmann, M. Orenstein, and M. Rutkowski. Washington, DC: The World Bank.

Posner, E. 2005. Sources of institutional change. The supranational origins of Europe's new stock markets. *World Politics* 58: 1.

Rose, R. 1987. *Ministers and ministries: A functional analysis*. Oxford: Clarendon Press.

Rose, R. 2005. *Learning from comparative public policy: A practical guide*. London: Routledge.

Shaffer, G. 2014. How the WTO shapes regulatory governance, regulation and governance. *Regulation & Governance*. doi:10.1111/rego.12057.

Weber, M. 1978. *Economy and society*. Berkley: University of California Press.

Wejnert, B. 2014. *Diffusion of democracy. The past and future of global democracy*. Cambridge: Cambridge University Press.

Zippel, K.S. 2006. Transnational advocacy networks and policy cycles in the EU: The case of sexual harassment. *Social Politics* 11: 57.

Chapter 7
Beyond Networks: The Interlocutory Coalitions and Globalization of Democracy

7.1 Three Concerns Related to Networking Within Civil Society

This book has developed from a deceptively straightforward question: are networks of GCS meaningful to the convergence of principles of democratic value between the European and other supranational legal systems? To answer this question, two lines of argument have been explored. The first line (Chaps. 2 and 3) is descriptive, in that identifies the conceptual underpinnings of the coalitions of non-state actors – named the ICs – that operate at the supranational level. The ICs, identified as a natural evolution of global civil society's advocacy, have had their structure, membership, governing rules and activities examined. In arguing for the relevance of such organised networks of civil society actors, the second line of argument of this volume has analysed their relationship with the EU and other supranational regulators. Chapter 6 in particular addressed the topic of the IC's influence on the relationship between GAL and EAS. Two different forms of administrative convergence were identified – namely: "by attraction" and "by imposition" – and it was postulated that the ICs combine these forms of convergence into a third one.

The final part of this volume will discuss the future of GCS' networks and related concerns. As previously stated, increased co-operation between the ICs and the IOs may show a pattern of harmonization of principles of democratic governance across legal systems. However, this is not a pattern without significant difficulties. Doubts regarding the existence of a pattern of harmonization of democratic principles arise in at least three areas. The first area relates to GCS' networking and substantiates in the following tensions: the functioning of GCS' coalitions; the competition among them; the issue of uniqueness (i.e. when a supranational regulator refuses to co-operate with a coalition of civil society actors on the basis of rules or standards formerly approved by a different regulator, assuming their uniqueness); and, finally, the issue of creativity – i.e. the loss of creativity and experimentation that might

G. Sgueo, *Beyond Networks - Interlocutory Coalitions, the European and Global Legal Orders*, Studies in European Economic Law and Regulation 8,
DOI 10.1007/978-3-319-28875-8_7

occur when the same legal standards and practices are massively recycled from different coalitions of civil society actors. Do these tensions influence negatively the impact of the ICs on the spread of methods of democratic governance at the supranational level? This question brings forth the second area of concern. Of particular importance is the impact that the ICs have on the reconfiguration of individuals' rights, entitlements and responsibilities in the global arena. An issue that leads directly to a third, and last, area of concern: the convergence between the EAS and the GAL.

The aforementioned areas of concern, and the problematic questions they raise, do not have a straightforward answer. It remains difficult, after all, to provide an exact measurement of how "determinant" the supranational coalitions of civil society actors are to the process of harmonization of regulatory schemes across supranational legal regimes. On the one hand, they may give the lie to this volume's original assumption of the relevance and meaningfulness of the GCS' coalitions in the supranational arena. These coalitions, in other words, may not be the 'brave new world' they may have appeared to be at first sight. Rather than the "transmission belt" of principles of democratic governance at the global level, their role could be scaled down to that of a mere compromise made among non-state actors and IOs. The former would merely liaise with IOs with the aim of capturing funds from international donors; instead, IOs would co-opt and capture the ICs, using them as a tool for legitimating their decisions and overcoming the critiques on their democratic deficit.

On the other hand, it is worth remembering that the alliances of civil society actors described in this volume are still a novel and changing phenomenon in the global legal arena. And this will be the central tenet guiding this chapter. While GCS' networking continues to grow relentlessly, with new alliances among non-state actors established everyday, existing coalitions continue to expand their membership and grow in relevance. Furthermore, it seems that GCS' networking is undergoing an evolution. New organizational forms – or meta-networks – are emerging. Existing coalitions of civil society actors are increasingly merging into meta-coalitions, apparently pursuing the same scopes that motivated their creation in the first place: to strengthen the advocacy positions of their members in supranational policy-making and to gain effectiveness in fundraising. The empirical picture seems to confirm this. Examples include the Steering Committee for Humanitarian Response – an alliance of nine of the largest international humanitarian organizations and networks working with the Office of the UN High Commissioner for Refugees – the NGO Working Group on the World Bank, the EPLO, the ATM – who admits as members not only individuals or organizations, but also networks of organizations (thus far, five of those networks joined the coalition) – and the Social Platform – an umbrella organization for Brussels-based social NGOs and networks of national NGOs in the various European Member States aimed at facilitating participatory democracy in the EU by promoting the consistent involvement of NGOs within structured civil dialogue with EU institutions. Significant is also the case of the GCAP, in respect to both its composition and advocacy strategy. The GCAP is composed not only of diverse non-state actors, ranging from trade unions to NGOs, but it also includes other coalitions as supporting members. Besides that, the GCAP chief strategy consists of creating smaller coalitions of civil society actors operating at the national level. In so doing, the GCAP turns into a meta-coalition, or meta-network, controlling and giving guidance to other domestic coalitions. Finally, to further exemplify the trend towards the creation of "networks of networks", one may also consider the ICs that take part in temporary *fora* for negotiation and discussion, including the QUANGOs described in Chap. 3 of this volume. Cases in point are the Joint Facilitation Committee and the European Habitats Forum. The former is a body established to facilitate the organization of the annual WB Civil Society Forum (where representatives of NGOs and other organized expressions of civil society convene).[1] This Committee is composed of both regional and international civil society networks and staff as well as senior managers of the WB. The European Habitats Forum, operating at the European level, assembles several European nature conservation organisations and ICs to provide advice on the implementation and future development of EU biodiversity policy.[2] Not just single NGOs are members of the Forum; ICs (e.g. the EEB) are also represented. The Forum is represented in the European Commission's Expert Groups, the Coordination Group on Biodiversity and Nature and the Nature Directors meetings.

7.1.1 Four Tensions: The Functioning of Networks

This brings us to a new question: is the evolution of GCS' networking described above helping to create new and increasingly complex networks? In answering this, some caution is required. In fact, while the paradigm of meta-networks demonstrates that civil society actors increasingly perceive networking as a necessity to advocate for their interests at the supranational level, it creates a number of tensions that – for the time being – remain unresolved. Four in particular can be identified: the first concerns the functioning of networks of civil society actors, the second regards the competition among coalitions, the third and the forth the uniqueness and creativity of GCS' networks, respectively. The current section will illustrate the tension related with the functioning of networks. Section 7.1.2 will discuss the issue of competition. Sections 7.1.3 and 7.1.4 will deal with the issues of uniqueness and creativity.

The most evident tension of GCS' networking is related to the functioning of networks. Previous chapters of this volume have shown that holding NGOs and other civil society actors together in a coalition constitutes a complicated enterprise. This problem is especially apparent when coalitions grow bigger and, in consequence, the likeliness of controversial positions among their members increases. The point is simple and yet central to the overall argument of networks' functioning.

[1] See Joint Resolution between the World Bank and the NGO Working Group, 6 December 2000, available at www.staff.city.ac.uk/p.willets/NGOWG/JNT-RES.HTM.

[2] See generally www.eurosite.org/en-UK/content/european-habitats-forum

On the one hand, associational forms like the ICs remain the best option to foster a broad range of interests of large constituencies and to contain the increasing number and diversity of their members. Also, the dimensions of the ICs matter to both their members and IOs. The former are aware of the fact that the more a coalition of civil society actors grows in size, the greater strength they gain in advocacy. IOs, in turn, understand that, at a time in which regulation increasingly concerns objects and situations whose heterogeneity and complexity escapes their cognitive capacities, cooperation with civil society actors becomes fundamental for sound policy-making. Consider the case of the EU. As EU institutions have expanded their regulatory competences into new areas (such as Freedom, Security and Justice, industrial policy and consumer protection), and policy proposals have become more complex,[3] increasingly they have come to rely on the technical expertise provided by pressure groups to draft legislation. Lobbying efforts towards members of the European Parliament almost doubled between 1994 and 2005, especially in the policy areas where co-decision applies,[4] creating a trust-based relationship between interest groups who want access to the EU legislative process and EU officials who welcome information to reduce uncertainties about policy outcomes and gain support for the policy process.

Bigger coalitions, however, are also weaker and less flexible, due to the wide range of adherents with different views, sizes, and strategies. Paradoxically, smaller coalitions may turn out to be stronger coalitions. As Mancur Olson (1982) explains, smaller groups are quicker in organizing themselves. In the nascent Westphalian system of sovereign states, for example, small interest groups "used" the states as instruments for obtaining a disproportionate share of resources for themselves. Eyal Benvenisti reports the case of the Dutch United East India Company.[5] This small group of Dutch merchants succeeded in securing access to the high seas commissioning a legal brief to Hugo Grotius, at the time a young lawyer. The notion elaborated by Grotius – i.e. that high seas were a shared resource – was crucial to transform the course of development of international law. Furthermore, big networks face a loss of flexibility, which constitutes a second paradox. The bigger is a coalition, the more formalized it will (probably) be. Instead, a coalition less formalised may turn out to be more effective in advocacy. Then, the question is: what brings the ICs to adopt formalised rules to govern their activities? Shouldn't the ICs settle on softer means of regulation in order to benefit from flexibility? As Chap. 3 explained, formalisation may not always be a choice. As it is often the case, the elevated number of members obliges a coalition of civil society actors to sacrifice some flexibility, and to adopt formal procedures to gather the view of all their constituents. Flexibility is renounced by the ICs not only for the sake of better advocacy, but also for reasons of governability and optimisation of costs/benefits. This explains why the large part of the ICs are governed by formal agreements (of type

[3] See H. Kluver, "The Contextual Nature of Lobbying: Explaining Lobbying Success in the European Union" (2011) 12(4) *European Union politics* 483–506.

[4] See D. Coen, *Lobbying in the European Union*, PE 393.266, 2007

[5] See E. Benvenisti, *Exit and Voice*, see chapter 3 n 39.

"A") or, alternatively, by a complex set of rules to define their functioning (agreements of type "B"), whereas only a few remaining ICs opt for being ungoverned by complex rules. Typically, informal ICs (i.e. those governed by agreements of type "C") are meant to exist only on a short or mid-term basis.

7.1.2 Coalitions in Competition

Competition is another issue between GCS' coalitions. While some scholars emphasise integration of organisations operating in the same field,[6] the majority of scholars emphasise the problematic aspects of competition. As noted by Kumi Naidoo (2006), cross-border activism has not yet successfully created a veritable GCS. This is because no civil society organization can truly claim representation in all of the countries of the world. The current situation, Naidoo argues, is better described as dominated by a large number of civil society cross-border groups who, to a greater or lesser extent, coordinate their activities depending upon their interest in similar issues. The assumption of Naidoo is very well exemplified by the case of European businesses in the early 1990s. Back then, the creation and liberalisation of the Single Market had increased the regulatory authority of European institutions. In consequence, legal firms and business groups increased their lobbying efforts to influence the European policies. According to Coen (2002), between 1985 and 1997, over 35,000 firms chose to develop direct European lobbying capabilities. Thus, in order to face the problem of balancing its informational needs and consultations requirements against a manageable number of interests, the Commission adopted an informal solution, i.e. it created a number of restricted entry industrial forums. Those *fora* included the famous "Bangemann telecommunications" – named after Martin Bangemann, Commissioner for Industrial affairs, Information and Telecommunications Technologies in the Santer Commission – as well as a number of pharmaceutical *fora*. The idea of the Commission was a success. Following the desire to have access to these *fora*, firms entered into fierce competition. They increased their efforts to build their European credentials, and to this extent created a number of ad-hoc business alliances.

Competition among the ICs is potentially ubiquitous. It may concern big coalitions, which encompass a great diversity of actors and are not guided by a clear leadership; but it may also affect small coalitions, since they are motivated by the necessity to remain competitive, in order to gain attention and thus secure access to funding and leverage on IOs' policy-making; competition may even concern single members of the ICs. In what follows, competition among coalitions will be first illustrated, and then discussed in the instance of ICs' competing among themselves.

Two cases exemplify competition among the ICs: the Infant Formula Action Coalition and the EEB. Between 1977 and 1984 the Infant Formula Action Coalition

[6] See, for instance, M. Warren, *Governance-Driven Democratization* see chapter 6 n 24.

promoted a global boycott of Nestlé products. The global boycott aimed at interrupting Nestlé's promotion of infant formula to poor mothers in developing countries, assuming that children would be healthier if breast-fed. After a few years, however, the Infant Formula Coalition split in two. At present, one part of the Coalition is based in Boston and for some time it retained the acronyms INFACT, but not the full name. Since 1993, it has focused on corporate accountability of organizations such as those linked to the tobacco industry and changed its name in "Corporate Accountability International". Another INFACT is based in Toronto, and it continues to boycott Nestlé. This latter INFACT is also part of a meta-coalition – the International Baby Food Action Network – where 150 NGOs are included.[7] The EEB is the oldest among the ICs considered in this book. As the European Parliament reports it,[8] right after its creation, the EEB had established a very close relationship with the European Commission, and specifically with the Directorate-General Environment. "For more than twelve years" – reports the European Parliament – "the EEB remained the only environmental organization dedicated to the EU arena". Things changed after the arrival of new environmental organizations in Brussels, a natural consequence of the increased importance of environmental regulation in EU (between 1967 and 1987 the European Commission produced over 200 directives and regulations concerned with the environment). This reduces the cosiness of relations between the European Commission and the EEB. The relevance of the EEB was further reduced by the presence of another IC, the European ECO-Forum, which also advocated on environmental matters.

This brings us to the second hypothesis of competition. As previously discussed, single members of the ICs may also theoretically compete against each other. However, this is unlikely to happen in practice. The ICs' members are less interested in competing against each other given the fact that, as Chap. 3 explained, membership to a coalition of civil society actors is rarely, if ever, exclusive. Members of the ICs may therefore decide to join more than one coalition and benefit from multiple memberships. After all, any member to a coalition contemplating the move into another IC will have to compare the value of accessing the latter against the costs of losing the current membership of the former. This will probably turn into the decision to remain in both coalitions. The only meaningful reason to leave a coalition has been discussed in Chap. 4. This consists of the hypothesis in which a member of a coalition perceives that this is not effective in advocating, and thus decides to abandon it.

One last point that should be mentioned in discussing competition among the ICs is that it may also be beneficial. Yet again, the EBB provides a good example. Even if the EEB progressively lost its grip on the European Commission because of the presence of many others environmental not-for-profit institutions operating in Brussels, this bought the EEB to enlarge the scope of its action and to enter into dialogue with other IOs, such as the UN and the OECD. Over the years the EEB

[7] See generally www.ibfan.org.

[8] See European Parliament, DG Research, *Lobbying in the European Union: Current Rules and Practices* Working Paper 04-2003.

increasingly advocated towards global IOs instead of just the European bureaucracy. The European firms reported above in this section provide a further example of the benefits of competition. Because the seats to the policy tables with the European Commission are limited, firms and business have begun to join into coalitions to the scope of enhancing their credentials. Networks like the "Transport Network Round Table" or the "Automobile Group" require firms wishing to join their membership to build credible and strong policy profiles in Brussels. Progressively, business coalitions have selected the most valuable members to build up their credentials towards the European Commission. This strategy paid back well. According to recent estimates there are 350 firms with European affairs offices in Brussels,[9] and more than 260 public affairs firms that are active in EU public policy.[10] Law firms in particular are considered among the most dynamic consultancies operating in Brussels, having doubled 5.3 times since 1995, and currently accounting for 53 % of the consultancy market in the EU.[11]

7.1.3 The Issue of Uniqueness

A third tension arising from networking within the GCS can be described as the "issue of uniqueness", and a forth as the "issue of creativity". These problems may be treated as two sides of the same coin. Both acknowledge the case in which, in spite of successful advocacy efforts, the ICs may experience negative outcomes. What differs between the first and the second issues (to be described shortly) is the perspective. The former issue – uniqueness – is problematic from the perspective of the supranational regulators; instead, the latter – creativity – sets on the viewpoint of the ICs.

Let's start with the issue of uniqueness. This may occur when IOs refuse to cooperate with a coalition of civil society actors on the basis of rules or standards formerly approved by a different IO, assuming their uniqueness, or the presence of important differences. While in fact supranational regulators may receive benefits from the development of common global standards, this does not mean that they will prefer any global standard. After all, the introduction of new rules or standards implies economic, political and administrative costs. Richard Stewart exemplifies this point when he describes competition among global regulatory bodies in providing regulatory standards to firms, governmental bodies, and other global regulatory bodies. In Stewart's analysis such competition is regarded as beneficial, because it can generate powerful incentives to respond to the interests and concerns of

---

[9] See D. Coen, "The evolution of the large firm as a political actor in the European Union" (1997) 4(1) *Journal of European Public Policy* 91.

[10] See C. Lahusen, "Commercial consultancies in the European Union: the shape and structure of professional interest intermediation" (2002) 9(5) *Journal of European Public Policy* 695.

[11] See C. Lahusen, *Commercial consultancies in the European Union* see text n 10.

consumers of regulatory standards.[12] However, the opposite may also be true. The efforts expended by global regulators to weaken the legitimacy of competing rules, standards or principles are problematic in two respects. To begin with, antagonism among global regulatory bodies may hamper or delay the process of harmonization of regulatory standards described in this volume, including those concerned with participatory democracy (e.g. transparency, participation and reason giving). Furthermore, such antagonism may negatively affect the ICs' capability to establish fruitful and lasting cooperation with IOs. Think as an example at the role that the ICs play in supporting the legitimacy of supranational regulators. As we know, the IOs' quest for legitimacy and accountability may vary to a great extent. Hence, the demand of the supranational regulators for tailored solutions to fill their accountability gaps. In such cases, the ICs are implicitly expected by the IOs with whom they cooperate to endorse their values and standards. More often than not, however, the ICs establish cooperative relationships with more than one supranational regulator. As a consequence, the more a coalition of non-state actors expands its range of cooperation, the more it is likely to face contradictory demands and/or expectations from their counterparts. These contradictions, in turn, may delay or even prevent the ICs from offering viable and efficacious solutions to IOs.

Having said that, it is important to stress that the issue of uniqueness differentiates from other tensions described in this chapter. While other issues can be treated and solved by the ICs themselves, uniqueness goes beyond the sole domain of the GCS. As an inherent problem of globalisation – i.e. the conflict of legal cultures – uniqueness concerns primarily supranational regulators and only residually GCS. The conflict of legal cultures in the global legal space, in fact, originates from the dominance of the executive branches of a handful of Western powerful states in global regulatory regimes, and it turns into the attempt from weaker states to oppose this dominance. Empirically, scholars point to the role of developing countries in supranational policy-making as embodiments of such inequalities. Patricia Nanz and Jens Steffek (2004), for instance, define the task for more inclusive deliberation in the WTO as a manifest unequal opportunity amongst actors, since the representatives from developing countries experience major disadvantages that prevent them from effective participation in the debate. Kristina Daurgidas (2013) points to the ability of the US Congress to influence global bodies such as the WB (but the same applies to the UN Human Rights Council and the UN Educational, Scientific and Cultural Organisation) by withholding funding. Grainne de Burca (2008) reports the criticism concerning the lack of representation of the IMF and the WB.

Now, being that the clash of legal cultures is a problem for supranational regulators, the solutions proposed to redress it inevitably point at IOs, leaving aside civil society actors and their coalitions. Of these solutions, two are especially notable. A first, general, answer to the problem of uniqueness is to strengthen the equal representation of different legal traditions within the decision-making panels of the various global bodies. A better balance in the distribution of power, scholars suggest, renders extra-state rules less vulnerable to the disapproval of actors from different

[12] See R. Stewart, *Remedying Disregard*, see chapter 1 at section 7.1.

legal cultures.[13] As an alternative, academics recommend that representatives to be involved in decision-making should be selected by IOs on the basis of their special expertise or competence. This option, it is assumed, would guarantee more reliability in interest-representation, and therefore would help to overcome the gaps between different legal cultures.

Both solutions, however, may be contested. If not only for the political obstacles that it would face, the first solution seems to ignore that the problem of unequal representation not only affects IOs, but it is an issue faced by GCS as well, even if only indirectly. Section 7.2 will take the endeavour to explain this problem in more detail. For the moment, it suffices to point out that, after all, coalitions of civil society actors are composed mainly of westernized members. One may assume that these coalitions are not the expression of a civil society of global stance, but rather are exclusive clubs who represent the sole interests of civil society actors from Western countries. Therefore, this argument goes, even in the unlikely case in which a global decision-making tailored to balance all existing legal cultures would exist, it is debatable that it would solve the problem of a substantially unbalanced GCS. The consequence of this could be the persistence of the issue of uniqueness (and the related effects on the harmonization of principles of democratic governance across different legal systems). The second solution proposed by scholars interested in solving the clash of legal cultures at the supranational level moves from this very point. The idea of improving supranational decision-making through the expertise from civil society may be confronted with three critiques. Firstly, a continuous selection process of civil society's representatives is risky, since it may result in co-optation (as we shall see in next section). Secondly, a selection process based exclusively on the technical skills of civil society actors may be opposed with the same critiques that regard the excessive influence of the epistemic communities (a topic already illustrated in Chap. 3 of this volume). Thirdly, one should not forget the reluctance from IOs to let civil society representatives have too much weight within decision-making processes, as a way to avoid limits on the effectiveness and rapidity of decisions.

7.1.4 The Issue of Creativity

A fourth, and last, tension to be considered is the loss of creativity and experimentation that may occur when the same standards and practices are massively recycled from different coalitions of civil society actors. Organizational theorists utilise the word "isomorphism" to describe the tendency of organisations to become alike. Isomorphism is not necessarily a negative phenomenon. However what follows will

---

[13] See M. Macchia, "The rule of law and transparency in the global space", in C. Cassese et al. (ed.), *Research Handbook on Global Administrative Law* (Cheltenham, Edward Elgar Publishing, 2016) see chapter 1 n 18 and chapter 2 n 3.

focus primarily on how it may negatively impact on creativity and experimentation of the ICs.

Three arguments can be used to elucidate the issue of uniqueness. The first was elaborated by David Meyer and Nancy Whittier (1994). Meyer and Whittier clarify how the "spill over" among SMOs (but the same, it is assumed in this volume, may be valid for ICs) poses disincentives to new SMOs for selection of issues to advocate for, when these issues have been already adopted by other SMOs. A second argument to explicate the issue of creativity links to the accreditation standards introduced in Chap. 5 of this volume. Ideally, the imposition of standards to civil society actors (including the ICs) from the IOs may benefit the selection of civil society actors equipped with the right skills and competences to deal with policy-making. A continuous selection process, however, may end up into co-optation. The distribution of EU funds is explanatory to this extent. It has been noted that in some cases (e.g. in the environmental policy) the variance of the recipients of these funds is scarce. As a further consequence of this, there is the unlikeness that civil society actors could experiment new strategies for advocacy or attempt to modify the existing practices. The third argument to explicate the issue of uniqueness concerns individuals as members of the ICs. As for any other professional sector, the members of civil society organizations also pass through a mechanism of "revolving doors" – i.e. the circulation of personnel within different organizations of civil society. Professionals moving from one organization, or IC, to another, bring together with them expertise and know-how in the new organization/coalition. Revolving doors are generally seen as an issue either because of concerns that insider knowledge of professionals may be exploited by their new employers to gain privileged access and influence, or rather because professionals could be improperly influenced by their former employees while carrying out their duties, thus compromising the integrity of public decisions.[14] However in the case of the ICs, the problem is one of creativity: organized networking in GCS may hamper cultural diversity and ultimately produces anonymous standards, since professionals that move from one civil society organisation to another may recycle their expertise and knowledge, with no efforts to experiment new practices of advocacy.

7.2 The Impact Factor

The four tensions illustrated in Sects. 7.1.1, 7.1.2, 7.1.3, 7.1.4 complete concerns related to the functioning of the ICs. When combined, these tensions produce a second area of concern, related to the impact of the ICs on the harmonization of methods of democratic governance in the global arena. The ICs may be good at

[14] A few studies oppose this criticism. See for instance J. Blanes i Vidal, M. Draca, C. Fons-Rosen, *Revolving doors lobbyists*, CEP discussion paper No 993, 2010. The authors find that lobbyists suffer an average revenue loss of 20 % (approximately USD 177,000 per year) when their former political employer terminates his or her political mandate.

influencing IOs' policies, but – it may be asked – can they truly encourage the spill-over of a method of democratic governance across supranational legal regimes? Further: should they? Drawing from these two questions doubts may be raised on, first, the role played by the ICs in the reconfiguration of individuals' rights, entitlements and responsibilities in the global sphere; and, second, on the desirability of a "global participatory democracy". Specifically, if such global democracy exists, doubts may be raised on the fact that such networks should drive it. The current section will try to respond to the first question, leaving to the following section the task to answer to the second.

When we talk about the ICs' "impact factor", we implicitly question whether the proliferation of these networks translates into the recognition of more participatory rights to individuals worldwide; and we question whether this process of recognition is equally distributed among citizens all over the globe, or rather if some individuals get more participatory rights than others, and why. This is the suggestion made by scholars such as Bhupinder Chimni. GCS, Chimni believes, could play a beneficial role in the democratisation of global rule making. However, as the theory – and to an increasing extent the practice – of the ICs' advocacy grows in importance, it has also shown to be unbalanced. Organised networks of civil society actors tend to embody asymmetric power relations in which powerful participants often play the dominant decision-making roles, rather than all members. The moment we assume that the ICs do not represent all interests, but only certain interests, we have to conclude that they are not capable of imposing democratic governance at the supranational level. Not that the issue of disparities among civil society actors is a novel one. There is a burgeoning literature that discusses how imbalances are an inner part of civil society. Written in 1960, the celebrated book by Elmer Schattschneider (1960) appears in retrospect as anticipating the current issue of the imbalances (that, if not instigated may be at least) accrued by networks of civil society. And the academic debate that some "voices" within IOs have a better chance of being heard than others has continued unabated to this day. "Stronger members get stronger" – writes Michael Walzer (2002) – "(while) the weakest and poorer members are either unable to organise at all – or they form groups that reflect their weakness and poverty".

It is not the purpose of this volume to dismiss scholarly opinions on imbalances in civil society as irrelevant, nor try to disavow their opinions completely. However, two reasons exist to be sceptical of their claims. Both reasons move from the same assumption: an increasingly networked GCS is still a novel phenomenon in the global arena, and it should be treated as such when discussing the impact it has on IOs' decision-making. While not directly "Cassesian" in orientation, this book suggests that, as reminded by Sabino Cassese (2016), in the global perspective legal concepts remain influenced by states and their rules. Administrative systems remain intrinsically divergent, because they still result from the overlap between the traditional Westphalian model of state and the newly emerged supranational regulators and their rules. In terms of participatory rights, then, this means that a mature participatory democracy is not yet developed at the global level. Rather, we observe principles and common rules that timidly spread across legal regimes. Inevitably, this causes tensions and divergences that reflect on citizens across the world. Having this in mind, we may assume that civil society actors coalescing into networks can help (albeit not yet solve) to overcome these tensions and to patch up the divergences.

A second, more wide-ranging, argument could be made that coalitions of civil society actors move a step forward to the construction of an infrastructure to support the voice of civil society in the development of a global democracy. On this point, it is worth recalling the work of Robert Keohane, one scholar who voiced his scepticism about the feasibility of democracy beyond the domain of national states (and, instead, has conceded to settle in practice for less demanding forms of accountability). When Keohane (2015) explicates his idea of "nominal democracy" – i.e. a façade democracy, embodying the appearance of democracy, but lacking the substance – he addresses three main gaps to substantiate his claim. It is not necessary to provide full account of all the three gaps – namely: the interest-public goods, the emotional and the infrastructure gaps. It is sufficient to acknowledge the third gap, this being directly related to this chapter. Keohane argues that a democracy requires an associative spirit from citizens, who coalesce in order to advocate for their rights. Hence, our question: do the ICs – described as transnational networks of civil society actors – provide a solution for this infrastructural gap? Not in Keohane's opinion. He admits that transnational, networks of civil society may provide some of the infrastructure for a global democracy, by nurturing civil society at the elite level. However, concludes Keohane, these networks are still far behind from building a "social capital". Much more energy and time has to be spent in building the multidimensional ties among civil society actors that could benefit the construction of a genuine, and not just nominal, democracy. Here, however, issue may be taken with the hypothesis advanced by Keohane, and it may be argued that the ICs offer the exact kind of infrastructure needed to develop more democratic governance at the global level. Indeed, it is tempting to conclude that with the ICs the issue of a quest for global democratic governance is solved. This temptation shall be resisted. Instead, it may be acknowledged that even if the ICs are missing the creation of social capital evoked by Keohane, they move a significant step forward the creation of (more) democratic supranational governance.

7.3 Beyond Networks

Indeed, the creation of supranational governance is a process that takes time. This brings us to our last question, which concerns the desirability of the ICs as drivers of principles of administrative governance across supranational legal systems. Despite their failings, are coalitions of civil society actors the best possible drivers of a global democracy? This cannot be easily answered. The concept of network evocated at the outset of this volume is inevitably hinged on the idea that it is entirely based on interactions among its members. And, admittedly, the concept of network fits well with the description of the coalitions of civil society actors that are described in this volume. Yet, the same term, network, seems less appropriate to address the array of relationships established between such coalitions and supranational regulators. Reflecting on what Anne Marie Slaughter describes as a network – i.e. the professional relationships between civil servants, professionals and activists – it remains evident that a certain degree of separation exists between the ICs and the global regulators. With very few exceptions, no IO has shown an effort to integrate coalitions of civil society actors within its decision-making, or to improve organizational connection with them. More than a single network, the ICs and the IOs constitute two overlapping systems of relations, which interact and cooperate in a manner that is mutually beneficial.

In fact, cooperation between coalitions of civil society actors and supranational regulators shows more of an affinity with the idea of regime complexes, as described in Chap. 1 of this volume. Two similarities and one difference exist between regime complexes and the cooperation between the ICs and IOs. The first similarity consists of this: in both cases we observe the overlap of different mixes of public actors, from the local to the global level. Differently from regime complexes, however, in the cases of cooperation between the ICs and IOs addressed in this volume no arrangement, nor a defined strategy towards a common goal seem to exist. In other words, the only (or, at least, the main) basis of the relationship between ICs and IOs is the practical benefits it produces. This brings us to a second similarity between regime complexes and the cooperation between supranational coalitions of GCS and IOs. In both cases supranational regulators may increase management costs without necessarily obtaining a wider set of choices.

Having in mind these similarities between the regime complexes and the cooperation established between IOs and the supranational coalitions of civil society actors we may conclude that, for the time being, the ICs remain the best possible drivers of harmonization of principles of democratic governance at the supranational level. What is going to happen in the next future is open to debate. Principles of participatory democracy are likely spreading across supranational legal systems. By the time the convergence among supranational systems of governance will be completed, however, organised networks of civil society actors could be already overcome by new organisational models. Global democracy evolves beyond networks.

References

Cassese, S. 2016. *Research handbook on global administrative law*. Cheltenham: Edward Elgar.

Coen, D. 2002. Business interests and European integration. In *L'action collective en Europe*, ed. R. Balme, D. Chabanet, and V. Wright. Paris: Science Po Press.

Daurgidas, K. 2013. Congress underestimated: The case of the World Bank. *American Journal of International Law* 107: 517.

De Burca, G. 2008. Developing democracy beyond the state. *Columbia Journal of Transnational Law* 46: 101.

Keohane, R.O. 2015. Nominal democracy? Prospects for democratic global governance. *ICON-S* Working Paper – Conference Proceedings Series 1, No. 4.
Meyer, D., and N. Whittier. 1994. Social movement spillover. *Social Problems* 41: 277.
Naidoo, K. 2006. Claiming global power: Transnational civil society and global governance. In *Transnational civil society. An introduction*, ed. S. Batliwala and D. Brown. Bloomfield: Kumarian Press.
Nanz, P., and J. Steffek. 2004. Global governance, participation and the public sphere. *Government and Opposition* 39: 314.
Olson, M. 1982. *The rise and decline of nations*. New Haven: Yale University Press.
Schattschneider, E.E. 1960. *The semi-sovereign people*. New York: Holt, Reinard and Wiston.
Walzer, M. 2002. Equality and civil society. In *Alternative conceptions of civil society*, ed. S. Chambers and W. Kymlicka. Princeton: Princeton University Press.

Synoptic Table

As is necessarily the case with a schematic presentation of a complex phenomenon, the only purpose of this table is to illustrate in a simple manner the basic elements of each interlocutory coalition. To this end, each case is sided by seven vectors that locate the essential common grounds of a Coalition. Namely: *(1) Europe or Global* indicates the main geographical area of activity of the interlocutory coalition; *(2) IO Concerned* regards the main institution that cooperates with the interlocutory coalition. When more than one institution is involved, an appropriate description is introduced (*e.g.* "European bureaucracy"). When no institution is showed in the box, it means that the IC cooperates with diverse IOs in different contexts; *(3) Date of Establishment* is the date from which the coalition has started to operate. When the interlocutory coalition is no longer operative, a date of ending is also indicated; *(4) Number of Members* indicates the number of members to a coalition. Not only full members are included, but also other typologies (*e.g.* supporting members, members in a observatory status). "NA" indicates that no information were available for the members; *(5) Type of Members* expressly refers to full members of the coalition, and defines the percentage of those that are NGOs and those who are not. "NA" indicates that no information were available for the members; *(6) Type of Agreement* specifies which kind of agreement (A, B, or C) governs the interlocutory coalition; *(7) Sector of Advocacy* provides information on the topic(s) of relevance to the interlocutory coalition.

G. Sgueo, *Beyond Networks - Interlocutory Coalitions, the European and Global Legal Orders*, Studies in European Economic Law and Regulation 8,
DOI 10.1007/978-3-319-28875-8

Name	Europe or global	IO concerned	Date of establishment	Number of members	Type of members	Type of agreement	Sector of advocacy
Alter-EU	Europe	European bureaucracy	July 2005	200	NA	B	Transparency of lobbying
Alternative trade mandate	Europe	Commission + Parliament	October 2011	50 (including other networks)	90 % of NGOs 10 % of other	B	EU trade policy
CIVICUS	Global	United Nations	1993	150	NA	A	Democracy
Climate action network	Global	–	1989	900	100 % NGOs	A	Ecological sustainability
Conference of international NGOs	Global	Council of Europe	1952	320	100 % NGOs		Democracy
Conference of NGOs in consultative relationship with the UN	Global	United Nations	1948	500	100 % NGOs	B	Human right Facilitate the participation of NGOs in the UN system
Consultative board on the future of WTO	Global	WTO	2001/2003	8	100 % of other	C	Strengthening WTO as an institution
Consultative committee of the universal postal union	Global	United Nations	2004	20	60 % NGOs 40 % others		Postal sector
Consultative platform	Europe	European food safety authority	2005	24	100 % NGOs		Food security
Euclid network	Europe	European institutions	2007	300	100 % others		Civil society
European energy and transport forum	Europe	European commission	2001	34	15 % NGOs 85 % other		Energy and transport
European environmental Bureau	Europe/ global	European bureaucracy + United Nations + OECD	1974	140	100 % of NGOs	A	Environment
European Peacebuilding Liaison Office	Europe	European institutions	2001	32	100 % of NGOs		Conflict prevention
Global call to action against poverty	Global	International institutions and states	2005	NA	NA		Advocacy campaign/ anti-poverty coalition
Global climate coalition	Global	International institutions and states	1989/2002	69 companies and trade associations	100 % other		Climate change

(continued)

Name	Europe or global	IO concerned	Date of establishment	Number of members	Type of members	Type of agreement	Sector of advocacy
Human rights and democracy network	Europe	European institutions	2004	47	100 % of NGOs		Human Rights
Informal council	Global	WTO	2001	NA	NA		Trade
NGO advisory body	Global	WTO	2003/2004	10	100 % of NGOs		Dialogue between WTO and civil society
NGO forum on ADB	Global	Asian development bank	1992	250	100 % of NGOs		Finance
Pan-European ECO Forum	Global	MoP – Aarhus Convention	1998	NA	100 % of NGOs		Environment
UNCAC coalition	Global	United Nations	2006	350	100 % of civil society organisations (CSOs)	A	Corruption

Index

G. Sgueo, *Beyond Networks - Interlocutory Coalitions, the European and Global Legal Orders*, Studies in European Economic Law and Regulation 8,
DOI 10.1007/978-3-319-28875-8

The manufacturer's authorised representative in the EU is Springer Nature Customer Service Centre GmbH, Europaplatz 3, 69115 Heidelberg, Germany. If you have any concerns regarding our products, please contact ProductSafety@springernature.com

Printed and bound by CPI Group (UK) Ltd, Croydon, CR0 4YY
25/09/2026
02222869-0006